FARQUHAR
to
FIELD DAY

Three Centuries of Music and Theatre in Derry~Londonderry

Nuala McAllister Hart

The History Press Ireland

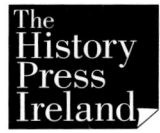

For Bill

Theatres are, above all, about people, people meeting people, people getting to know each other, people sitting down together to watch a conspiracy of actors with their magic articulate their own, secret unspoken thoughts.

Tom Mullarkey, theatre architect, 1985.

First published 2012

The History Press Ireland
119 Lower Baggot Street
Dublin 2
Ireland

www.thehistorypress.ie

© Nuala McAllister Hart, 2012

The right of Nuala McAllister Hart to be identified as the Author of this work has been asserted in accordance with the Copyrights, Designs and Patents Act 1988.

All rights reserved. No part of this book may be reprinted or reproduced or utilised in any form or by any electronic, mechanical or other means, now known or hereafter invented, including photocopying and recording, or in any information storage or retrieval system, without the permission in writing from the Publishers.

British Library Cataloguing in Publication Data.
A catalogue record for this book is available from the British Library.

ISBN 978 1 84588 735 3

Typesetting and origination by The History Press

CONTENTS

	Acknowledgements	4
	About the Author	6
	Abbreviations	7
	Introduction	8
One	Earliest Beginnings, 1677-1788	9
Two	The Golden Age, 1789-1833	30
Three	Contrasting Fortunes, 1834-1858	55
Four	'The Glitterati', 1859-1886	79
Five	'Calm Sea and Prosperous Voyage', 1887-1914	111
Six	Wars and Divisions, 1914-1945	142
Seven	Against the Odds, 1945-1979	173
Eight	The Foyle Renaissance, 1980-1995	200
Nine	Epilogue: An Embarrassment of Riches? 1996-2009	226
	Appendix 1 Derry~Londonderry Cultural Calendar	237
	Appendix 2 Drama and Music Societies in Derry~Londonderry	242
	Notes	244
	Bibliography and Further Reading	250
	Index	252

ACKNOWLEDGEMENTS

Thanks are due to a host of friends, colleagues and of course, the many musicians and drama enthusiasts who provided help, information, guidance and archive material, including:

Martin Agnew of First Derry Presbyterian church
Tim Allen and Donal Doherty and of the Two Cathedrals' Festival
Iain Barr of the Waterside Theatre
Dr Sean Beattie of the Macklin Festival
Francine Bull of the West Australian
Jonathan Burgess of Blue Eagle Productions
David Burke of Fourth Derry Presbyterian church
David Byers of the Ulster Orchestra
Roma Cafolla, daughter of Orlando Cafolla
Harry Christophers of the Sixteen
Pat Coull of the Red Cross
The late Professor Basil Deane
Gordon Douglas, former organist of Ebrington Presbyterian church
Dr Ken Hamilton of Birmingham University
Matthew Hendry of the Arts Council of Northern Ireland
Donald Hill and Jim Goodman of the Londonderry Amateur Operatic Society
Celia Herdman of the Londonderry Feis
The late Bob Hunter of Magee College
Ethan Ladd of the Tarisio Auction House, New York
Scott and Elma Marshall
Cathy McCafferty of the *Derry Journal*
Pat MacCafferty and Una O'Somachain

Acknowledgements

Mickey McGuinness of the Brow o' the Hill Choir
Mary McLaughlin, Jo Mitchell and Joe Tracey of the Foyle Civic Trust
Finola O'Doherty of the Foyle Arts Centre
Lieselotte Pohle of Siegfried's Mechanisches Musikkabinett, Rüdesheim, Germany
Mrs Maureen Phillips
Pauline Ross and Niall McCaughan of the Playhouse
Marie Elaine Tierney and staff of Derry Central Library, Foyle Street
Bernadette Walsh of Derry City Council Museum and Heritage Service
Staff at the Linenhall Library, the National Library of Ireland, the Public Record Office of Northern Ireland (PRONI) and the University of Ulster

Special thanks are due to:

Sean Doran of Impact '92 and Octoberfest '93.

Mrs Margaret West for the gift of the programme collection of her late husband, Billy, chorister, organist and choirmaster of Christ Church and St Columb's Cathedral over many years.

The late Fred Logan for his theatrical notes, guidance and many lively conversations.

Nigel McDowell for his photographic work.

The late Professor David Sturdy for supervision of early research.

And my husband, Dr Bill Hart, to whom I owe everything.

ABOUT THE AUTHOR

Dr Nuala McAllister Hart is a musician with a passionate interest in the history of Derry~Londonderry about which she has published widely. Her career has included university teaching, being a church organist and working for the Arts Council of Northern Ireland. She is married to philosopher Bill Hart who shares her love of music and theatre. They live just outside the city.

She once appeared as a dancer in a Kathleen Watson *Matinée Dansante* in the Guildhall.

ABBREVIATIONS

ACNI: Arts Council of Northern Ireland
CDDC: City of Derry Drama Club
CEMA: Council for the Encouragement of Music and the Arts
DCC: Derry City Council
The Feis: The Feis Ceoil, later the Londonderry Feis, finally the Londonderry Musical Festival
The Feis Dhoire: The Feis Dhoire Colmcille
First Derry: First Derry Presbyterian church, Magazine Street
Fourth Derry: Fourth Derry Presbyterian church, Carlisle Road
Guardian: *Londonderry Guardian*
Journal: *Londonderry Journal*, later *Derry Journal*
LMA: The Londonderry Musical Association
LAOS: Londonderry Amateur Operatic Society
The Long Tower: St Columba's Catholic church at the Long Tower
The Philharmonic: The Derry~Londonderry Philharmonic Society
Second Derry: Second Derry Presbyterian church, Strand Road
Sentinel: *Londonderry Sentinel*
Standard: *Londonderry Standard*
Third Derry: Third Derry Presbyterian church, Great James Street
TAG: The Theatre Action Group
VAC: The Verbal Arts Centre

INTRODUCTION

This book was originally envisaged as the story of Derry~Londonderry's theatrical and musical life and times told through the history of the rise and fall of its public places of entertainment, from the Exchange Building in the seventeenth century, through the Shipquay Theatre of the 1780s and the much-loved Royal Opera House on Carlisle Road (1870s-1940), to the present-day Millennium Forum. Something of that structure remains in the book, but in the writing the focus moved from places to people and their stories. It became more a social history of music and theatre in the city, in which the people of Derry, as audiences and as performers in their own right, took centre stage, alongside the visiting artists.

On the other hand, one of the things that emerged from this study is a rebuke to the city's sense of self-sufficiency. The more one knows about its history, the more aware one becomes of how much music and theatre in Derry has owed to incomers – Dublin-born and English theatre-managers, Scots Presbyterian precentors, European immigrant musicians – quite apart from the major celebrity figures – the Edmund Keans, the Jenny Linds, the Madame Albanis, the Paul Robesons, the Harry Christophers – who brought their talents and the breath of a larger air to Derry's stages and concert platforms.

Another thing that became apparent is that the cultural apartheid between Catholics and Protestants that was the norm in Derry's theatre and music for much of the twentieth century (institutionalised in its two Feiseanna) and which, of course, had its roots in the religious, social and political differences between the two groups, was a departure from the tradition of an earlier era when members of the different religious denominations in the city came together in their acting and music-making, performed in each other's churches and shared each other's facilities.

In the aftermath of the Troubles and on the eve of Derry's 2013 Year of Culture, this may be the most important message of the last three centuries of theatre and music in the city.

One

EARLIEST BEGINNINGS, 1677-1788

In 1657, about twenty years before the birth of playwright George Farquhar, there was a riot in the Market Place in Derry when William Edmundson, a travelling Quaker preacher, was embroiled in a fracas with strolling actors and their audience. He was trying to dissuade a gathering and enthusiastic crowd from watching a group of English 'Stage-players and Rope-dancers' who were staging an impromptu show of drama and acrobatics. Edmundson loudly proclaimed that actors were a source of 'corruption and iniquity', the view held by the Puritan government in England at that time. A row then broke out between the preacher and onlookers, but Edmundson fared worst: to the cheers of the crowd, he was imprisoned in the city gaol. Undeterred, he continued to preach loudly through the bars of the gaol while the actors carried on their performances. Edmundson was only silenced when local people demanded that the Mayor intervene; he blocked the cell window and locked the prisoner in a leg-iron, thus quelling Edmundson's protests.

In his *Memoirs* published in 1720, Edmundson records his disgust at local entertainments, 'Profaneness was rampant: on Sundays their main entertainments were football or kales and nine-pins, shooting at the butts, quoits and bowling … stool-ball leaping and the like'. Some religious leaders in Derry no doubt shared his view and were just as forthright in expressing their disapproval of theatrical and musical entertainments, thus establishing a pattern – one which was to endure for over 200 years – whereby travelling actors, entertainers and showmen enlivened Derry's cultural life to the chagrin of its religious leaders.

This English troupe of 'Stage-players and Rope-dancers' was the first recorded mention of actors in Derry, and during the later seventeenth century more groups of strolling players came in search of work to Ireland, where anti-theatre attitudes were less rife. Their 'tours' had no pre-determined route or timetable, rather the actors, singers and dancers travelled on horseback or by stagecoach in an *ad hoc* fashion,

From Farquhar to Field Day

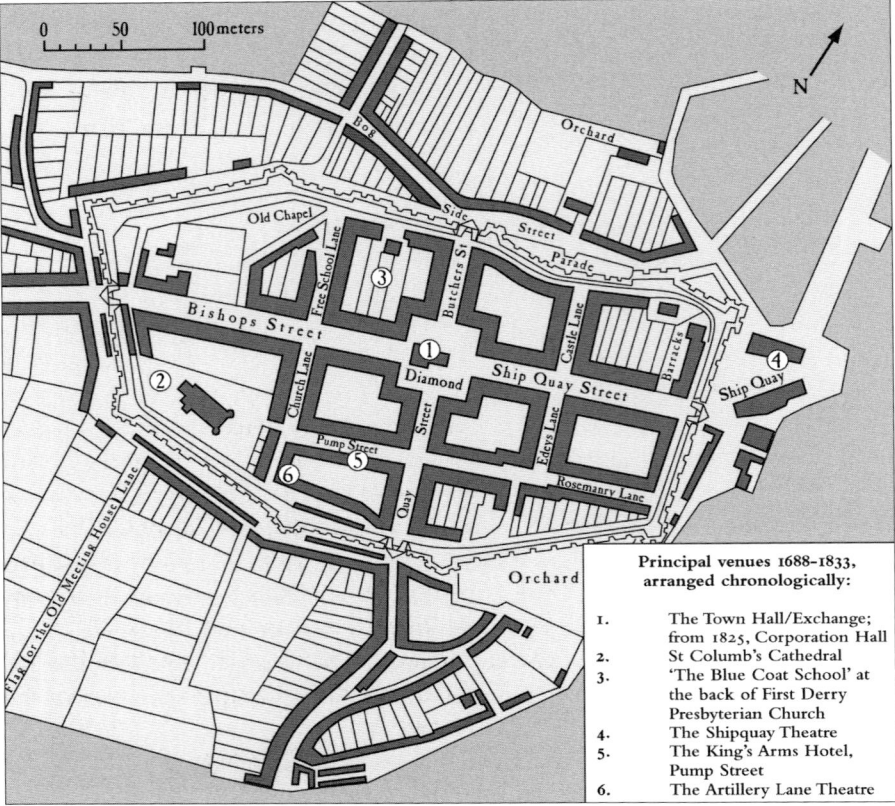

The approximate locations of the principal cultural venues between 1688 and 1833. All were clustered in and around the walled city.

moving from town to town in search of new audiences as interest in their performances waned. The pattern was illustrated in a rousing chorus of the time, sung by a group of travelling actors:

> Gallants, this Thursday night will be our last,
> Then without fail we pack for Belfast.

As there was no permanent theatre building in Derry, the entertainers used the Market House and surrounding square for performances of dramas, comedies and farces. The Market Place was in the centre of the walled city and lay at the junction of the four main thoroughfares: now Bishop Street, Butcher Street, Ferryquay Street and Shipquay Street. Older street names were then used: Bishop Street was originally in two parts, called 'Queen' and 'King' Streets, Butcher Street was 'The Shambles',

Earliest Beginnings, 1677-1788

and Ferryquay Street was known as 'Gracious Street'. Shipquay Street, then 'Silver Street', led north-eastwards from the Market Place, down a steep slope towards the Shipquay Gate and the quays. And it was reputedly here, in a narrow alleyway now known as Bank Lane, that Derry's first known playwright and actor was born.

George Farquhar

George Farquhar always claimed that he was born in Derry, and it is said that his mother had travelled to Derry toward the end of her pregnancy to give birth near family and friends. George was one of seven children of John Farquhar, Anglican curate of Stranorlar, a small town about twenty-five miles south-west of Derry. As a ten year old, the young George was a boarder at Derry's Free School, a forerunner of the present Foyle College, and he was thus at school in the city during the famous Siege. In December 1688, the local Apprentice Boys closed the city gates against the Jacobite forces, and the inhabitants of the walled city then held out for 105 days against the troops encamped outside. At this time Derry came into its own as a garrison town, and Farquhar's experience of living in this military environment no doubt gave added reality to the soldiering themes which later permeated his plays.[1]

After his father's premature death, Farquhar enrolled at Trinity College Dublin, following in the former's footsteps in training for the ministry. As the income of a curate's widow was quite meagre, Farquhar's studies were subsidised by Bishop Wiseman of Dromore, a relative on his mother's side. But the temptations of Dublin's social life intervened and soon Farquhar was combining his studies with visits to the Theatre Royal in Smock Alley, a favourite haunt of the 'college wits'. He quickly decided that his career did not lie within the Church and he abandoned his theological studies; thus began an association with drama which lasted for the rest of his life.

George Farquhar (c. 1677-1707), playwright and actor.

Farquhar became an actor in Smock Alley in 1696, on a weekly wage of 20s, and made his debut as the lead in *Othello*. But he was considered 'unpromising' as an actor, and as he also suffered from intense stage fright, he was thereafter given only minor roles. This, combined with an accident onstage, in which he seriously injured a fellow actor by forgetting to change his sword for a foil, led Farquhar to abandon live performance and turn instead to writing. He set off for London, at that time the centre of theatrical life. His first two plays, *Love in a Bottle* and *The Constant Couple*, were staged in London theatres to considerable acclaim, but Farquhar failed to benefit financially from them in any substantial way. This was a recurrent pattern in Farquhar's life, with the increasing success of his plays failing to be reflected in his monetary situation. His marriage in 1703 to a penniless widow with two children – apparently undertaken, not unlike one of his heroes, in the mistaken belief that she was an heiress – further drained his already perilous finances.

London audiences enjoyed Farquhar's plays because of their fresh blend of warmth, humour and country life, all of which were innovatory for city theatre audiences unaccustomed to such tales of simple, rural life. As was the norm at that time, Farquhar's dramas were interspersed with songs, musical interludes, dances and recitatives, all held together by witty dialogue, satirical comment and humorous plots.

Farquhar's most popular plays, *The Recruiting Officer* and *The Beaux Stratagem*, were written in the closing years of his life and have proved the most enduring of all his works. *The Recruiting Officer* explored the romantic adventures of soldiers in the provinces, and drew upon both Farquhar's acquaintance with the Derry garrison and his own – albeit limited – later military experience. Being perennially short of money, he had accepted a temporary post in 1704 as a recruiting lieutenant for the Grenadier Guards. The comedy was premiered in the Drury Lane Theatre on 8 April 1706 and was an immediate success, but Farquhar received only £16 2s 6d for the manuscript, and within a few months he was again seriously in debt.

His final play, *The Beaux Stratagem*, was written when he was terminally ill with tuberculosis. Again, this play was hugely successful on the London stage but Farquhar outlived the premiere by only eight weeks. He died on 20 May 1707 – ironically on the night of his own benefit as author – leaving a widow and two stepdaughters penniless and destitute. Farquhar had achieved popular acclaim as a playwright but financial success eluded him throughout his career.

After he had discovered the attractions of the London stage, Farquhar returned to Ireland only once: in 1704 he came to Dublin to take the title role in a benefit performance of *The Constant Couple* in the Smock Alley Theatre. He did not return to Derry after his school days. Nonetheless, it is with Derry that the name of George Farquhar is often associated, not just from birth but also from his most successful play, *The Recruiting Officer*, which derived much of its popularity from its military and provincial themes, reminiscent of Derry's own position as a defensive military outpost at the end of the seventeenth century.

THE
Recruiting Officer.
A
COMEDY.

As it is Acted at the

THEATRE ROYAL

IN

DRURY-LANE,

By Her MAJESTY's Servants.

Written by Mr. FARQUHAR.

—— *Captique Æolis, donisque coacti.*
Virg. Lib. II. Æneid.

LONDON:

Printed for BERNARD LINTOTT at the *Cross Keys* next
Nando's Coffee-House near *Temple-Bar.*

Price 1*s.* 6*d.*

Title page of George Farquhar's play The Recruiting Officer, *published in 1706. It was often performed in Derry, where its military themes struck a chord with local audiences.*

During the Siege, there had been considerable death and destruction in Derry and its hinterland. At least 7,000 people perished in the locality, through hunger, disease and battle, and the Town Hall in Market Place was destroyed beyond repair by 'ye enemies bombes'. In 1692, it was rebuilt on the same site, but in a more grandiose style, and it was here that the city's first scheduled drama performances took place in 1741.

Theatre in the Exchange

The new Market House, or the Exchange, as it was also known, dominated the main square within the walled city, and was built with money given to the city elders by King William III in reward for the city's resolute defence during the Siege. Designed by a Captain Neville, a military engineer, it was an impressive stone building on two floors, with the upper storey supported by seven pillars. The 1837 *Ordnance Survey Memoir* recorded that over 120 tons of timber and 40,000 laths were used in its construction.

Drama performances, concerts, grand balls, civic dinners, coteries and drums[2] were held in the elegant upper room, which had views over the four gates of the city, the River Foyle, Shipquay Place and the surrounding countryside. Bishop Pococke visited Derry in 1752 and remarked upon the 'handsome structure' of the Exchange, which was by then the regular venue for theatre performances and social entertainments for the gentry and elite. Local traders used the lower, open-air arcade as a market place and the basement was used for prison cells. These cells replaced the small gaol on the corner of Butcher Street, where the preacher Edmundson was imprisoned on his fateful visit to Derry.

In 1741, the Dublin newspaper *Faulkner's Journal* published the itinerary for Lewis Duval's company from the Smock Alley Theatre. The troupe were to perform in Derry's Exchange Building for a few days in late summer, probably during 'Race Week', when the annual races were held at the Ballyarnett Racecourse, and the city was filled with gentry from the surrounding area. Thereafter there are only fleeting references to theatre in Derry, as in 1755 when the actor and theatre manager Richard Elrington brought his English company to play in the Exchange. The company performed in Belfast and Lisburn, before arriving in Derry on Monday 24 March, their engagement coinciding with the Spring Assizes, another highpoint of the social season which drew the elite to the city. The company no doubt performed the same programme which they had given in Belfast: a variety of farces, pantomimes, tragedies and comedies, combined with 'popular' songs and dances. These productions included Shakespeare's *Romeo and Juliet*, *Julius Caesar* and *Hamlet*, Thomas Otway's perennially popular domestic tragedy *The Orphan: or, The Unhappy Marriage* and Colley Cibber's comedy *Love Makes a Man*.

Earliest Beginnings, 1677-1788

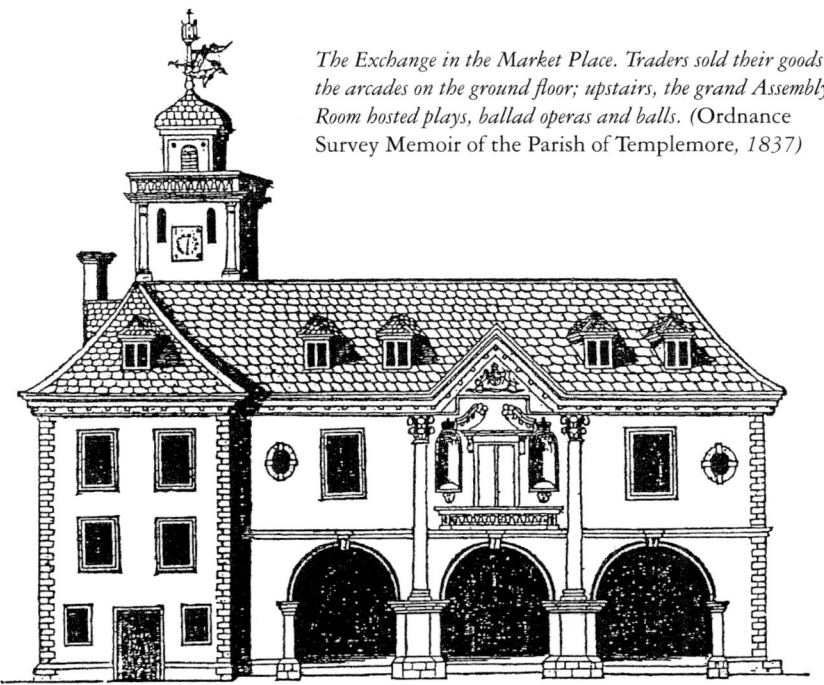

The Exchange in the Market Place. Traders sold their goods in the arcades on the ground floor; upstairs, the grand Assembly Room hosted plays, ballad operas and balls. (Ordnance Survey Memoir of the Parish of Templemore, *1837*)

Elrington's troupe consisted of eleven actors and singers – seven gentlemen and four ladies – and was fairly typical of the smaller eighteenth-century touring companies. Of the company, three were married couples: the Elringtons, the Longfields and the Wards. The remaining members were Mrs Mozeen, principal singer of the party, and Mr Pitt, a dancer and 'harlequin', who offered dancing lessons in Derry during the theatre run. In his press advertisement, Mr Pitt promised not to 'defraud' potential pupils, as had previous visiting dance masters to Derry – presumably he had heard that the profession of dancing master was not held in the highest regard in the city.

Thomas Ryder's company came to Derry for a four-month run in the winter of 1769/70. Ryder seems to have benefitted from the paucity of theatre in the country towns at that time, finding that 'the general business was excellent, and the benefits lucrative'. The company drew large audiences, especially as the party included the well-known, versatile actor and singer John O'Keeffe who delighted audiences with his songs and improvisations on standard plays. He gave the city one of its first 'tailored' pantomimes, *Harlequin in Derry: or, the Dutchman Outwitted*, appropriately adapted from his earlier comedy *Harlequin in Waterford*.

It was around this time that Charles Macklin, the renowned actor and playwright, is supposed to have played the Derry stage.

Charles Macklin

Macklin was born in Culdaff, County Donegal, allegedly the son of a Donegal publican. However, his exact origins remain shrouded in mystery, as it has also been claimed that he was descended from gentry who had lost substantial lands in Donegal for their support of the Jacobite cause. What is known is that the family moved to Dublin in the early 1700s, where the young Macklin became enamoured of the stage. Around 1716, he moved to London to begin acting, having changed his name – originally 'Cathal McLaughlin' – to Charles Macklin to make it more acceptable to English audiences.

There followed a lengthy career on the London stage, in the Covent Garden and Drury Lane Theatres, where one of his early leading roles was in Farquhar's *The Recruiting Officer*. However, it was Macklin's portrayal of Shylock, a role which he made his own for over fifty years, which was to be his lasting memorial. His masterful characterisation of Shylock, in which it was said that 'he rescued the character from the clutches of the low comedian', was such that Alexander Pope said of Macklin:

Charles Macklin (c.1699-1797) as 'Sir Gilbert Wrangle'. (By kind permission of Dr Sean Beattie, Macklin Festival)

> This is the Jew
> That Shakespeare drew.

Macklin had a lengthy and acrimonious career on the London and provincial stages, in the course of which he controversially converted from Catholicism to Protestantism. In mid-life he began to write his own plays, producing *Love a La Mode* in the later 1750s. It proved to be an outstanding and lasting success, and was repeatedly produced in London theatres and on the Derry stage (there in a musical version) for several decades. Like Farquhar, however, Macklin died penniless, leaving his third wife to deal with the effects of his bankruptcy, and to struggle on with a young family.

The Shipquay Theatre

Travelling companies continued to visit Derry during the early 1770s, developing the public's appetite for plays, ballad operas and pantomime, and attracting full houses at the high points in the social calendar, the Quarterly Assizes and Race Week. But a visit by Michael Atkins' Belfast theatre company in 1773 was a turning point in two respects: it was the first time that a Northern-based company had given a theatre season in Derry, and its manager, Atkins, was subsequently instrumental in establishing Derry's first purpose-built theatre. Thus began a link in theatre management between Belfast and Derry which was to last for over 100 years.

In summer 1774, the *Journal* advertised that a new theatre would soon open on the Shipquay. It was to be built on reclaimed land, roughly on the site of the present Guildhall. This, the city's first theatre, was a collaboration between local builder William Stewart and theatre manager Michael Atkins. Stewart owned and built the theatre, and leased it to Atkins for use when his theatre company was in Derry. The theatre itself was a simple wooden structure with a single room as the auditorium, and the *Journal* described the interior as having 'pit and gallery laid together'. The visiting actor John Bernard was less generous, derisively describing it as 'merely a temporary erection'. In spite of its basic simplicity, the Shipquay Theatre hosted hundreds of dramas, operas, farces and pantomimes during the next fifteen years, replacing the Exchange as the new home of elite entertainments. On 10 June 1774, the *Journal* added to the sense of anticipation in the city by publishing Atkins' promise that he would be bringing 'a company of players ... superior to any that have performed in this city for several years'. This was followed by a warning from the manager, Michael Atkins, that he expected a rush on the opening night and therefore 'no gold coin would be changed at the door'.

Atkins chose Farquhar's play *The Constant Couple* as the main attraction on the opening night, 5 August 1774. The significance of this particular play was not lost upon local theatre-goers: they recognised the staging of Farquhar's comedy as a fitting tribute to his association with Derry, in much the same way as later Derry audiences appreciated the premiere of Brian Friel's *Translations* in September 1980. Admission on the opening night was a uniform 2*s* to all parts of the theatre, and the auditorium was packed by 7 p.m. with people keen to see Farquhar's play, which was paired with George Colman's two-act farce *The Deuce is in Him*, and additional songs and dances. For this opening night there was no 'half-price admission' after 9p.m., which was the norm on all other evenings.

The opening performance was prefaced by a forty-four-line address by a Mr Wilmot, one of Atkins' actors, in which he drew comic parallels between the ending of the Siege and the opening of Derry's new theatre:

> Then spite of walls – or you in martial plight,
> E'er prompt for Life and Truth and Vict'ry to fight …
> Each gate shall open to dramatic laws
> And crowding hands shall greet us with applause.

Michael Atkins

By 1774, Derry's new theatre manager, Michael Atkins, was already a veteran of the Irish stage. He had been an actor in the Smock Alley Theatre in Dublin since he was fifteen, and had toured in Belfast and other provincial towns since his early twenties. His ambitions, however, quickly extended beyond acting and he took over as manager of the Belfast theatre in 1773, where he established his own troupe as the first resident theatre company in the north of Ireland. Atkins' company had about a dozen players but was also a family business, as it included his Belfast-born wife, the former Catherine Hutton, an actress and singer, and his daughter; both sang and played the harpsichord onstage. Atkins' son, also named Michael, acted and built the scenery. Atkins himself was theatre manager, stage director, financial controller, singer and actor; in addition, he was reputedly a good violinist.

The first season lasted for four and a half months, between 4 August and 26 December, with performances three times a week, on Mondays, Wednesdays and Thursdays. This increased to nightly during Race Week in early August, when Derry's streets bustled with fashionable crowds. Newspaper advertisements for the races in 1777 and 1778 advertised 'public ordinaries, balls or plays each night', and Atkins' company returned to Derry every August during the later 1770s, confident of attracting 'bumper houses' to the theatre. In return, theatre patrons were presented with lengthy and varied performances; two plays per night were the norm, with dances, songs and musical interludes, and an evening's entertainment rarely ended before midnight.

For the next fifteen years, Derry audiences enjoyed repeated performances of their favourite plays, such as Farquhar's comedies, dramas by Molière and a masque by

Milton. Shakespeare's plays remained especially popular with presentations of *As You Like It* in December 1774, *The Merchant of Venice* in June 1782, and *Hamlet*, *Macbeth* and *Romeo and Juliet* during the 1783 summer season. But these productions differed from the modern dramatic norm; they were loosely adapted musical versions of the plays, interwoven with songs, dances and instrumental interludes. Contemporary legislation forbade the performance of purely dramatic performances in theatres other than in London's Drury Lane and Covent Garden, so theatres in the provinces staged their own musical versions of the popular plays of the dramatic repertoire. As a result of this, theatre seasons in Derry between 1774 and 1788 were exceedingly musical in tone and content, with performances on the harpsichord and songs by Michael Atkins' wife and daughter, and guest appearances by amateur 'Gentlemen' flautists.

Ballad operas became particularly popular in Derry, with the first advertised staging of *The Beggar's Opera* on 18 August 1779, the beginning, perhaps, of a love for operetta in the city. Bickerstaffe's musical interlude *The Recruiting Serjeant* and Dibdin's operetta *The Quaker* were also presented to great acclaim in autumn 1782 and then given repeat performances in the same season – an unusual accolade in a city where the newness of a production was a major attraction. Opera enthusiasts could buy copies of the opera libretti for 6½*d* and opera glasses in George Douglas's bookshop in the Diamond. At this time, Douglas was also proprietor of the *Journal* and his early knowledge of the content of theatre seasons probably enabled him to stock his bookshop in advance. In addition, Douglas sold music paper, music books and German flutes, and was the first music retailer in the city before 1800.

In 1782, there was competition between the rival theatre companies of Michael Atkins and Myrton Hamilton, who vied for tenancy at the theatre during the profitable summer season. An agreement was reached, with Hamilton's company having the theatre during June, while Atkins' troupe had an extended autumn season between August and early December. For this run, Atkins offered season tickets at a guinea each, with guaranteed admission to all performances. Theatre tickets cost 2*s* in 1774 but had risen to 2*s* 2*d* by 1782. In view of this price increase, Atkins' subscription ticket offered a good bargain to theatre patrons and endeared him to his Derry public. But notwithstanding Atkins' apparent generosity, the Shipquay Theatre was a profitable enterprise. During June 1783, for example, Atkins' share of the theatre takings amounted to £25 after all expenses had been paid. At this time, an agricultural labourer or a manual worker could expect to receive only 9*d* for a day's employment.

In autumn of that same year, a weak beam in the roof of the Shipquay Theatre made the building unsafe. The fault was rectified within two weeks, however, and the theatre declared ready for business again on 27 October. In the meantime the actors had gone to Sligo to perform but they reassembled in Derry to continue another sparkling season which lasted until February 1784. Derry was by then a 'staging post', with touring companies playing in the city *en route* to Sligo and the West of

Ireland, and then performing again on the return leg of the journey. This arrangement received advance billing in the press, with the promise of more performances in the city within a few weeks.

The presence of the garrison was also an important stimulus to theatre seasons. The *Journal* often commented upon a strong military presence amongst the audience and performances were often held 'Under the Patronage' of the officers and men of the garrison. The local Volunteers also played their part in Derry's theatrical life: during the 1783 season, their band was the resident orchestra at the Shipquay Theatre.

By 1784, the hastily built, wooden-framed theatre had been open for ten years and the likelihood of it becoming increasingly unsafe no doubt prompted Atkins to look for a new venue in Derry. In September of that year he announced that he would open 'a new theatre on an elegant plan', which could accommodate 'the polite audience of Londonderry'. But it was another five years before this theatre opened, and in the meantime Atkins worked at increasing the audience that he had already drawn to the Shipquay Theatre. During the 1785/6 season, he again offered subscription tickets. Although more expensive, at one and a half guineas, they were for a season lasting seven months, between November and May.

Within ten years of the opening of the Shipquay Theatre, 'the drama in Derry' – as the press referred to it – had been established on a secure and popular footing. Atkins had provided his Derry audiences with varied entertainments and fulfilled the promise made in 1774 to include 'all the new pieces that have appeared in London and Dublin theatres'. More importantly, he had secured enough finance to begin planning a new theatre, this time housed in a more substantial structure and in a central location within the walled city. This new theatre, which opened in October 1789, built upon Atkins' early achievements and brought drama and music in Derry to new heights.

Concerts

Concerts were rare in Derry before 1830, as in most Irish provincial towns during the eighteenth century. Some 'concerts' were advertised in the press but they were actually hybrid entertainments by visiting musicians which relied upon novelty features, dramatic interludes and freak-show elements to attract audiences. The musicians were diverse and unusual, and their musical accomplishments were usually secondary to their other attractions. In 1777, there were 'concerts' by a singing and dancing male giant and female dwarf, and in 1782, 'concerts' by the nine-year-old Master Jackson, who was 'skilled in Music both Theory and Practical and [had an] agility in Dancing'. In spring 1784, Derry had a lengthy stay by a certain 'Don Diego Decepio Visus' a self-styled 'Bee-keeper' from Lapland. Don Diego stayed in Derry for six weeks, benefiting from the crowds drawn by the Spring Assizes, giving daily performances of his 'Grand Medley of Entertainments'. He promised 'A Good Fire and Good Music in the Room' – with the precise nature of his 'act' (surely it didn't involve bees?) left tantalisingly unclear.

In all, there were about ten 'novelty' visits of this kind before the end of the 1780s, providing audiences with more of a 'curiosity-show' than a musical experience. Local musicians, who were few in number, do not seem to have given concerts. Instead, most music was heard in the theatre: in the songs and dances in the plays, in musical interludes between the acts, and in the perennially popular ballad operas. Surprisingly, therefore, out of this concert vacuum sprang Derry's first known music society, the Londonderry Musical Society, which was active for a brief yet concentrated period in the early 1780s.

The First Londonderry Musical Society

Only fragmentary details can be gleaned about this first society, drawn from a handful of advertisements for four concerts between 1780 and 1781. The members of the society must have been part of a small, close-knit group and would have known practice times and venues without the need for notification in the press. This type of small music society, in which professional men gathered together to 'sing glees', was common at the close of the eighteenth century. John Bernard, an Irish actor who often attended music society meetings in the larger provincial towns, said that the meetings were convivial social occasions when an exclusively male membership got together regularly 'to smoke a pipe and sing a song'. The Londonderry Musical Society was probably formed along these same lines.

Only four names appeared in press advertisements for the music society: James Acheson, the treasurer; Dr Gordon; John Shannon, the Cathedral organist, and John Augustus Kalener, a foreign musician. Acheson was a local merchant and an office-bearer in other local charitable bodies as treasurer of Derry's infirmary and poorhouse committees. Dr Gordon and John Shannon were jointly responsible for supplying subscribers' tickets to members, and as Cathedral organist, Shannon was one of the two professional musicians in the ranks of the society. It is probable that both he and Kalener gave musical leadership and received fees in return. These four members were a microcosm of the society as a whole, representing its three separate component strands: the city's professional and merchant classes, church musicians and a resident foreign musician.[3]

The music society gave several concerts during its first year, but only advertised at the start of an 'ensuing quarter' (as in July 1780) or the 'first of the ensuing half year' (as in December 1780), thus precluding any accurate estimate of the number given. But there seem to have been regular concerts between July and September 1780, followed by a second season from December 1780 to May 1781. Admission to the concerts was by subscribers' tickets, with concertgoers being warned that 'tickets could not be purchased at the door'. This might, however, have been a device to encourage ticket sales in advance. The repertoire at the concerts was probably the usual fare for this type of society: glee singing, duos, trios and some instrumental items, for which the menfolk would have been heartily applauded by their largely female audience.

The first and last of the four advertised concerts provide insights into this early music society. Both concerts were benefits for Kalener, the first probably as a reward for services already rendered. For the first concert, on 17 February 1780, tickets were available from Dr Gordon and John Shannon at 3s 3d each. This was expensive – the costliest theatre tickets at this time were 3s and the cheapest, 1s – underlining yet again the elite membership and patronage of the Londonderry Musical Society. The second benefit concert was an entirely different occasion, organised by Kalener for himself. In February 1781, he suddenly announced that he had become 'desirous of returning to his own country' but was 'unable to go for want of money'. There was no mention of the music society, and, in contrast with the earlier concert, tickets were priced much lower (at 2s 2d) and were available only from Kalener himself. This was a solo venture by Kalener, who was hoping to benefit personally from the financial generosity of society members whom he had tutored. After this concert, nothing further was heard of Kalener; his sudden departure probably meant that the society disintegrated without his professional guidance, since after February 1781 there was no further mention of it.

There was a single concert of 'Vocal and Instrumental Music and Ball' in February 1784 by local amateurs in aid of the 'Poor of the City'. The performers were not mentioned as music society members, but it is likely they were the remnants of the city's first music society giving a final charitable performance.

Social Entertainments

Derry also had a vibrant round of social entertainments which were designed to appeal to the gentry and garrison. These entertainments included music, plays, recitations and dance, and made their own contribution to the richness of the city's cultural life.

The *Journal* was first published in July 1772 and its advertising columns give a glimpse into the social life of the gentry and upper classes who lived in the nucleus of streets within the walled city. A notice appeared in September 1772 for a 'Public Ball' organised by a Mr Morris, a dancing master from Dublin, and he promised a full evening's entertainment, 'Tea, Cakes and Cards' and a performance of 'Part of a Play', followed by a 'Dance, to begin at six o'clock in the afternoon'. The event was in the Town Hall on 1 October, with tickets at 2s 2d for adults and 1s 1d for 'Young Masters and Misses', a cost far beyond the reach of the working classes of the city. The same edition of the *Journal* advertised a 'Charitable Assembly' in the Town Hall on Monday 14 October, this time organised by a Revd Mr Blackall, for 'the Benefit of the Widow Dunlap', with admission of 2*s* 2*d*. The early appearance of these two advertisements indicates that Derry, like other provincial towns in Ireland, already enjoyed a frequent round of balls, assemblies and coteries during the eighteenth century.

This activity increased during the five highpoints of the social calendar: Race Week in August and the Quarterly Assizes, when social entertainments were held daily. The city buzzed, with the upper classes keen to enjoy themselves. Only the wealthy elite in Derry could afford to attend these social events, which were modelled upon the larger and grander events held in London and Dublin. To keep themselves up to date with the latest songs, dances and plays from the two capital cities, Derry's aspiring socialites could buy copies of *The Fashionable Songster* and *The Gentleman's Magazine* in George Douglas's bookshop in the Market Place. Both these publications contained sheet music and verses of the latest popular songs.

Derry's larger balls and assemblies were held in the Exchange Building, while Neilson's Hotel in Pump Street[4] was used for the smaller balls and coteries held in the winter months. As with the theatre, it was the upper classes and the officers and men of the garrison who flocked to the dances. Members of leading Derry and Donegal families – the Ash, Ferguson, McCausland, Knox and Alexander families – were named as stewards at the balls, coteries and drums, alongside the captains and officers of the garrison.

From 1781, the Derry Assemblies were held fortnightly between December and February, when the services of the local garrison proved invaluable. The regimental band stationed in the city provided the 'Musick' for dancing at eight assemblies during the winter of 1784/5, and was paid 17*s* 4*d* per night for their services. Of course, this arrangement benefited the musicians of the garrison by providing additional income for the individual soldiers.

Another new entertainment was added during the winter of 1785, when a card-room opened in the Exchange on Thursday evenings. Here the 'Ladies and Gentlemen' of the city could meet to play cards and to dance from 7p.m. onwards for the relatively inexpensive admission of 1*s* 1*d*, a cost on a par with theatre tickets. The 'Company' was requested to appear 'in half dress', suggesting that a certain air of formality was still to be observed, even in these quieter winter months.

As with the theatre, the presence of the garrison was a key element in Derry's social life. The officers and men of the garrison not only provided audiences for the theatre and dance partners at the balls and coteries, but were themselves key guests at dinners and civic celebrations. Grand dinners were regularly held in the Exchange for the officers of regiments departing the city, complemented, of course, by equally 'Grand Dinners' for the officers of incoming regiments. In May 1782, the 'Gentlemen' of Derry held a Grand Dinner for Colonel Frazer and the officers of the

'Royal Regiment' who were about to leave 'to march to Dublin'; the following week this regiment was replaced by the entire 49th Regiment from Belfast, for whom more celebratory dinners were held. Of course, the men of the garrison made their own contribution to Derry's unique local celebrations, as in December 1786, when they 'fired three vollies' at the 'Shutting of the Gates' commemorations in the city square and then hosted 'a most elegant ball and supper' for the 'Ladies and Gentlemen' of the city. This was reciprocated the following week by an equally 'elegant' dinner given by a number of Derry's 'Gentlemen' for the officers of the 13th Regiment.

This range of social entertainments in Derry changed little during the later eighteenth century, except for an occasional increase in frequency when new regiments arrived at the garrison and the city's young ladies were keen to meet the new officers. These entertainments and the theatre remained the central focus of cultural life, providing social contact for the gentry, middle classes and the officers of the garrison.

Derry's social and cultural life was also periodically enlivened by visits from its celebrated – if eccentric – Anglican Bishop, Frederick Hervey, who was an ardent devotee of theatre and the arts.

The Earl Bishop, Frederick Hervey

Frederick Hervey was appointed Bishop of Derry in 1768, at that time the richest diocese in Ireland; eleven years later he succeeded to the title and estates of the Earl of Bristol, which made him a wealthy man in his own right. His family connections were also with the highest in the land – the Prince of Wales had attended his christening – and the wealth he inherited funded what was, even for those days, an extravagant lifestyle. Latterly he spent little time at his official Palace in Bishop Street in Derry, preferring instead to travel throughout Europe on the Grand Tour, collecting art treasures for the great houses he was building in Suffolk, Ballyscullion, and Downhill outside Castlerock.[5] The many 'Bristol' hotels in Europe today, which take their name from him, show the impression left on contemporaries by this flamboyant, worldly cleric, as he travelled with his entourage from place to place.

Hervey had diverse interests in Derry. He became passionately involved in the Volunteer Movement, which was set up during the later 1770s to defend Ireland against invasion by the French. Hervey manoeuvred himself into the position of Colonel-in-Chief of the Londonderry Volunteers, who invariably turned out in strength to greet him warmly on his returns to the city. Although no model spiritual leader of his own Anglican flock in Derry, Hervey was generous towards the city in material terms. He contributed £1,000 towards the construction of the new wooden bridge over the Foyle and donated towards the building of both First Derry Presbyterian church[6] and the Catholic Long Tower church. In return, when he died in 1803 and was buried at Bury St Edmunds, the 'people of Derry' showed their gratitude by

Portrait of the Earl Bishop, Frederick Hervey (1730-1803).

having an obelisk erected there in his memory. It was inscribed with details of his good works towards the people of all religions of the city, and ended with the tribute, 'He was the friend and protector of them all ... After thirty-five years' occupancy of the See of Derry, all hostile sects which had long entertained feelings of deep animosity towards each other were gradually softened and reconciled by his influence and example.'

For St Columb's Cathedral, Hervey paid for the erection of a lofty spire in 1798, but it proved to be unstable and had to be dismantled four years later. Hervey, however, had little interest in the music of his own Cathedral, which suffered from comparative neglect during the later eighteenth century in that the full choral service was infrequently performed. Nonetheless, it was in Derry's churches where the poorer people of the city, excluded from the theatre and social entertainments by the high admission costs, could enjoy some music.

Music in St Columb's Cathedral

St Columb's Cathedral was completed in 1633, the first Anglican Cathedral to be built in Britain after the Reformation. Like the Exchange, it was built with the financial help of the London Guilds, and their contribution of £3,800 is acknowledged in a tablet in the porch of the Cathedral, with the words:

> If Stones Could Speake
> Then Londons prayse
> Should sound who
> Built this church and
> Cittie from the grounde.

The earliest recorded musical performance in St Columb's Cathedral was in December 1789, during a three-day celebration of the centenary of the Siege. A procession of dignitaries and townspeople, led by the Earl Bishop, paraded to the Cathedral for a special service, where selections from Handel's oratorio *Judas Maccabeus* were sung by the Cathedral Choir. The choice of this particular oratorio for the Siege commemoration service was significant, given its allegorical theme of victory over the enemy and its anti-Jacobite origins.[7] The Cathedral Choir was probably augmented for the occasion, as it was quite small at this time. It was, however, unusual in having both boys and girls in its ranks.

Although the music in St Columb's was undistinguished during the eighteenth century, visitors to the city did note that the Cathedral had a 'fine organ'. It was a good instrument for its time, with three manuals, nineteen stops and 'In all One thousand one hundred and eighty pipes.' The organ was installed in 1748 by Dublin organ-builder Philip Hollister and was a gift from the then Bishop of Derry, George Stone, later Archbishop of Ireland. Local folklore has it that the original mahogany case, which still stands in the west gallery of the Cathedral, was carved from wood salvaged from a ship of the Spanish Armada which had foundered off the north coast of Ireland in 1588. The quiet life of the Cathedral was interrupted by an unexpected incident in November 1778, when 'some evil-minded persons' vandalised the new organ. Several organ pipes were broken and the intricate carved casing was damaged, prompting a newspaper advertisement offering a £5 reward for information leading to the arrest of the culprits.

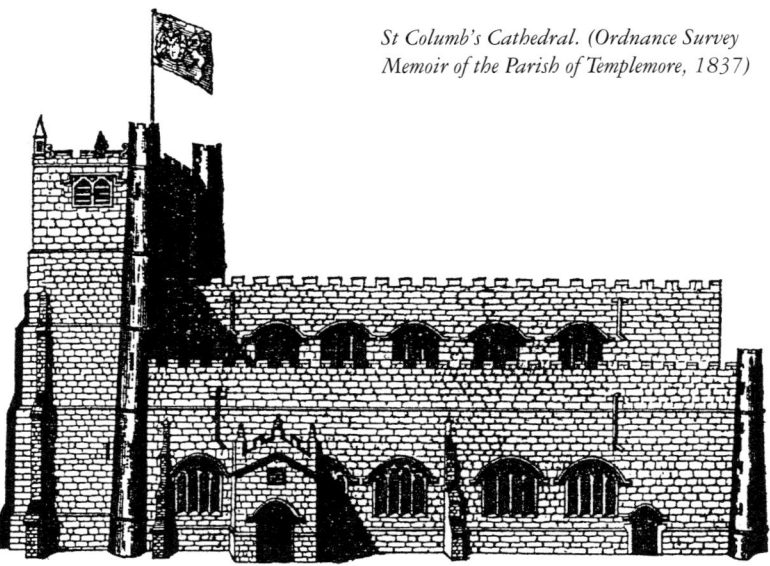

St Columb's Cathedral. (Ordnance Survey Memoir of the Parish of Templemore, 1837)

Between 1699 and 1817, the position of Cathedral organist was concentrated in two local families: the Garraways (father and son) and the Shannons (father, John, followed by son William around 1800).[8] The post was a joint appointment from 1791 onwards, with the organist taking on responsibility for training the choir as well. John Shannon, organist since 1770, was paid an additional £10 per annum for this new duty. But Shannon had always augmented his organist's salary with other sources of income: he gave private music tuition in Derry and, as previously mentioned, was singing tutor to the Londonderry Musical Society. Shannon was one of the first private advertisers in the *Journal*, selling harpsichords, spinets and guitars, and, by 1796, the first pianos to reach the Derry market.

After the 1789 centenary service in the Cathedral, the procession of city notables moved to First Derry on the West Wall, home of the singing 'Blue Boys'. There, the minister, Revd Robert Black, preached a sermon and the congregation joined with the boys in the singing of unaccompanied psalms.

The Singing Blue Boys

The 'Blue Boys', or the 'Singing Boys' as the *Journal* sometimes called them, were the first known leaders of church singing in Derry. Their name came from their uniform: a blue coat with a yellow collar worn with boots, hats and breeches. The use of local 'charity children' (i.e. orphans and street urchins) to lead congregational singing was common in Anglican churches during the early eighteenth century, and similar types of 'singing schools' were also found in Scottish Presbyterian congregations.

Apart from Derry's school, there was only one other known 'Blue Coat' school in Ireland – in Dublin – but no links are known between the two institutions. However, they both employed the same educational model: the boys were housed, clothed, fed and educated in return for singing in church. After a boy's voice had broken, he was apprenticed 'to a Protestant Master' with the opportunity to learn a trade. The Derry schoolhouse did not have the architectural splendour of its Dublin counterpart, or its longevity, but it was a unique institution within Derry in laying the foundations of choral singing in the city. Derry's four Presbyterian congregations and their choral societies built upon this tradition during the nineteenth century.

The exact date of the establishment of the Blue School in Derry is unclear: the records of the First Derry Church suggest 'about 1773', but the City Corporation records mention a payment of £12 'To ye Charity boys' in February 1744. Samuel Lewis's 1837 *Topographical Dictionary* dates the foundation even earlier, to the 1730s. Regardless of the precise date of inauguration, the Blue School was already operating in a small building at the back of First Derry in Meeting-House Row when the *Journal* began publication in 1772, as the first edition of the paper mentioned a hymn which the boys had sung at a service and said that the school had become a charity five years earlier.

The school grew from small beginnings: it had just eight boys in 1773; five years later there were two more boys, and by 1798 the number had reached 'twelve singing boys'. The *Journal* provided detailed accounts of the costs of feeding, clothing and teaching the boys. In 1773, the finances of the school were in a healthy state, testament to the value which the city inhabitants attached to it. The accounts recorded a credit balance of over £22, even before inclusion of two years' contributions of £24 due from the City Corporation. However, little is known of the musical accomplishments of the Blue Boys, except that in addition to their singing of unaccompanied psalms in the Presbyterian church, they occasionally sang anthems in the Cathedral to organ accompaniment.

Between 1778 and 1820, the Blue School was funded by charity sermons, held alternately in First Derry and the Cathedral, and after each service the *Journal* listed the names of those who had attended and contributed to upkeep of the school.[9] The newspaper also mentioned sizeable donations from those absent on the day. The contributors included most of Derry's leading citizens, showing that the Blue School had financial support and goodwill from both its own Presbyterian congregation and from the Anglican Church. In 1794, the *Journal* commented upon this harmonious relationship between the two major denominations in the city and described the success of the charity sermons as evidence of 'the amiable intercourse between the Church and the Presbyterian Congregations in Derry'. The sermon in February of that year was in the Presbyterian church and was attended by 'The members of the Corporation, the colonel and officers of the Donegal Militia and the principal families of the Established Church.' The Mayor and clergy acted as collectors and the sermon raised over £77. Contributions rose steadily in following years to reach £93 in 1799.

The final charity sermon was in 1820 and was accompanied by an appeal for extra generosity; it raised over £150. But musical practices had changed with the new century, and within two years the Blue Boys Choir had been disbanded and a precentor appointed to lead the psalmody in First Derry. By 1824, the school had lost its privileged charitable position and was opened to all Protestant children upon payment of one penny a day. The musical dimension of the school also declined; the advertisement for the new schoolmaster's post did not specify the ability to teach vocal music as a particular requirement.

Thus ended Derry's first School of Music, the Blue School, which attained a unique status in the city, being the single sphere in which church music, education and charitable benevolence intertwined for the benefit of Presbyterianism, which was to remain the dominant religious force in Derry during the next fifty years.

John Wesley in Derry

By the end of the 1780s, Derry was a prosperous city with a population close to 4,500 people. Houses within the walled city now accommodated fashionable gentry and the upper classes, alongside an expanding merchant class eager to see the city grow in prosperity. The quays buzzed with commercial activity, both in goods and passengers trade, such that the Shipquay area was no longer an appropriate location for the city theatre. In addition, the steep incline of Shipquay Street, which led towards the Shipquay Theatre, was difficult terrain for the coaches that transported the 'Ladies and Gentlemen' to the theatre. The increased popularity of the visiting theatre companies and musicians also meant that the small Shipquay Theatre had become inadequate for the needs of the elite classes, merchant families and the men of the garrison. The theatre in Artillery Lane that opened in 1789 was to become the new elite venue for visiting artistes and their audiences.

There were, however, other visitors apart from travelling actors and musicians. John Wesley, the founder of Methodism, made his first visit to Derry in May 1765 and claimed that he had preached in Linenhall Square to 'the largest congregation [he had] seen in the North of Ireland'. He returned for nine more visits, the last being in 1789, when he preached at the newly built Methodist chapel on the East Wall, within earshot of the new theatre. Wesley's views on theatre were well known: he regarded the theatre as 'the sink of all profaneness and debauchery', a view which may have found support among many of his Derry listeners. By 1802, the author Robert Sampson noted 'a remarkable vein of piety' in the city's inhabitants. He also perceived 'an air of superiority' among the Presbyterian congregations, which he attributed to their industry in the manufacture of linen.

Not all clerics shared Wesley's views on theatre. Within a year of opening, the new theatre in Artillery Lane hosted a visit by the Bishop of Derry, Frederick Hervey, Earl of Bristol. In November 1790, on his last visit to Derry, Hervey rode through the city to attend a Grand Dinner and then a performance at the theatre. At that time he was Colonel-in-Chief of the Londonderry Volunteers and it was they who formed a Guard of Honour for his triumphant procession towards his palace, where he dined before his evening's entertainment in Artillery Lane. Hervey's visit to the theatre confirmed its status as the new home of elite entertainments for the gentry, garrison and upper classes. The Artillery Lane Theatre was soon to fulfil its early promise during Derry's 'Golden Age' of drama.

Two

THE GOLDEN AGE, 1789-1833

In the summer of 1796, an exotic figure passed over Derry's wooden bridge towards the city. It was the 39-inch Polish dwarf and self-styled 'Count' Joseph Boruwlaski on his way to give a concert in the Artillery Lane Theatre. His guitar playing – and probably the novelty of his size – proved such an attraction that he gave a second unplanned concert, this time under the 'Patronage of the Officers of the Garrison'. Boruwlaski visited the city again in July 1798, by which time Derry had a much-increased garrison as a result of the heightened political and social tension caused by the rebellion of the United Irishmen. This had already brought about the closure of the Belfast theatre, but in Derry the presence of the garrison held the peace and allowed its theatre to remain open and relatively unaffected. Nonetheless Boruwlaski's touring party would have been noticed immediately as strangers by the fearful city inhabitants who, wary of outsiders, closed the city gates at nightfall.

On both visits, Boruwlaski provided a diverse programme: he played the guitar and sang, held a 'Concert and Ball', sold his 'memoirs' and 'exhibited himself'. His audiences were drawn from the upper classes of Derry and Donegal and the officers and men of the garrison, who thronged the theatre for entertainment and company. Perhaps they were intrigued by the story that Boruwlaski's wife, a woman of normal stature, would lift him onto the mantelpiece when she was annoyed with him and leave him there to struggle down alone.

During Boruwlaski's first visit, the French traveller De Latocnaye was on a walking tour of Ireland and stopped for a few days in Derry, where he was impressed by the city's apparent wealth. He commented that, 'Londonderry does not have the air of an Irish town', referring to the evidence of commerce and industry which he had not found elsewhere. At the close of the eighteenth century, Derry was a thriving port with a population approaching 5,000 people and newer houses extending outside the walled city.

The Golden Age, 1789-1833

John Kay's later eighteenth-century engraving of Joseph Boruwlaski, drawn while he was in Edinburgh. (Author's collection)

The Artillery Lane Theatre

The Artillery Lane Theatre, where Boruwlaski performed, had opened in 1789 and was Derry's most popular, successful and profitable theatre before the opening of the New Royal Opera House in August 1877. Programming at Artillery Lane included concerts, dramas, ballad operas, variety shows, lectures, and even equestrian displays. From the first, the local press provided a wealth of information in theatre advertisements, previews and reviews, reflecting the favoured position which the theatre held in the city's social life. Grand balls, assemblies and coteries were also held at the nearby King's Arms Hotel in Pump Street, and after 1826 in the new Corporation Hall in Diamond Square. Between 1790 and the early 1830s, this rich variety of entertainments gave Derry its first Golden Age of theatre, when the Artillery Lane Theatre was always 'filled to overflowing' and patronised by all the 'fashion and beauty of the city'.

The new theatre was located in a corner site in Artillery Lane at the junction of Widow's Row and London Street, and within easy walking distance of the houses of the gentry in Pump and Ferryquay Streets. The theatre was quite small – only 70ft long by 40ft broad by 23ft high – but audiences at that time preferred small auditoria with an intimate atmosphere where they could comfortably see and be seen by their friends and acquaintances. In spite of its compactness, the theatre could hold 300 people; at least that number attended in March 1802, when the evening's takings amounted to over £51. The theatre had boxes, the gallery and the pit; the boxes the most expensive, followed by the pit and then the gallery. There was half-price admittance after 9 p.m. and servants could physically reserve seats for their masters. Alternatively, tickets could be bought in advance in George Douglas's bookshop in the Diamond, where a box office opened in 1790.

As at the earlier Shipquay Theatre, Michael Atkins was the proprietor and was greatly beloved by his Artillery Lane audience. By June 1802, he had been associated with theatre in Derry for over thirty years and the *Journal* paid tribute to his 'conduct ... both in his private and public character', which had earned him 'the approbation of the polite and generous audience of Derry'.

His first season in Artillery Lane was a lengthy run, lasting from August 1789 until the end of June the following year. Music featured prominently, with performances on the German flute (by an unnamed local 'Gentleman'), songs by a young lady 'lately returned from America' and harpsichord pieces by Mrs Atkins, in addition to the usual round of operas, songs and dances. 'Benefit nights' for the actors and singers alone lasted through May and June. Benefits were a crucial source of income for individual actors, as the theatre manager did not pay them regular wages. The financial arrangements were complex in that the takings, after costs were deducted, were divided equally amongst the players, but with the manager having four additional shares on account of the scenery and costumes. Thus the benefit nights provided

The Golden Age, 1789-1833

a much-needed bonus for the players, when their individual popularity and their resourcefulness in 'rounding up' an audience determined their incomes. Frequently the actors would call at the houses of the gentry and with local shopkeepers to invite them to attend their benefits. Usually Derry audiences did respond with 'bumper houses', but sometimes attendance was disappointing, as in April 1798 when Mrs Caulfield thanked the 'small, but truly respectable audience' which had turned up for her benefit.

During the 1790s, Atkins had presented his Derry audiences with much the same repertoire as he had provided in the Shipquay Theatre, but in more lavish surroundings. An evening performance was still wide ranging and lengthy, with various combinations of drama, farce, ballad opera, musical interludes and dance. Ballad operas were especially popular in Derry; during every season there were repeated performances of *The Beggar's Opera*, *Inkle and Yarico*, *Love in a Village* and *Rosina*, providing a familiar diet which the theatre-goers must have enjoyed. Each evening, two, and sometimes three, plays were presented with interludes of songs and dances between the acts, requiring the players to be versatile. In a single evening a player might be onstage as a dancer, singer, musician and actor. Folk dances were particularly popular, with Highland flings, clog dances, reels and strathspeys drawing huge applause and calls for encores. Performances could last four hours or longer, beginning in the early evening and ending just before midnight. Again, as in the Shipquay Theatre, the seasons were unpredictable in length; in 1793 the season lasted eight weeks, in 1803 it extended to eighteen weeks. The only certainty was that performances would increase from thrice weekly to nightly during Assizes and Race Weeks to accommodate visitors flocking to the city.

Atkins occasionally subleased the theatre to other managers, as in the 1794/5 season, when Robert Owenson, father of Sydney Owenson the author (the later Lady Morgan), took over the theatre for a few weeks. Owenson had been touring in the provinces, including Kilkenny, Sligo and Cork, on his travels. He was a renowned singer and musician, as well as an accomplished actor, and he was accompanied on tour by the talented young actress Miss Walstein. In Derry, Owenson did not advertise his performances in the local papers, relying instead upon daily handbills. His daughter recalled poor audiences, with the company playing to rows of 'empty benches'. Owenson himself explained the poor turnout by the political turbulence at the time, in that many areas of Ulster were being terrorised by the 'Peep O'Day Boys'.[10] But perhaps Derry audiences just preferred the familiarity of Atkins and his Belfast troupe, with whom they had their own particular rapport.

The 1790s were a time of social and political turbulence in Ireland, but in Derry the garrison provided protection from the ongoing dangers. The city and surrounding area had several volunteer companies, including the Londonderry Fusiliers, the Londonderry Independent Company and the 'Blue Volunteers'. These formations, in addition to the regiments stationed in the garrison, ensured a high military presence in the city, and as in the 1780s, the garrison, its regiments and local volunteer units continued to make their own contributions to cultural life.

The Derry Garrison

The 1798 and 1799 theatre seasons in particular strengthened the link between the theatre and the local military. Due to political unrest, Belfast actors were reluctant to travel to Derry, so the officers from the garrison stepped into the breach and undertook the male leads in some productions. In January 1798, the officers donned theatrical costumes to appear in the comedy *The Wheel of Fortune* and three months later the actors and several 'Gentlemen of the City' were joined by the officers in the plays *The Beaux Stratagem* and *No Song, No Supper*. The press commented that 'the most brilliant audience ever witnessed in this place' attended that evening, indicating that the social standing of the theatre-goers and the spectacle they presented was as important a measure of a theatre's success as the quality of its productions. An entire cavalry company, in full uniform, attended another performance in April, held in aid of the 'Derry Volunteer Cavalry' and the services of the garrison were employed again in January 1799 when the French Band of the Somerset Regiment contributed musical interludes between the plays. Quite often, the theatre manager returned the favour by presenting plays and ballad operas with military themes. *The Poor Soldier*,

> **THEATRE.**
> By Permission of the Worshipful Andw. Ferguson, Esq; Mayor.
> On Friday Evening the 26th Inst will be presented a Celebrated new Comedy (never performed here) called
> *A Cure for the Heart-Ache.*
> The Principal Characters by the
> OFFICERS OF THE GARRISON.
> With a Farce as will be expressed in the Bills.

Press advertisement for Derry's Artillery Lane Theatre, where the officers of the garrison frequently appeared as actors. (Londonderry Journal, *23 January 1798*)

THEATRE, L:DERRY.

By Permission of the Worshipful THOS. LECKY, Esq. Mayor.

On THURSDAY EVENING Sept. 8, 1808,
(The Fourth Night of Mr. GORDON'S Engagement,)
Will be presented the COMEDY of

LOVER'S VOWS.

Baron Wildenhaim,	—	Mr. HAMERTON
Count Caffel,	—	Mr. GORDON;
Frederick,	—	Mr. MUNRO;
Anhalt,	—	Mr. KELLY;
Verdun,	—	Mr. THOMAS;
Landlord,	—	Mr. PITMAN;
Cottager,	—	Mr. TROTTER.
Agatha Friburgh,	—	Mrs. MOURTON
Amelia Wildenhaim,	—	Mrs. SKINNER;
Cottager's Wife,	—	Mrs. TROTTER.

Between the Play and Farce a comic Song by
By Mr. ADAMSON.

To which will be added the favourite FARCE of The

Irishman in London.

Murtoch Delany,	—	Mr. HAMERTON
Edward,	—	Mr. GORDON
Captain Seymour,	—	Mr. KIRK;
Collooney,	—	Mr. KELLY;
Old Froft,	—	Mr. THOMAS;
Simon,	—	Mr. TROTTER
Caroline,	—	Mrs. SKINNER
Louifa,	—	Mrs. MOURTON
Cubba,	—	Mrs. TROTTER.

Tickets to be had at Mr. M'Corkell's, Diamond.—Places for the Boxes to be taken at Mr. Strickland's, Hair-Dreffer, Pump-ftreet.

To prevent any Confufion arifing from particular Tunes being called for during the Performance; the following Arrangement will be attended to, viz:—At the End of the fourth Act of Play, "God fave the King" will be played; End of the Play, "St. Patrick's Day;" and at the End of the firft Act of the Farce, "Rule Britannia," which Mr. Skinner hopes will meet the Approbation of the Audience.

An 1808 playbill from the Artillery Lane Theatre. Note the compromise reached on contentious 'party songs'. (By kind permission of the Deputy Keeper of the Public Record Office of Northern Ireland, PRONI, T2591/1)

The Soldier's Daughter, *The Serjeant's Wife* and Farquhar's *The Recruiting Officer* were popular choices, which undoubtedly raised Atkins' stock with the local garrison. Overall, these two seasons were outstanding in terms of attendance, it being fashionable to be seen at the theatre in the company of the garrison, which enjoyed a privileged social position amongst the gentry and business people of Derry.

Nonetheless, underlying political tensions occasionally came to the surface. During the 1808 season, some members of the audience made requests for particular 'party' songs. These requests were at first discouraged by the theatre management, which was anxious to avoid confrontations. Then, in an attempt to be seen as even-handed – or, as was printed on subsequent handbills, 'to prevent any Confusion' – there was a change of tactics. Instead, the precise order in which a number of 'Irish' and 'English' songs would be sung was published: 'God Save the King', followed by 'St Patrick's Day' and finally, 'Rule Britannia'.

In autumn 1808, Atkins retired as theatre manager, after thirty-five years' involvement with Derry, during which he had opened two theatres and established an unrivalled tradition of drama, opera and music. He sold his theatre leases to Thomas Bellamy, son of English musician and composer Richard Bellamy. Atkins returned to Belfast, where he died in April 1812 aged sixty-five; he is buried in Friar's Bush Cemetery on Stranmillis Road.

Atkins' Successors: Thomas Bellamy and Montague Talbot

Bellamy (1770-1843) was the only Derry theatre manager to have a musical rather than a theatrical background, having started his career as a boy treble in the choir of Westminster Abbey. A move to Ireland in 1794, in search of property which he had inherited from his Irish maternal grandmother, took him to Dublin, where he became involved in theatre. This early flirtation with the stage led to his purchase of the leases of the Belfast, Newry and Derry theatres, which Bellamy attempted to run single-handedly for the next two years. Bellamy's lack of contacts in the Irish theatrical world, combined with his musical rather than dramatic background, probably led to the failure of his speculations in theatre management. By mid-1810, he had sold the leases to another Englishman, Montague Talbot, an experienced actor on the Irish stage. Talbot remained manager of the Belfast and Derry theatres for the next ten years. Bellamy returned to London and became a leading singer in the Covent Garden and Drury Lane Theatres. The remainder of his life was devoted to music, in public performance and in the foundation of a Logierian Academy of piano tuition.[11]

Talbot, the new manager, had an unusual background. Born in Boston, USA, he came from a respectable English family background with Irish connections. He initially trained for the Bar at Trinity College Dublin, but then decided to abandon law and go on the stage, acting at first under the name of 'Montague'. This change of career cost him a £30,000 legacy, since he was disinherited by a wealthy uncle who disapproved of theatre. (Even at the end of the eighteenth century, the view of actors as 'rogues and vagabonds' was still widely held.) Unabashed, Talbot made his debut in Covent Garden in 1794, and then performed throughout England and Scotland, becoming well known as a comic actor. He moved to Dublin, allegedly to avoid being implicated in the 1795 scandal of the so-called 'Shakespeare Forgeries'. Talbot had discovered a close friend, William Henry Ireland, in the act of forging what purported to be 'new' and unpublished plays by Shakespeare, with a view to touting them to the highest bidder. Whatever Talbot's motives, he then joined the Irish theatre circuit and toured the provinces, and it was while acting in Derry in October 1800 that he married a young actress called Emily Coore Binden.

Talbot (1773-1831) took over as manager in 1810, and, like Atkins, soon developed a close rapport with his Derry audiences, such that the theatre became popularly known as 'Talbot's Theatre at the Newgate' rather than by its proper name. After a few months he closed the theatre for 'some alteration and entire new painting and decoration', but he was soon entertaining his theatre-goers again with lengthy seasons of opera, drama and farce.

The 1813 season, which lasted between 28 August and 1 December, was particularly brilliant in terms of visiting actors and musicians, and bore the hallmarks of Talbot's connections with the Dublin stage. He brought a fifteen-strong company to Derry, soon joined by other Dublin performers. In November, Mr Montgomery, already a well-known singer from the Theatre Royal, arrived and took the lead role in ballad operas for the remainder of the season. Talbot produced two outstanding musical events during autumn 1813: Michael Lacy, the Spanish-born violinist, and the opera *Brian Boroimhe (Brian Boru), or the Maid of Erin*. Unusually, both were held in November after the larger audiences drawn by the autumn race meeting had departed the city.

Lacy performed on 22 November 1813, on a bill that included *Julius Caesar*, two 'Comic Songs' and a farce, *Killing, No Murder*. He was a celebrated violinist who had first performed in Dublin as a child prodigy with Madame Catalani in 1807; this 1813 tour was his second visit to Ireland. The Derry press described him as a 'Pupil of Kreutzer, leader of the Grand Opera at Paris' and said that the highlight of his performance would be 'a concerto on the violin, into which [he] would introduce the favourite Irish Airs of "Molly Astore" and "Paddy Carey", the last arranged as a Rondeau by Himself'. This concerto was the *pièce de resistance* of Lacy's tour, the wording of the advertisement being exactly that used in *Faulkner's Journal* to advertise his Dublin concerts a few months earlier. Lacy's appearance was a spectacular coup for the theatre manager, but *Brian Boroimhe* proved an even greater success.

The opera's first performance in Derry was preceded by a detailed press advertisement which listed the forthcoming attractions of the opera, 'The Dresses, Warlike Instruments, Banners, Arms, etc., after the Costume of the Ancient Irish and Danes. The Music and Songs selected from the Ancient Irish Airs, and the Whole of Irish

Manufacture.' The opera had a libretto by Samuel Del Mara and music by the German-born, Dublin-based composer Johann Bernhard Logier. It was advertised as the first opera based on events from Irish history. It had been premiered in Dublin in January 1810 to mixed press reviews but had enjoyed popular success in Dublin, Cork and Belfast in the years that followed.

Its Derry premiere was on 17 November 1813 and the local press was ecstatic, with the *Journal* declaring that the production 'afforded [us] more satisfaction than any other play we ever witnessed'. 'The performers', it said, 'seemed animated with a zealous spirit to support the piece.' The high praise and the superlatives of the review were the more notable given that the storyline – the defeat of the Danes by the Native Irish – might have been expected to strike a discordant note in this garrison town. But Derry theatre-goers seemed to share the reviewer's opinion and a repeat performance was demanded a week later, the only production to be repeated during the entire season. Logier's opera was staged again in the Derry theatre in 1814, and also during the 1820 season, this time with a new libretto by James Sheridan Knowles, a cousin of Richard Brinsley Sheridan. The Derry audiences of 1813 could not have foreseen that thirty years later, the composer's son W.H. Logier would arrive in Derry to become one of their leading music teachers and performers.

Montague Talbot continued as manager of the Derry theatre for another seven years, but faced two major challenges in early 1820. Firstly he found it increasingly difficult to get enough actors together to mount productions in his Belfast, Newry and Derry theatres. Many actors, it was said, had left for the United States, whose theatres offered new, unheard-of opportunities. In addition, the physical fabric of the Derry theatre had deteriorated and required constant attention. Talbot temporarily closed the theatre that summer to allow for a 'complete repair' before the arrival of the 'bumper' audiences of Race Week. But shortly after this, he decided to give up the lease of the theatre, and in September 1820 the *Journal* mourned his departure, attributing it to 'the finding of his theatrical property of late an unprofitable concern'. He was assured that, 'Wherever he goes, the best wishes of Londonderry will attend him.' Talbot returned to Crow Street Theatre in Dublin, where he continued to act until his death eleven years later. Like Atkins, and appropriately, in view of his links with theatre in Belfast and Derry, Talbot was also buried in Friar's Bush Cemetery in Belfast, but in an unmarked grave. George Benn, historian of early Belfast, later described his resting place, 'No memorial, no stone of any kind, marks the spot where Talbot lies: the green sod alone covers his remains.'

The Artillery Lane Theatre lease was sold to a Mr Mason from Glasgow, who ran the theatre for a couple of years. Of the managers who succeeded him, none lasted more than a few seasons. Attempts were made to refurbish the interior, and during the next few years successive managers advertised substantial 'improvements' and 'new comforts' for their patrons. The frequency of such claims suggests that the theatre was finding it harder to attract an audience, even for the celebrated actor

The Golden Age, 1789-1833

German-born Johann Bernhard Logier (1777-1846), composer, inventor, theatre and military musician, and father of William Henry Logier, one of Derry's émigré musicians. (Author's collection)

Title page of Johann Bernhard Logier's Brian Boroimhe *(Brian Boru), a popular opera in the Artillery Lane Theatre in 1813. (Author's collection)*

THEATRE, LONDONDERRY.

By Permission of the Worshipful Richard Young, Esq. Mayor.

The Manager has the honour of announcing that he has engaged
MR. WEEKES,
THE CELEBRATED IRISH COMEDIAN,
FOR NINE NIGHTS ONLY,
Who will make his Fourth appearance
ON MONDAY EVENING, AUGUST 15, 1831,
When will be performed (first time here) an entire new Grand Historical Drama, founded on the late Triumph of Liberty in France,
ENTITLED THE
FRENCH REVOLUTION, 1830,
Embracing an Historical Outline of the memorable events of the three days, July 27, 28, and 29,

(WITH NEW SCENERY, DRESSES, AND DECORATIONS,)

Dramatized by T. R. Haines, Esq.

(Of the Theatres Royal, London and Liverpool,) who was an eye-witness to the Revolution.

Jacqueline, ... Mrs. F. CONNOR.
Terry Regan, (an Irish Traveller,) . . Mr. WEEKES.

ACT I.—Exterior of a Parisian Inn—River Seine by moonlight—Suspension Bridge of the Place de Grave—the City of Paris in the distance—Commencement of the Revolution—La Place Vendôme, with Trajan's Pillar.
ACT II.—La Grange—Chateau of Lafayette.—He accepts the command of the National Guards. *Scene 2.*—House in the Rue St. Honore—Popular Tumult. *Scene 4.*—Guard House—Place de la Bourse—Battle between Swiss and Citizens—The Guard House bursts into flames—Lafayette falls on his knees—Jacqueline waves the Tri-coloured Flag above his head.

THE PIECE CONCLUDES WITH
Shouts of Vive La Liberte.

In the course of the Evening Mr. Weekes will Sing several new Irish Songs.
A DANCE BY MISS VILLARS.

To conclude with the Laughable Farce of the
IRISHMAN IN LONDON.
Murtock Delany, ... Mr. WEEKES.

Doors to be open at Seven, and Performance to commence at Eight o'clock.—Tickets to be had at the Theatre, from Eleven to Three o'clock, where places for the Boxes may be had.—Boxes, 3s.—Upper Boxes, 2s.—Pit, 1s.

*Press advertisement for the Artillery Lane Theatre. (*Londonderry Sentinel*, 13 August 1831)*

Edmund Kean in 1823. Press interest in the Derry theatre also declined, with fewer advertisements and reviews of performances. In January 1823 and yet again in 1829, the building was offered 'To Let'.

Decline in theatrical terms, if not in numbers attending, was temporarily arrested in 1829-30, when the theatre was taken over by the Connors, father and son. Someone who attended the theatre at that time later remembered it nostalgically as offering 'every variety of drama, opera and ballet'. The services of well-known actors from Drury Lane and Covent Garden (Miss Paton, Miss Jarman and Mr Henry Johnston) were secured to supplement the local company. Nevertheless, as the theatre-goer recalled:

> The great theatrical feature of the Derry theatre in those bygone days occurred as the curtain fell, when the united audience used to call vociferously for 'MacTaggart', – a gentleman who was always present, who invariably responded to the call, and, in a comic-heroic, serio-macaronic way, entered into a full and unsparing criticism of the play, players, and intelligence and judgement of the audience.[12]

Last Seasons at Artillery Lane

The theatre was then leased to Englishman Frank Seymour, who reopened it during 1832 and 1833. Seymour was another veteran of the Irish stage, first appearing as a young actor in 1813 and then briefly as theatre manager in Derry in 1823. He later managed theatres in Glasgow, Tralee and Belfast, which gave him an opportunity to build up friendships in the theatre world.

His last two seasons in Derry were a glorious swan song. Seymour presented novelty, spectacle and excitement in a wide variety of operas, plays and ballets, and the press resumed its former, supportive role providing frequent previews and reviews. It was loud in its praise of the theatre manager and offered him 'congratulations on the fashionable audiences he [has] already attracted to the theatre'. Seymour was deemed to deserve 'that encouragement and support which his merits as a manager, an actor and a gentleman, so well entitle him to'. He was also praised for having 'rescue[d] the theatre from a state of comparative ruin and neglect', an indication of how much the fabric of the theatre had deteriorated during the 1820s.

Opera featured strongly in the 1832 theatre season. The lengthy season, between 4 April and 13 August, had at least thirty different musical productions, with repeats a comparative rarity. There was still a strong reliance on the ballad operas of the eighteenth century, with performances of *The Highland Reel* (first performed 1788), *The Turnpike Gate* (first performed 1799) and of course, *The Beggar's Opera*. But Derry audiences were also introduced to newer works, such as Henry Bishop's operas *Clari, or The Maid of Milan* (1823) and *Guy Mannering* (1816), the latter based on Walter

THEATRE, LONDONDERRY.

By permission of the Worshipful GEORGE HILL, *Esq. Mayor*

LAST NIGHT BUT ONE
OF THE COMPANY'S PERFORMANCE THIS SEASON.

For the Benefit of Mr. DYOTT,

Who most respectfully solicits the patronage and support of the Nobility, Gentry, Garrison, and Public of Londonderry and its vicinity on the occasion.

On MONDAY EVENING, SEPT. 30, 1833,

Will be presented Shakspeare's Tragedy of

ROMEO AND JULIET.

Romeo, ... Mr. DYOTT.
Juliet, ... Mrs. CAMPBELL.

END OF THE PLAY,

A Double Comic Dance, in character, by Mr. M'Gowan, as *Dame Gurdy*, and Mr. *Thompson*, as her man *Hodge*.

A FAVOURITE SONG BY MISS KELLY.

To conclude with the popular and laughable Farce of

THE LANCERS.

Captain Lenox, ... Mr. ROBSON.
Captain Belton, ... Mr. DYOTT.

Tickets to be had of Mr. DYOTT, at Mr. M'MENEMY's.

On TUESDAY, OCTOBER 1,

POSITIVELY THE LAST NIGHT,

FOR THE BENEFIT OF PIERCE EGAN,

When will be performed, of course for this Night only,

THE DERRY THEATRE IN AN UPROAR,

OR THE MANAGER IN DISTRESS.

" It is true! and true; 'tis pity!" Hem! SHAKSPEARE.

And the much admired Petite Comedy, called

THE MIDNIGHT HOUR,

WITH SONGS, &c.

The whole to conclude with the laughable Farce of

THE VILLAGE LAWYER.

Scout, ... Mr. ROBSON.
Sheepface (for this Night only) ..... PIERCE EGAN.

Tickets to be had, for the Last Night, and no mistake, at the Theatre, Italian Saloon, &c.

Press advertisement for the final performances at the Artillery Lane Theatre in September 1833 when a riot closed the final season. (Londonderry Sentinel, *28 September 1833*)

Scott's novel. The highlight of the season was the Derry premiere of Weber's opera *Der Freischütz*, on 13 June. The first performance was received with 'enthusiastic applause' and then repeated by 'popular demand' the following Monday, at the unusual time of 1 p.m. This same season also saw the Juvenile Corps de Ballet from the Theatre Royal, Covent Garden, in dancing interludes between plays and in several new ballets. These were the first complete ballets to be presented in Derry, at a time when ballet still carried a whiff of libertinism. It would take Queen Victoria and Prince Albert's patronage of the ballet in the 1840s to make it thoroughly respectable.

The short 1833 season ran from mid-August to the end of September and featured a wide variety of operas, plays and ballet, with the Juvenile Corps de Ballet making a return visit for a second season. London actor Pierce Egan, originally a sports journalist and novelist, joined Seymour's company for the season, and put on a comic burletta based on his novel *The Adventures of Tom and Jerry in the Great Metropolis* on 26 August.[13]

Operas, plays and ballet were always accompanied by 'popular songs', such as the 'Much admired National Airs', Moore's Melodies, Irish and Scottish songs and the 'popular ballads of the day', performed by Mr O'Callaghan and the Misses Kelly from Dublin in September 1833. Press advertisements from 1832 and 1833 suggest that evenings at the theatre were even longer than before.

In spite of Seymour's ambitious programming, theatre audiences continued to fall, as Derry's elite moved from the Georgian houses in the city to their leafy estates in the county and in Donegal, and increasingly sought their amusements within their own social circle.

The final night of the season, on 1 October, was also the theatre's death knell. The play being put on for Pierce Egan's benefit, *The Derry Theatre in an Uproar*, was the occasion of a real-life riot. Whatever the reason – whether it was the title of the play that put the idea into people's minds or knowledge that the theatre was closing its doors for the last time – the attendants were showered with stones and refuse. Inside, 'lawless persons' in the audience tore up the benches and threw them onto the stage, scattering the orchestra and causing the actors to cower backstage, so that 'the house was one scene of tumult, confusion and terror'. It was a sorry end to Derry's Golden Age of theatre.

Behaviour in the Theatre

The mayhem of 1 October was an extreme case, but the behaviour of theatre audiences at this time was frequently disorderly. Horseplay, catcalls, jibes and the firing of missiles were common occurrences in the Artillery Lane Theatre, as they were in theatres throughout Ireland and England. Indeed, during the 1820s, a visitor had remarked that 'the most striking thing to a foreigner in English theatres is the unheard-of coarseness and brutality of the audiences'. It was the same in Derry – in

1802 a theatre-goer was fined two guineas by the Mayor of Derry for throwing a bottle from the gallery onto the stage.

And trouble did flare up from time to time. In 1819, the *Journal* identified the occupants of the gallery as troublemakers, and one of the principal offenders as 'the son of a respectable inhabitant who boasts that it is fashionable to row in Dublin, where he has lately resided'. The gallery, with the cheapest seats in the house, provided an ideal vantage point from which to heckle, jeer and throw whatever came to hand. The *Journal* suggested remedies to the problem, 'that the prices of pit and gallery should be reversed and that the gallery should be opened as a middle lettice' at the pit price. On the newspaper's advice, the theatre management adopted this approach during 1819 and for two further seasons. And for part of the 1825 season, the gallery of the Derry theatre was closed, although the management discreetly gave no reason for the closure. By this time, theatre audiences were in decline, so the manager may not have wished to draw attention to disturbances. However, Derry could consider itself fortunate that it did not have the 'annual theatre riots' that Dublin theatres experienced.

Derry was also fortunate in that there were no theatre fires, common occurrences elsewhere. Artillery Lane Theatre was heated by open fires lit a week in advance of the season, and kept alight in the lobby and in the auditorium during performances. Additional fire risks were the tallow and later wax candles used to illuminate the auditorium, as gas lighting was not introduced until 1832. Yet no theatre in Derry was lost to fire until the Opera House was destroyed in a dramatic blaze in 1940.

The Artillery Lane Theatre attracted some of the most famous performers of the age. Thomas King, creator of the comic roles of Lord Ogleby in *The Clandestine Marriage* and Sir Peter Teazle in *The School for Scandal*, appeared there in the former role in June 1791, and 'met with the most marked approbation of a numerous audience'. Singer Charles Edward Horn, composer of 'Cherry Ripe', sang at the theatre and then gave a concert in the Coterie Rooms of the King's Arms Hotel in 1819. The great dramatic actor Edmund Kean played Othello in Artillery Lane in October 1823. Ira Aldridge, the gifted African-American actor and so-called 'African Roscius', also impressed as Othello and was 'inimitable' as Mungo in *The Padlock* when he visited Derry in August 1829.

In addition, the theatre provided entertainments of a different kind. Tightrope dancing 'on a pair of real skates' was an attraction in 1815, and a troop of horses provided equestrian displays in April 1823, accompanied by 'a slack and tight rope-walker' performing acrobatic feats. Many patrons were disappointed in being unable to gain admittance to this show, as the 'gallery overflowed at an early hour'. There were clog dances, highland reels and ballets, musical interludes on harpsichord and piano, and countless performances by singers, violinists, cellists, flautists, regimental bands and players of musical glasses, who 'graced' the stage and delighted city audiences.

The Golden Age, 1789-1833

Mr IRA ALDRIDGE as AARON

"He dies upon my scimetar's sharp point,
That touches this my first-born son and heir!"
TITUS ANDRONICUS. Act 4. Sc. 2.

Ira Aldridge (1807-1867), the 'African Roscius' who visited Derry four times, his first visit being in 1829.

The secret of the Artillery Lane Theatre's success before the 1820s was that its managers gave their audiences what they wanted. The theatre-goers of the time looked for excitement, music, novelty and the opportunity to mix socially with other members of the audience. In the coming decades, Derry's middle classes were to find these in 'popular' and 'subscription' concerts.

Concerts

Concerts, in the modern sense, were rare in Derry before the 1820s. Boruwlaski's performances in 1798 were advertised as 'concerts' but his popularity probably derived as much from his size as his musicianship. His visits had been preceded in 1791 by a group of 'gymnasts' [sic] who 'played select Airs and Tunes on the Much Admired Musical Glasses'. Novelty concerts of this type, where the freak-show element was present, remained popular in Derry for several decades. Signor Rivolta gave 'An Extraordinary Vocal and Instrumental Concert' in 1822, during which he played on eight instruments simultaneously. Even more arresting were the concerts in 1833 by the blind Professor Watson from Scotland, who played the 'Musical Glasses and the Psaltery', and produced, 'by his own efforts, the effect of a whole band, by performing at once on two violins, a violoncello and Pan's Pipes'.

From around 1800, however, theatre musicians, military bands, touring sopranos and male instrumentalists began to give concerts with more obvious musical content. In January of that year, the band of the York Regiment held a 'Concert of Vocal and Instrumental Music' in Neilson's Hotel, but even this concert included dance routines: a 'Clog Dance in Dresses Suitable' rounded off the evening. It was Mr Haigh, a theatre musician from Artillery Lane, who gave the first concert proper in Derry in November 1800, performing a 'cello concerto' in the Town Hall. Haigh gave two concerts on evenings when the theatre was closed, but even he felt obliged to advertise his events under the banner of a 'Concert and Ball', to conform to the demands and expectations of his audience. Like theatre, concerts were viewed by Derry's elite as an opportunity for 'socialising' as much as a cultural experience.

The price of concert tickets in Derry was relatively high between the 1770s and the later 1830s. Boruwlaski's 'Concert and Ball' in July 1798 was moderately priced at 3s 3d for gentlemen and 2s 8d for ladies, but other concert-givers charged more. Tickets for Mr Haigh's 'Concert and Ball' were 4s 4d and 2s 8d respectively, greatly in excess of theatre prices, where 3s, 2s, 1s, and half-price admission after 9 p.m. were the norm. In his pricing policy, Haigh showed himself one of a new generation of professional musicians, quick to maximise his opportunities for earning and determined to be properly paid for his work.

James May

In the winter of 1816/7, there was a short burst of local musical activity when Scotsman James May organised a series of concerts and set up Derry's second music society. May had first arrived in the city as a theatre musician during the 1809 theatre season but he decided to settle in Derry to teach piano, violin and flute. He became music tutor to the daughters of the wealthy Alexander Family of Boom Hall, to whom he dedicated his 1813 composition 'The Fairy Bower Ballad'.

However, May maintained his links with theatre and concert-giving outside Derry, for he announced two concerts with performers 'brought from a distance and consequently attended with Great Expense'. He claimed that he had engaged a 'celebrated band' of musicians drawn from the Dublin and Belfast theatres, concert platforms and music societies for two concerts on 31 January and 2 February. An extra concert of 'sacred music' in St Columb's Cathedral was added later; this concert, on 1 February, included the earliest documented performance in Derry of excerpts from Handel's *Messiah*.

James May's ballad song, composed in 1813 and dedicated to daughters of the local gentry, the Alexanders of Boom Hall. (By kind permission of the National Library of Ireland)

The promotion of concerts was not without risk and May had to make several appeals to the Derry public for support. Eventually, in order to cover his expenses, he organised a committee of 'local gentlemen to assist' in what he described as 'this novel and spirited attempt' to bring concerts to the city. Tickets, at 7s, were costly; more than double the price of the most expensive theatre tickets. In spite of his early worries, May was obviously pleased with the success of the concerts, for within a year he had formed the Londonderry Musical Society, the second of its kind in the city.

The Second Londonderry Musical Society

The society's first concert was held in spring 1817, followed by two more annual concerts in May 1818 and March 1819, with the net proceeds of all three donated to the 'Ladies' Penny Society', a local charity. Given their benevolent nature, the Mayor of Derry acted as Principal Steward at the concerts, assisted by several leading merchants. The concert programmes had a broad appeal, mainly drawn from the popular songs and melodies of the day, but also with some music of a more serious character.

At the March 1818 concert, the gentlemen of the society sang glees, trios and choruses, as had the all-male membership of Derry's first music society. Ladies were admitted to membership of this second society and 'their performances thrilled the audience with delight'. At this time, ladies played only keyboard instruments – stringed instruments being deemed unladylike because of the supposedly inelegant physical postures required to play them. Similarly, the playing of brass and woodwind instruments by women was discouraged because of the puffing and blowing involved, not to mention the probability of a reddened face, which in a woman was considered unsightly.

The 'Full Band' consisted of professional musicians who played symphonies by Haydn and Gyrowetz, and also accompanied the male choruses. The 1819 concert was attended by over 300 people: the elite of the city and county – those who could afford the hefty 6s 8d ticket prices. The concerts always ended with enthusiastic singing of 'God Save the King'. Later that year, James May left Derry to return to his native Glasgow and the second Londonderry Musical Society fell into abeyance. Local music-making stagnated during the next three decades, until Derry's third music society emerged in 1849.

However, concerts took on a new lease of life from 1829, as more renowned 'outside' performers started to include Derry and the nearby towns of Strabane, Coleraine and Omagh in their concert timetables. The practice of flexible concert-giving, whereby performers stayed as long as they had audiences, all but disappeared; visiting musicians now adhered to strict schedules advertised well in advance. Admission prices remained high in relation to theatre tickets, but those charged at Madame Catalani's concert in 1829 surpassed anything previously known.

Angelica Catalani

The concert by Angelica Catalani charged the highest admission prices – 8s tickets with no concessions whatsoever – for what was the greatest single event in the musical life of Derry until the later 1850s, when it was equalled only by that of the other renowned nineteenth-century Prima Donna, Jenny Lind. Italian-born Catalani was the foremost soprano of the early nineteenth century, popularly known as the 'Prima Cantatrice del Mondo' because of her ability to captivate audiences with her trills, chromatic runs and *bel canto* singing. She had a rich and powerful voice of such amazing strength that it was described by the contemporary French novelist Stendhal as, 'filling the soul with a kind of astonished wonder, as though it beheld a miracle'. The sheer volume which she could produce prompted a London critic to remark that he need not go to York to hear her sing as he 'could hear her well enough where he was'. Catalani was also known for her arrogant and unpredictable behaviour, although this was not uncommon for a Prima Donna accustomed to having European audiences in thrall. In Munich, she was criticised for sitting in a church pew reserved for the Royal Family. Her response was to cancel her concert in the city and never to return there again.

By the later 1820s, Catalani's career was in decline and her voice had lost some of its more glorious tones, but she continued to tour throughout Europe, exchanging the opera house for the concert hall, where she sang the operatic arias of her former glory days. At her concert on 30 June, Catalani was accompanied by a 'Full Band' of musicians from Belfast, led from the piano by organist John Willis. She sang mainly operatic arias, for which she was heartily applauded; the packed and enthusiastic Derry audience then demanding several encores. Catalani ended with a rousing rendition of 'Rule Britannia' – a popular choice of finale in this maritime city.

The celebrated Italian soprano Madame Angelica Catalani (1780-1849), who sang in Corporation Hall in 1829.

Corporation Hall

Madame Catalani was among the first musicians to perform in Derry's new Corporation Hall, which had opened just three years earlier. Although initially planned as a 'thorough repair' of the older Exchange, the Town Hall emerged as a substantially new building after construction work lasting three years. It cost over £5,500 – more than double the original budget – with an additional £400 for 'furniture'. The building measured 120ft by 45ft, with the main entrance through a circular facade in Bishop Street. Corporation Hall was a much grander building than its predecessor, with three large rooms upstairs, including an assembly room, which was 75ft by 36ft. On the ground floor there was a smaller, more intimate 'Round Room', which became a public reading room in 1835, and a kitchen. The more luxurious character and accommodation of the new Assembly Room was probably a major factor in attracting the larger number of more 'high-class' concerts in the 1830s.

Social Entertainments

Corporation Hall took over the role of the Exchange Building in hosting 'Grand Balls' and assemblies during Race Week and the Assizes, still the highpoints of Derry's social calendar. But social life of all kinds flourished during Derry's Golden Age, with the round of entertainments for the elite expanding steadily from 1798 onwards. The increased garrison strength was a stimulus for more balls and coteries, organised to entertain the regiments and to enable captains and officers to mingle with eligible young ladies from local families.

The city's main hotel in Pump Street offered more select and, at the same time, more intimate surroundings for the genteel courting rituals observed at these balls and coteries. The hotel had different names and owners: from 1798 it was Neilson's Hotel; from 1810 to 1814 it was renamed Dobie's Hotel, and thereafter it was the King's Arms Hotel, owned by the Birch family.[14] It hosted a wide range of events, from the smaller winter-time coteries, as in January 1818 when the presiding hosts, Mrs Hammond and Major Maxwell, were described as the 'Queen' and 'King' respectively, to the larger prestigious dinners held annually in December to commemorate the 'Shutting of the Gates' by the Apprentice Boys at the time of the Siege. The 'Public Dinner' on 18 December 1815, held after a day of 'beating of drums and other demonstrations of joy', was a lengthy and protracted affair. The *Journal* recorded that, 'In the evening, the Officers according to annual custom, together with the Officers of the Garrison, the Nobility and Gentry of this neighbourhood, dined together at the King's Arms, where the greatest conviviality prevailed during the night.'

New pleasures were continually added to the social calendar, as in April 1800, when the Bishop's Gardens were opened during the summer months for 'Ladies and

Gentlemen to walk in' for a subscription price of 6s 6d. Derry's walls were also a popular area for strolling, prompting the contemporary historian George Sampson to comment that the walls of Derry, 'once its strength', had now become 'its ornament' – a reference to the wide promenade they now provided for the 'fashion and beauty of the city'.

The circus was another novel amusement, which came for the first time in August 1801, when Philip Astley's Dublin circus took over a timber yard on Derry's quayside for eight days. Admission was 2s 2d and 1s 1d, comparable to theatre prices but still well beyond the financial reach of the lower classes. Labourers in Derry at this time usually earned between 8d and 13d a day.

The River Foyle became a new focus of attraction, with boat races starting in August 1815, followed soon after by boat launches and annual regattas. Pleasure cruises, with band music on board, became all the rage in the summer months, with steamer trips along the Donegal coast and to the Giant's Causeway. More distant excursions to Iona and Staffa then joined the list of attractions for the social elite, again with band music and convivial company to complement the passing scenery. A local boat company even advertised that it would transport dancers to and from a 'Charity Ball' in Portstewart. However, having explored and perhaps exhausted the city's pleasures, Derry's elite began to look elsewhere for its amusements.

From about 1819, advertisements appeared for balls and coteries in the nearby seaside towns of Moville, Greencastle and Bundoran. An advertisement from even earlier, in the 1790s, by a travelling musician called Mr O'Donnell, indicated that the services of musicians were in demand for private parties and balls. He described himself as a 'celebrated performer on the Irish Pipes [and] offered to provide music for dancing for Parties in City and Country on the shortest notice'. The reference to 'the country' suggests that O'Donnell was hopeful of being asked to play at dances and balls in the large stately houses which had been springing up along the banks of the Foyle, towards Muff and Moville. What O'Donnell offered was typical: music for dancing in private homes was normally provided by a single musician who played on the harp, violin or pochette.[15]

The Music Trade

By the early nineteenth century, the elite of Derry still had a keen appetite for theatre, music and dancing, around which their social life had revolved during the previous half-century. Alongside this taste for the arts, there developed a desire to perform themselves, for family and friends in their own drawing rooms. There was no specialist music shop in Derry, but instruments and sheet music were available from a variety of sellers: church musicians, music teachers, booksellers, and of course second-hand from private individuals. Advertisements for music or instruments appeared only occasionally, when sellers returned with fresh supplies from London or Dublin, or when a new consignment had just arrived. In this small city, word-of-mouth was probably the usual method of obtaining instruments and sheet music, as regular and competitive advertising in the music trade did not begin in Derry until the early 1850s.

The range of instruments for sale was small: some keyboard instruments (spinets, harpsichords, and early wooden-framed pianos), violins, German flutes and guitars. Trade in these was concentrated principally in the hands of William Shannon, organist at St Columb's Cathedral. The main sellers of sheet music were the city booksellers, such as George Douglas, the first proprietor of the *Journal*, who ran a bookshop from the early 1770s, where he stocked music tutors for harpsichord, violin and flute. In the 1790s he expanded his stock to include *The Fashionable Songster* (with 'all the New Songs sung at Ranelagh [Gardens], Vauxhall [Gardens] and the Theatres') and collections of minuets ('from the Castle and Rotundo, Dublin'), as well as guitars and German flutes. Douglas also sold *Walker's Hibernian Magazine* and *The Gentleman's London Magazine*, both of which included music and songs. His stock was obviously targeted at Derry's gentlemen and lady musicians keen to keep abreast of the latest London songs, dances and fashions. Douglas was in a particularly advantageous position: as the proprietor of the *Journal* he was able to devote considerable space on the back page of the newspaper to advertise his own book and music sales.

But by the early 1820s, music sellers from outside Derry began to appear, setting up stalls in hotels and vacant shops. The more up-market 'bazaars' were held in the King's Arms Hotel, as in July 1823, when Mr Mosley from Anglesea Street, Dublin, brought selections of his stock, 'supplied by his agents in England and France', for a two-week sale. He did not quote prices for his instruments and sheet music in press advertisements, relying instead upon their novelty value, exclusiveness and exotic appeal to attract buyers. Thereafter, on an almost annual basis, he was followed by a series of specialist music firms and bazaar traders, keen to capitalise on this new, untapped market. Then prices began to appear in press advertisements, allowing the Derry public to choose between cheaper and more expensive instruments. Variety and competition had at last reached Derry.

One interesting local shop then entered the music trade, albeit in addition to its normal range of foodstuffs. The Birch family, proprietors of the King's Arms Hotel, owned the exotically named 'Italian Saloon' adjoining the hotel (the outline of the shop windows can still be seen in the building in Pump Street). The Saloon was advertised as a general 'Emporium' and sold a variety of goods, including sauces, spices, cheeses, pickles, liqueurs, medicines and tobacco. By 1833, the shop had diversified, selling smaller musical instruments: violins, clarinets, flutes, fifes, flageolets and musical boxes. The Saloon also stocked a wide range of music accessories, such as strings, bridges, piano wire and violin bows. It was the first local shop to set out its prices, for example: 10*d* for a fife, 2*s* for opera glasses, 14*s* for a silver-keyed clarinet, and musical boxes from 40*s* to 10 guineas.

The Golden Age, 1789-1833

Corporation Hall in the Diamond as viewed from lower Shipquay Street. (Author's collection)

By the mid-1830s, Scottish firms had started to make forays into the Derry music trade, and one salesman in particular, James Hunter from the 'Mackellar and Robertson Piano Manufactory', made repeated visits to Derry. Hunter was a piano tuner by profession, which he combined with being the manufactory's travelling salesman. After several visits, Hunter finally settled in Derry and was to set up the city's first music shop. Thereafter, the constant availability of cheaper pianos and 'popular' sheet music ensured that, although music was no longer heard in the city theatre, it would be heard in the drawing rooms of Derry's upper and middle-class homes.

In 1837, the author of the *Ordnance Survey Memoir* commented upon the lack of social entertainments in Derry: the theatre had closed, concerts were few in number and fashionable balls were no longer held in the Town Hall or in the King's Arms Hotel. Advertisements in the local press confirm this. Seven balls and coteries had been advertised in 1830; there was only one in 1834. The King's Arms Hotel no longer hosted 'Grand Balls', but instead housed piano and instrument sales by visiting traders for a new middle-class clientele. The once fashionable theatre lay derelict.

The author lamented that he had encountered in Derry, 'a prevailing indifference to public amusements, to polite literature and to the fine arts'. Again, press advertisements in the *Journal* confirm this observation, and also provide a more exact timetable for the change in attitudes. By the early 1820s, balls and coteries in local seaside towns had replaced those once held in Derry. Grand Balls were no longer advertised in the press but were instead private events attended by invitation only. Audiences in the Artillery Lane Theatre were down and theatre seasons less frequent. The succession of theatre managers who took over the theatre failed to win back former patrons among the gentry. When the theatre finally closed in 1833, it became part of a coach-house and later Fourth Derry Presbyterian church. Theatre did return in the early 1840s, but with a more plebeian audience in the louche surroundings of the Theatre Royal in Fountain Street.

By the early 1830s, the gentry and upper classes had completed the process of withdrawal from Derry. They had removed themselves physically from the city's entertainments and drawn a veil of privacy around their newfound pleasures. The Golden Age of elite entertainments in Derry had passed, and by the end of the Georgian age, the Grand Balls, assemblies and dances once 'presided over by a King and Queen of the night … had died away'.

Three

CONTRASTING FORTUNES, 1834-1858

On 29 October 1836, a letter appeared in the *Sentinel* denouncing theatre as 'contrary to the spirit of true religion'. The writer expressed outrage at the reintroduction of theatre in Derry and claimed, 'it was considered by all sober-minded persons a matter of thankfulness when symptoms of distaste for theatrical entertainments were evinced and when the old theatre was converted by its proprietor into a coach-house'.

What had provoked the writer was a series of plays put on at Corporation Hall by the officers and men of the 92nd Highlanders. The Artillery Lane Theatre had been sorely missed by the garrison, and they decided to fill the gap themselves. Starting in September 1836, they performed a succession of comedies, farces and dramas similar to those previously seen there. Old favourites reappeared, like Macklin's *Love a La Mode*, Colman's *The Wags of Windsor* and Townley's *High Life Below Stairs*. Farces and comedies predominated, although Scottish and military plays were also popular: *Cramond Brig, or The Laird of Ballangeich* and *The Lancers* giving, one suspects, as much enjoyment to the cast as to their local audiences. The *Journal* claimed that amateur theatricals were 'the rage in most of the garrison towns in Ireland', and added, as if in their defence, that the performances complained of were in aid of charity.

The last of these plays closed in January 1837, and from that time until the 1860s Corporation Hall was rarely used as a theatre. In any case, Derry's theatre-goers were unhappy with the hall's facilities: it lacked a proper gallery, where – as was said of Artillery Lane – 'the inhabitants of the gods' could give lively expression to their 'free and independent spirits'. When another theatre did open, it lacked the atmosphere, public patronage and central location of its predecessor.

Conversely, during this period, musical events took over from the theatre in popular esteem. European musicians continued to visit, but increasingly alongside concerts by Derry's own choral and instrumental music societies. New forms of musical enter-

From Farquhar to Field Day

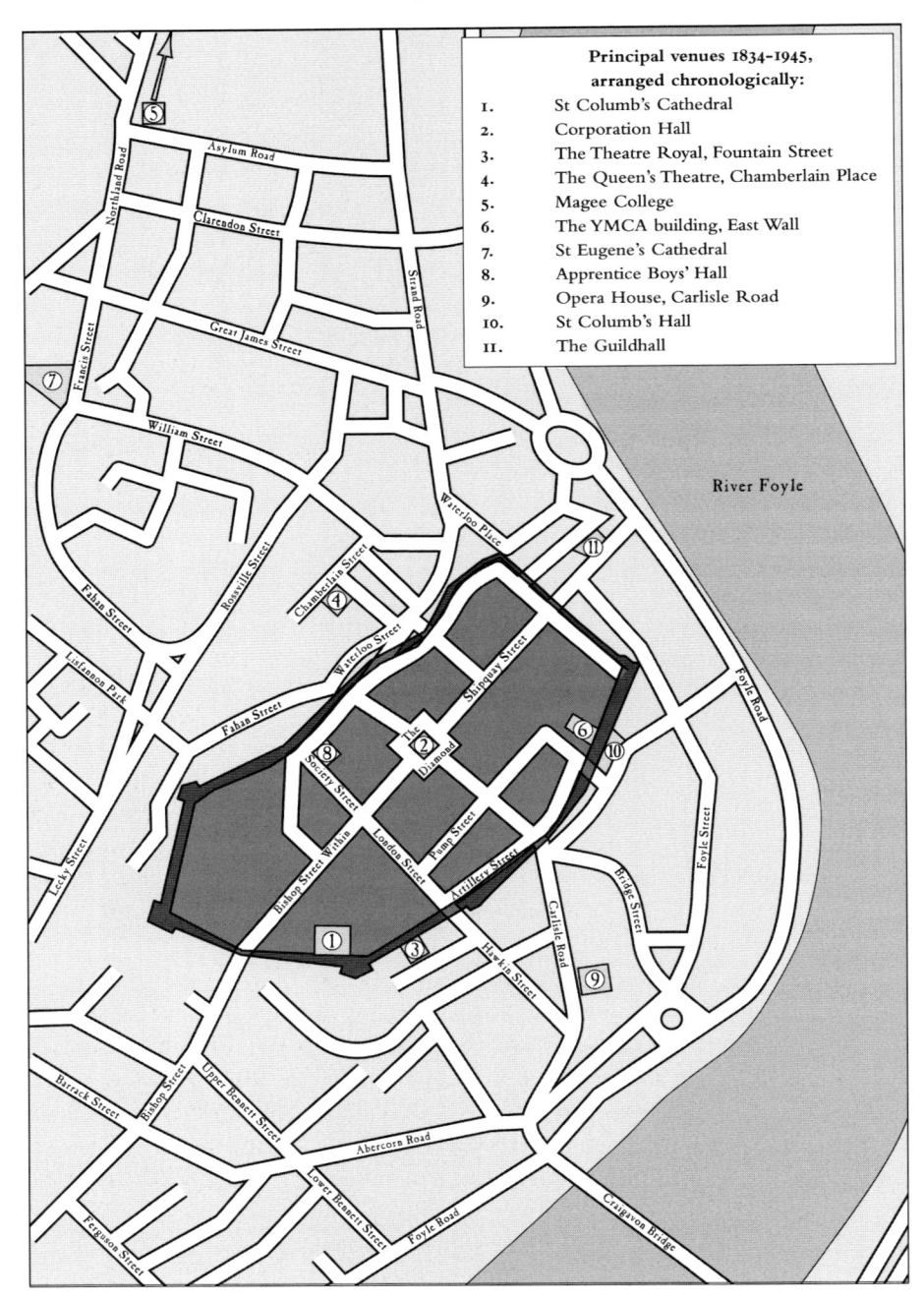

Principal venues 1834-1945, arranged chronologically:

1. St Columb's Cathedral
2. Corporation Hall
3. The Theatre Royal, Fountain Street
4. The Queen's Theatre, Chamberlain Place
5. Magee College
6. The YMCA building, East Wall
7. St Eugene's Cathedral
8. Apprentice Boys' Hall
9. Opera House, Carlisle Road
10. St Columb's Hall
11. The Guildhall

The principal cultural venues between 1834 and 1945. By the later nineteenth century the physical parameters of cultural life had moved outside the walled city to include Magee College, the Opera House and the Guildhall.

tainment emerged, in factory soirées, band concerts, Apprentice Boys' events and boat trips with music provided. And in 1843, James Hunter opened Derry's first music shop to satisfy the rising demand for pianos and sheet music. Set against this quickening in the city's musical life, there was, on the theatre side, only a poorly supported and uneven diet of drama, burlesque and pantomime. At first these were staged outdoors, for want of a proper auditorium, and then in a makeshift theatre in a less fashionable area, which, it was claimed, attracted only a 'lower class' of patron.

Derry had a taste of outdoor theatre in the early 1840s, when visiting companies set up 'booths and caravans' in Shipquay Square. To alert local people to their presence, the actors marched around the city 'in full costume', drumming up support. Then, in the evening, oil burners were lit to illuminate the square and their shows began. The travelling actors usually presented excerpts from Shakespearean plays – always popular with Derry audiences – but performances were often enlivened in the wrong way by the actors being the worse for drink. Naturally this did nothing to allay the prejudices against theatre in the city.

The Theatre Royal

In the mid-1840s, a few advertisements appeared in newspapers for a theatre in Fountain Street which had already been open for some time. The 'Theatre Royal' – a rather grand name for a ball-court converted into a makeshift theatre – was owned by a Mr Meehan and situated in Wapping, a run-down area of the city adjoining the walls. At first, Meehan ran it as a 'fit-up' theatre himself, but it was then leased to a succession of short-term managers who had the building redecorated, brought in actors from Belfast and further afield, and claimed to have converted it into a 'small and comfortable theatre'. This included the addition of 'private boxes', which could be reached directly by an entrance from the walls.

Despite these improvements, the new theatre was not highly regarded in Derry. The 1844 *Parliamentary Gazetteer* was scathing in its description of it, dismissing it as 'a paltry structure in an obscure situation'. An illustrated map by James O'Hagan (1847) contained engravings of the city's principal buildings but omitted the theatre. And in July 1849, the *Londonderry Standard* provided a detailed survey of the city's buildings, describing the earlier theatre in considerable detail, but again the Fountain Street theatre was not mentioned. It did appear on an 1849 map, identified improbably as the 'Teatro', perhaps an attempt, like the title 'Royal', to lend it the glamour of a foreign name to offset the disadvantages of its location.

The few advertisements that appeared in the local press give no titles of the plays produced nor names of performers; presumably these details were in the 'daily handbills' posted prominently around the city. As the 1843 Theatre Act had relaxed the requirement that provincial theatres include musical interludes in all performances,

> **THEATRE ROYAL, LONDONDERRY,**
> **FOUNTAIN STREET.**
>
> THE MANAGERS beg leave to inform the Ladies and Gentlemen of Londonderry, that on MONDAY Evening, 15th NOVEMBER, 1847, will be Performed, (by desire,) Shakspere's Tragedy of
> **MACBETH, KING OF SCOTLAND,**
> WITH OTHER ENTERTAINMENTS.
> To conclude with the laughable afterpiece of the
> **RENDEZVOUS.**
> Boxes, 2s.; Pit, 1s.; Gallery, 6d.—half prices to Boxes only at 9 o'clock. A private entrance to the Boxes from the Walls, back of the Theatre.

*One of the few press advertisements for the Theatre Royal in Fountain Street. (*Londonderry Sentinel*, 13 November 1847)*

the repertoire in the Theatre Royal may have been quite different from that of its predecessor and more like theatres of the present day, with greater emphasis on the plays themselves and music given a much lesser role. This move of music from the theatre to the concert hall was a development in Derry's cultural life that became more pronounced as the century progressed. The little information we have about programming suggests that Shakespeare's plays were a popular choice of actors and theatre-goers alike.

The Theatre Royal did attract one famous name. The celebrated Dublin actor Gustavus Vaughan Brooke (1818-1866) appeared in lead roles in *Hamlet* and *Richard III* during a one-week engagement in July 1843, and drew capacity audiences for every performance. Sadly he wasn't rewarded for this success, as the theatre manager not only failed to pay him for his week's work, but refused to repay a loan Brooke had given him. After fruitless attempts to obtain what was owing to him, Brooke was reduced to borrowing money to travel to Carlisle for his next engagement.

In June 1854, when Vivian Ryan took over as manager of the Theatre Royal – at least the sixth in its short history – he took out a press advertisement assuring Derry audiences that 'all profane allusions would be carefully avoided' in his productions, and asked them to return to his theatre. The fact that Ryan felt he had to appeal to the public directly in this way, with a promise not to offend the sensibilities of a respectable audience, was both a reflection of the difficulty he was having in reversing the decline in attendances and of a change in the moral tone of society since 1820, when the *Journal* had commented that the theatre was 'filled to overflowing with all the rank and fashion of the city'. This decline is all the more striking when one considers that Derry's population had more than doubled to 20,000 by the mid-1850s.

Ryan made the point that in other places, theatres were attended by 'the sovereign, the nobility and the body of the people', arguing that theatre still commanded wide public support, even in the highest ranks of society. He was well aware that in Ulster in particular, theatre-going faced strong opposition on grounds of immorality from a powerful – and vocal – religious lobby. Had not Henry Cooke, a Belfast Presbyterian minister of the time who commanded a huge following, declared theatre-going to be only one step above prostitution? Such ideas fell on fertile ground in Derry. The *Standard* didn't hide its hostility to the Theatre Royal, 'The theatre will not exhibit its bait [*sic*] until 8.30 p.m. We earnestly exhort our young friends … not to be seen in such a place … and to endeavour to employ their few spare hours in the acquisition of useful knowledge.'[16]

Managers and Audiences

The behaviour of the audience in the Theatre Royal was probably rowdy by modern standards. Disturbances in Irish theatres were so common in the middle of the nineteenth century that *The Belfast Newsletter* once commended an audience in Newry for its restraint in allowing performances to continue without violent interruption. The *Sentinel* found less to praise in the Derry theatre-goers, among whom it criticised 'the rough element' and 'the rude gods whose boisterous manners are obnoxious', adding that the entertainment on offer was 'the lowest burlesques and farces'.

There were various reasons for crowd trouble in Irish theatres of the period, from lateness in raising the curtain to dissatisfaction with the performances of drunk and incompetent actors. The presence of soldiers from the local garrison was sometimes resented by Nationalist elements in the audience, especially at times of political tension. Heckling from 'pitties' – the groundlings in the front section of the theatre – at critical moments in the dramatic action often resulted in one or more being ejected, audience and actors joining forces to expel the guilty party. The pit and the gallery were frequently at odds, as in a Belfast theatre in January 1864, when the simultaneous hissing from one area and applause from the other forced the theatre band to 'retire with precipitation'. What complicated matters further were the cross-currents in the audience's reaction to what was happening on stage: actors at one moment being hissed at, only to be promptly forgiven and encouraged to go on again. Among the pit-dwellers, fights sometimes broke out between those who had only just previously been united together against those in the 'gods'.

Some of the heckling had a humorous side, when the actors on stage had to play second fiddle to the amateur comedians in the auditorium. Theatre managers, whom all sections of the audience took against at different times, were the frequent target of complaints and abuse, prompted by accusations of mismanagement or objections to sudden, unheralded changes in programming. Even in the best-regulated theatres of the time, all stage performances took place against a background of smoking, drinking, loud conversation and gross inattention.

It is a measure of how far theatre had sunk in public esteem in Derry by the 1850s that newspaper advertisements for performances are few and far between, and drama reviews disappear almost completely. The few press notices by theatre managers, setting out their optimistic hopes for increased public patronage, usually stressed that ticket prices were low. Admission costs were just 1*s* 6*d* and 3*d*, down sharply from 3*s*, 2*s* and 1*s* during the 1830s. Half-price admission after 9 p.m., which remained a feature in Irish theatres until the 1870s, lowered the cost further. In 1856-7 there was no mention of the theatre in the press, and in 1858 the building itself was offered for sale or rent, described as a 'tenement ... lately used as a theatre'. It would be another five years before a new theatre, the Queen's Theatre, took up the challenge of presenting live drama on a Derry stage.

Musical Rebirth

While theatrical performances were in eclipse throughout the period 1833-58, the opposite was true of the city's musical life, which saw exceptional growth, much greater participation by the general public, and the appearance of new kinds of musical events. And it was to Corporation Hall, formerly Derry's premier theatre venue, that the middle-classes flocked to concerts, musical evenings and soirées. It hosted concerts by visiting artistes, music society meetings and concerts, singing and Tonic Solfa classes, and was at other times used for the increasingly popular Temperance meetings. By the later 1850s, Derry was alive with music, largely stimulated by foreign musicians and Scottish Church precentors who led and directed its musical life. If the years between 1789 and the 1820s were Derry's Golden Age of theatre, then the middle decades of the nineteenth century have a claim to be its first Golden Age of music, when the foundations of its future musical life were laid. Growth was slow to start, however, with concert performances in the 1830s still infrequent and irregular.

Five groups of musicians visited Derry between 1834 and 1840: three Italian, one Polish guitarist and one each from Scotland and England. Madame D'Alberti was first, on 23 May 1834. She had arrived several days early to make arrangements for her two 'Grand Concerts of Vocal and Instrument Music' on 28 May and 10 June. D'Alberti was a lesser-known soprano – not in the same starry category as Catalani or, later, Jenny Lind – but her concerts nonetheless drew 'highly respectable audiences' to Corporation Hall, enticed perhaps by a press preview claiming that she was 'a celebrated pupil of Rosini [sic]'. The concerts, of course, focused on Madame D'Alberti's soprano voice: her compass of three octaves, 'the brilliancy of her cyncopated [sic] and staccato passages and the clear rapidity of her chromatic scales'. She sang mainly operatic arias, including the 'Cavatina' from Bellini's *Norma* – a *tour de force* for any soprano. The D'Alberti concerts also had instrumental pieces by the band of the First Royals, stationed in the city, and by the Perois Family. Admission was a hefty 5s, prohibitive for all but the well-off, but her concerts provided a unique opportunity for Derry audiences to hear something of Italian opera, albeit in a concert setting.

Visits by other European musicians took place through the 1830s. They fell into three categories: child prodigies, family groups and novelty acts. The concerts by Italian-born virtuoso Giulio Regondi (1822-1872) in June 1835 combined all three. He was a child prodigy, he travelled and performed alongside his 'father' (in reality, his guardian and step-father), and he played the concertina, guitar and mellophone. The concertina was a relatively new instrument, invented just seven years earlier, and had a curiosity appeal for provincial audiences. From advance publicity in the press, concert-goers learned that Regondi had played in Milan and Paris at the age of seven, and had already earned the admiration of Paganini. His three concerts featured guitar and concertina solos, and – always a popular item with a Derry audience – 'Irish and Scotch Airs'. His father had a supporting role; he sang duets with his son and several solos, including a favourite, 'Laughing Song'. The young Regondi also gave a solo performance of the overture to Rossini's opera *The Italian Girl in Algiers*, a challenging showpiece. A year later, the Valentini family (father, son and daughter) performed 'songs, dance and ventriloquism', a similar mixture of novelty and variety.

By the 1840s, the visits of celebrity performers were more frequent and usually involved giving several concerts. Another change was that, towards the end of the decade, local musicians themselves began to give concerts and set up music societies. Despite this increase in performances, however, the number of venues dwindled. Up to 1833 there had been four venues: the Theatre, Corporation Hall, the King's Arms Hotel and the Cathedral. By 1850, there was only Corporation Hall. The theatre had closed, the Cathedral no longer held concerts, and in 1849 the King's Arms Hotel had become the Convent of Mercy. A solo concert by the Polish guitarist Mr Szczepanowski ten years earlier was the last concert there.

The Royal Agricultural Society Concerts

A major event for city audiences occurred in the week beginning Monday 9 August 1847, when the Royal Agricultural Society of Ireland (RASI) held its annual meeting in Derry for the first time. The local newspapers went to town in their coverage, the *Sentinel* publishing a special supplement on the celebrations, which included a 'Grand Ball', 'Grand Banquet' and of course, a 'Grand Concert'.

The concert was held on 11 August in Corporation Hall, with a special band brought over from Glasgow, and soloists from the 'Glasgow and Edinburgh Concerts' and the 'London Dress Concerts'. This was the biggest musical event in Derry since Catalani's visit in 1829, and the first professional orchestral concert ever in Derry, with music by Balfe, Mozart, Bellini and Labitzky. Tickets were priced at 4s 6d for the Body of the House and 2s 6d for the Gallery, and the gentry were advised that, 'Carriages [were] to be ordered for half past ten o'clock.'

But then a second concert, billed as a 'Promenade Concert', was advertised for the following Saturday at 12 noon in a pavilion in Bishop Street. This concert seems not to have been held under the auspices of the RASI but to have been organised by the musicians themselves, seizing the opportunity to use the society's pavilion before it was dismantled. It had been specially erected for the 'grand' events earlier in the week, but the Saturday concert-goers were assured that it would 'be lighted with Gas, and appear in the same splendour as at the Grand Ball'. For this – Derry's first promenade concert – all tickets were 1s. The band and soloists were the same for both concerts, and the Saturday programme included orchestral items too, with overtures by Rossini and Mozart. But it had more popular items as well, in the form of songs, glees and choruses, instead of just solo instrumental pieces. This opportunistic use of the Bishop Street pavilion marked the beginning of popular concerts in Derry, a development which was to make concerts more affordable to city people in the following decades.

During the week of the RASI meeting, all the official events in Corporation Hall and Bishop Street were widely supported by the local well-to-do and the festivities were described in lavish detail in the press. They served to divert attention from a very different event, an agricultural and human calamity on a national scale, which was taking place in Ireland at the same time: the *Sentinel* noted that between 1 and 18 June 1847, 2,400 people emigrated from the port of Derry, as the ravages of the Great Famine reached their height. The contrast between the scenes of conviviality in the specially erected pavilion in Bishop Street and the harrowing scenes on Derry's quaysides, throws into sharp relief the yawning gap between the lives of the elites, and their entertainments, and those of most ordinary people.

Unsung Émigrés: Foreign Musicians in Derry

Major influences on the development of the city's musical life at this time were musicians who settled in Derry from Scotland and mainland Europe. In Derry, Madame D'Alberti had been accompanied on piano by Madame Perois, her husband, Caesar

Augusta, contributing a violin solo. The Perois family ran a boarding school at 34 Bishop Street, where they also gave music and dancing lessons.[17] Another French family named D'Acosta, new to the city in 1831, were music and dancing teachers as well. The young son of the family had danced at the Artillery Lane Theatre during its final 1833 season.

There was a steady stream of these musician immigrants throughout the 1840s, and it was principally they who transformed the musical scene in Derry in the middle of the century. Church precentors and organists, bandmasters, dancing masters, pianists and instrumental teachers, from Germany, Italy, Poland and France, held concerts, set up music societies and bands, and taught music. In the thirty years after 1830, no fewer than fifteen European families of musicians and about a dozen Scottish musicians arrived. Amongst the Europeans were the Polish Bartowski couple; Henry Logier (Irish born, but whose father, Johann Bernhard Logier, was a German of Huguenot origin); the Italian singing teacher Signor Rivelli; and later, the German Waldemar Malmene and another Pole, Captain Jerzy Renczynski. Now largely forgotten, they brought hitherto lacking innovation and variety to the musical life of their adopted city. Of these, the most long-lasting contribution was from three generations of the Logier family.

The Logier Family

William Henry Logier (1802-1870), known simply as Henry, was involved in music teaching, concerts, music societies, social entertainments and church music for over a quarter of a century in Derry. His children and a grandchild followed in his footsteps: Elizabeth and Joseph, between 1861 and 1922, followed by his granddaughter Harriette. They became Derry's longest-lasting musical dynasty. Henry Logier's many-sided career in Derry serves as a kind of microcosm of its musical life and its expansion from that of a small provincial town based on trade to that of a newly industrialised city of the mid-Victorian age.

The family's connection with Derry began with Henry Logier's arrival in the city in November 1843. He was well travelled and had a cosmopolitan background, having previously taught in Prussia, London and Dublin.[18] From the beginning, Logier had a high public profile, placing frequent advertisements in the press for his 'Logierian Academy' in Richmond Street, for his wife's boarding school on the East Wall, and offering sales of instruments.[19] He had pupils in Derry, Strabane and Donegal. But the scope of his contribution to Derry's musical life widened in the 1850s.

Being a more than competent pianist and violinist, he was increasingly in demand as accompanist and bandleader. In December 1856, for example, Logier played the harmonium at the Apprentice Boys' Anniversary Soirée in Corporation Hall, in a programme of party songs, glees and choruses. A few days later, he was accompanist, on piano this time, at a celebration soirée for the opening of the new Tillie & Henderson shirt factory in Foyle Road. Logier played at every type of social event, from Literary Association meetings and temperance meetings to Presbyterian Sunday school soirées. He preferred, it seems, to accompany others, rather than take centre stage as soloist. These freelance engagements provided him with extra income and also helped establish his reputation as a central figure in Derry's musical life.

In an unpaid capacity, he was a founder member of the Londonderry Musical Association (LMA) in 1849 and his skills as an accomplished violinist were frequently praised in their concerts. Then in the 1860s, Logier organised his own 'Annual Concerts' in both Derry and Strabane, using the 1862 concert in Corporation Hall to launch the musical career of his eldest daughter, Elizabeth. The most unusual of his concerts was in June 1864, when he played a 'grand band piano' of ten instruments, including drum and triangles, all of which he offered for sale afterwards.

Logier's contribution to Derry's music received public recognition in December 1858 with a benefit concert in Corporation Hall. The range and quality of the musicians who took part reflected the esteem in which Logier was held within the city: the Cathedral organist, the precentor of Third Derry Presbyterian congregation, and members of both the LMA and the Londonderry Choral Union all united to perform alongside him. Logier himself led the orchestra of forty instrumentalists in a programme of choruses, and vocal and flute solos. According to the newspapers, the audience was both 'numerous and fashionable', and the 'general effect of the music, grand and magnificent'.

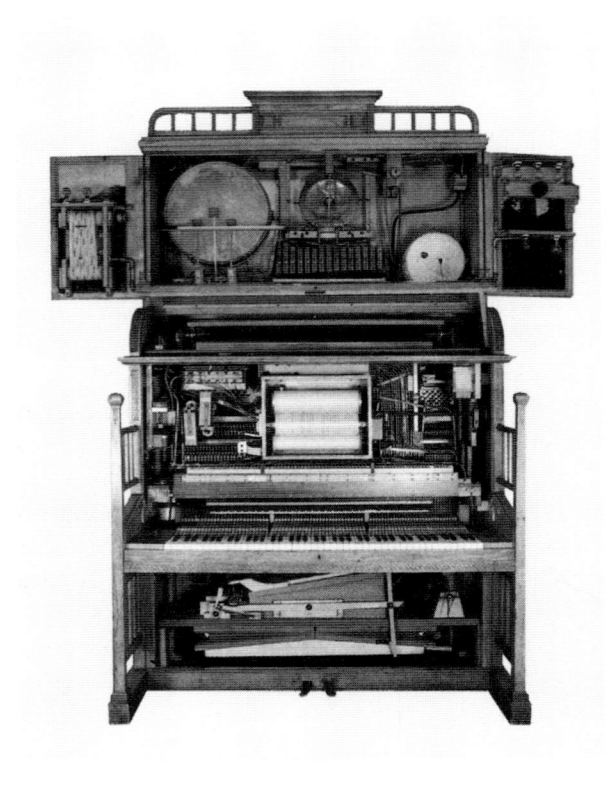

Logier's last public appearance was in April 1867. By then he was an elderly man, struggling to maintain teaching com-

A multi-instrument piano of the type 'played' by Henry Logier at his concert in June 1864. He later offered it for sale. (By kind permission of Siegfried's Musikkabinett, Rudesheim, Germany)

mitments alongside his duties as organist at Christ Church, a post he had taken up the year before. He died on 15 May 1870, leaving his family in dire straits. An indication of this is a small notice that was posted in the *Sentinel* some months later by the curate of the Cathedral, appealing for financial help for Logier's family, 'now reduced to great poverty'.

Of Logier's twelve children, two, Elizabeth and Joseph, stayed on as musicians in Derry; two older sons, Henry and Frederick, both military musicians, emigrated to Bermuda and America respectively. Elizabeth was a gifted soprano and pianist. When she was still only fifteen, the press described her performance of Beethoven's *Moonlight Sonata* as 'faultless ... her fingering proving her to be a perfect mistress of the instrument, her singing of great compass, flexibility and sweetness'. Elizabeth's income as a music teacher supported the family in the ten years following her father's death.

Joseph Logier (1861-1922) was a pupil at the Model School when his father died. In 1892, he became organist at St Augustine's church, a part-time post. His main job was as production manager in a Derry shirt factory.[20] The Logiers' long musical connection with Derry ended in 1934, when Joseph's widow Rebecca and daughter Harriette, both music teachers, moved to Belfast. In contrast with her father, Harriette was a flamboyant figure, revelling in the Logier name and her Huguenot lineage. She was fondly remembered in Derry as wearing bright red lipstick and smoking French cigarettes. Henry Logier, her grandfather, is buried in Lone Moor Cemetery with his second wife, Margaret, son Joseph and four grandchildren.

Concert Beginnings, 1849-1853

Logier was a frequent performer at concerts in Derry, but in comparison with other Cathedral cities, local musicians were slow to put on concerts of their own. Cathedral organist John Walsh had lived in Derry since 1818 but only held his first concert in March 1849, and then it was given jointly with William Watson, the Glasgow-born precentor of First Derry. The programme included Scottish songs by Watson, Italian and English songs by Walsh's daughter, and interludes by the band of the 95th Regiment. There was no press review, but the concert must have been successful, as it was repeated two months later. The same performers reappeared, but now joined by Mr Cordner, 'an eminent Professor from the Cathedral of Armagh'. A brief review in the *Standard* mentioned attendance by a 'numerous and highly respectable assemblage' and a concert programme 'exceedingly well selected'. These were the first locally organised concerts in Derry since the final Londonderry Musical Society concert in March 1819, and were a new development on the musical scene. They were followed up in the 1850s by a series of regular concerts by William Watson and by the LMA.

William Watson, Precentor of First Derry

After his initial collaborative ventures with Walsh, Watson organised his own series of concerts over the next two years, becoming the first church musician to make a significant impact on musical life in the city at large. One of these was 'A Concert of Sacred Music' in Glendermott Presbyterian church (Waterside) on Tuesday 11 February 1851, with a chorus of 'Two Hundred Voices'. This concert marked the beginning of large-scale choral singing in Derry.

Watson's choir was assembled from his weekly public vocal classes in Corporation Hall, taught through Tonic Solfa.[21] But he did not restrict his teaching to Derry; he also held classes in Coleraine, Limavady, and at churches at Banagher and Upper Cumber. Many of his concerts were linked to his singing classes and were as much showcases for his teaching as public concerts. A press review of a January 1853 concert began with a reference to Watson 'having concluded his classes for the season', and added that in the concert itself he was 'ably assisted by his pupils' in psalm tunes. A Scottish element was added to the concert by the inclusion of some solo Scots Gaelic airs of Watson's own composition.

Watson's departure from Derry, in April 1853, to become 'Conductor of the Psalmody' in Regent-Square Free church, London, was marked by a concert of sacred music in First Derry and a presentation in formal recognition of his 'assiduous and skilful training' of the choir.

The concerts of Walsh, Watson and, as we will see, the LMA, fundamentally altered the pattern of concert provision in Derry, in that, for first time, local perform-

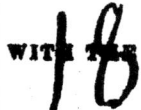

> **MR. WATSON,**
> WITH THE CONCURRENCE OF THE REV. MR. BUCHANAN AND SESSION,
> WILL GIVE A
> **CONCERT OF SACRED MUSIC,**
> IN THE
> **FIRST PRESBYTERIAN CHURCH, GLENDERMOTT,**
> **ON TUESDAY EVENING, 11th FEBRUARY INST.,**
> On which occasion he will be Assisted by Two HUNDRED VOICES.
> Mr. W. will introduce a number of GAELIC AIRS during the course of the Evening.
> *Tickets of Admission, Sixpence each, to be had at the*
> *STANDARD* OFFICE.
> Londonderry, February 4, 1851.

Derry's first choral concert: William Watson's Chorus of 200 Voices at Glendermott Presbyterian church. (Londonderry Standard, 5 February 1851)

ers outnumbered visiting ones. There were also two new major players on the musical scene: the church musician and the music society. Together they dominated concert life in Derry for the remainder of the nineteenth century.

The Londonderry Musical Association (LMA)

The LMA was Derry's first 'inclusive' choral and instrumental music society. At first it was a 'closed' society, holding musical 'meetings' in Corporation Hall which were neither open to the public nor advertised in the press. But within eighteen months it had thrown off these hangovers from earlier gentlemen's music clubs and developed a broader membership. By March 1852, even ladies were encouraged to join, 'to lend their sweet voices' to the society's chorus.

The LMA was formed in the latter half of 1849 from the city's professional musicians: the McCloskie family (father Michael and two sons, military musicians); a dancing master, 'Old Jack' Laughlin; organist John Walsh; the precentor of First Derry William Watson, and Henry Logier. All had come to Derry from elsewhere. At first the chorus was made up of young men from 'merchant families' who sang glees, 'robust songs and hearty choruses' accompanied by the band. But from early 1851, there was a new openness about membership, the society band and concerts. The *Standard* claimed that it was gaining 'new members daily', and by March 1852 it numbered 130, although many were 'honorary', non-performing members. The band had a core of eleven players, mainly the original professional musicians with a sprinkling of amateurs: a local doctor, James Eames; a retired army sergeant, Mr McCullough, and the (unnamed) bandmaster of the 54th Regiment from Ebrington Barracks. Walsh was conductor, with Laughlin and Logier on violins; the McCloskie family, all three wind players, completed the ensemble.

Two concerts were advertised for early in 1851. The first, in February, featured Walsh and his daughter (a singer) alongside society members. In the second concert, in May, they were joined by members of the longer-established Belfast Anacreontic Society. At both concerts, members sang glees and choruses and the band played short instrumental interludes. Then the LMA took the step of advertising its first 'Monthly Concert', set for 2 December 1851. This concert was the first in three winter seasons (of five concerts each) which ran until April 1854. The concert programmes were not advertised in advance, but printed copies were available at the door. In the 1850s, the Derry press began to give more detailed concert reviews, allowing a glimpse of the LMA's repertoire and main performers.

The January 1852 concert had an ambitious programme, featuring a Haydn symphony, an overture by Boildeau, several polkas, galops, quadrilles and glees, and other unnamed vocal and instrumental items. Soloists included singers, wind players and a string quartet (drawn from the band) which played a quartet by Stamitz.

This became the standard format for the concerts, with each including a symphony (usually by Haydn), shorter orchestral items by Rossini, Bellini, Reeves, D'Albert or Mozart, and a wide selection of 'popular airs' and dances. This repertoire was similar to that of the Belfast Anacreontic Society, and their advice on programming may well have been sought at the joint concert in 1851. Sacred music and oratorio selections were excluded from the concert programmes of both societies. Instead, they focused entirely on secular music, with repeat performances of popular operatic melodies, Irish and Scottish songs, and orchestral pieces by the 'full band'.

At first, the local press could barely contain its pride in having an active music society in the city. In December 1850, with the society still in its infancy, the *Standard* spoke of the 'rich treat' afforded by their concerts 'which would reflect credit on any musical society in the kingdom'. The newspaper's glowing descriptions of the concerts, akin to that given to theatre performances in the 1820s, was characteristic of the early press coverage and was a valuable asset to the society in encouraging recruitment and providing free publicity. But then the reports became less adulatory, criticising not only the amateur performers but also the responses of the audience. The latter was blamed for demanding too many encores and so prolonging concerts. Concert reviews in the *Sentinel* could be particularly biting. Its review of the February 1952 concert singled out an unfortunate (and unnamed) cornet-à-piston soloist for special mention, declaring tartly that, 'He has not yet acquired sufficient confidence for solo playing in public, his intonation being hurried and indistinct.' The review did, however, praise the strings for displaying 'accuracy and brilliant execution'. This was the start of more mature and discriminating – if at times unflattering – reporting of musical events in Derry.

The LMA provided a platform for younger talent, with the children of professional musicians as recurring soloists. These included: Walsh's daughter, a singer and pianist, and son Billy, an 'entertaining singer'; Laughlin's daughter on piano, and the two McCloskie sons on flutes. The McCloskie boys' father Michael 'arranged' medleys of 'popular airs'; in December 1853, a quartet played his 'Scotch Medley', followed four months later by his 'Irish Medley' for full band. The audience's instinctive reaction to these pieces provoked the *Journal* to comment austerely on 'the offensive efforts of some persons to beat time with their feet'.

LMA concerts were always well attended and supported by 'an assemblage ... of the elite of the town'. At an 1854 concert, the *Sentinel* reported that 'the anxiety to obtain places was so great that a large number of persons holding tickets assembled in front of Corporation-hall before the doors were opened, and when the performance commenced the room was crowded to overflowing with a most respectable audience'. Notwithstanding this popularity with the public, the LMA, for reasons which are unclear, was beginning to break up. Its last scheduled concert was a May 1954 benefit for Michael McCloskie and John Laughlin; no concert season was announced for 1854/5. That might have been the last heard of it but for the stimulus of 'The Patriotic Fund' that same winter.

The Patriotic Fund Concerts

The Patriotic Fund, set up to aid the Crimean War effort, led to a frenzy of national fundraising. Derry newspapers joined in, urging donations and publishing lengthy lists of local contributors. Then in December 1854, a letter from 'A Citizen' appeared in the *Sentinel* requesting the city's music society give a concert in aid of the fund. A reply from the LMA secretary confirmed that, in spite of their 'current difficulties', a concert would be held in January. Mention was made of 'several of the performers having left town' and the society needing 'a few weeks to practise'. The resulting concerts on 25 and 26 January, which were augmented by outside soloists and members of the gentry, saw the LMA give its final and crowning performances.

The orchestra was twenty-two strong, equally divided between amateur and professional players. The chorus was largely drawn from the principal merchant families in the city but local gentry on this occasion lent their support because of the patriotic and charitable character of the concerts. The press had announced in advance that 'Ladies of respectability, and of high accomplishments, intend ... to assist'. While the concert programme was broadly similar to that of previous LMA concerts, there was a 'Patriotic Medley' of melodies from England, Scotland, France and Ireland for 'full band', specially arranged for the occasion by Michael McCloskie, which was deemed both the musical highlight and the 'charter piece of the evening'. It provoked 'tumultuous applause and loud cheers' from a 'most brilliant and fashionable assembly'. Concert reviews were detailed and fulsome in praise of the performers, the sole exception being a visiting musician, Mr Gray from Westminster Abbey, who was criticised for the 'falsetto effeminacy of his tones'; his solos, it was said, were only 'fairly sung'. The concert was repeated the next day but with ticket prices considerably reduced, 'in order to afford all classes the opportunity of attending'.

After these concerts, the LMA disappears from view. It had lost two key members through the death of John Laughlin and Michael McCloskie's appointment as bandmaster of the Donegal Artillery. And although one newspaper wrote about 'a short rest' by the society in later 1855, there was, in the event, no further revival of the concerts given in its name.[22]

Instead, Derry acquired its first choral society, which had been set up the previous year by Glasgow musician James Peterkin. He was the third Scottish-born precentor at First Derry Presbyterian church and yet another of the many well-qualified 'outsiders' who played a crucial, if now largely forgotten, role in Derry's musical development. What set the precentors apart from others was their Scottish Presbyterian background and their consequent insistence on choral, rather than instrumental, music. Indeed it was claimed that by 1800, 'Scotland had more vocal societies to her credit than the remainder of the British Isles put together.' (It was also hinted at by sceptics south of the border that singing was a good deal cheaper than buying a musical instrument.) Whatever the reason, the Scottish Presbyterian

GRAND CONCERT
IN AID OF
THE PATRIOTIC FUND.

THE COMMITTEE of the LONDONDERRY MUSICAL ASSOCIATION, beg to announce that they purpose giving a Concert, in the CORPORATION HALL, on THURSDAY Evening, JANUARY 25th, 1855.

PROGRAMME.

PART FIRST.

HAYDEN's Symphony in C.
GLEE—" Up, Clansmen, up," .... C. F. Bird.
SUITE DE VALSES—" Le Moulin des Tilleuls," Strauss
SONG—With Orchestral accompaniment. " Let the bright Seraphim," .... Handel.
    Mrs. WILLIAM HARVEY.
PATRIOTIC MEDLEY—Arranged by Mr. M'CLOSKIE.
SOLO—PIANO FORTE—" When the Swallows hasten home," .... Oesten.
    Miss H. DAVIDSON.
BALLAD—" Sweet Home," .... Bishop.
    Mr. GRAY.
DUET—HARP and PIANO FORTE—" Io Ludia Torquato Tasso," .... Donizetti.
    The Hon. Mrs. HUNTER and Miss HUNTER.
TRIO—" Perfida Chlori," .... Cherubini.
    Mrs. WILLIAM M'CLELLAN, Mrs. J. SMYTH, and Mr. GRAY.
QUADRILLE—" Como," .... D'Albert.

PART SECOND.

OVERTURE—" Le Nozze di Figaro," ...... Mozart.
    Piano accompaniment by Miss LAUGHLIN.
GLEE—" Hail Smiling Morn," .... Spofforth.
POLKA—" Review," .... D'Albert.
ENGLISH SONG—" The Young Soldier," .... Balfe.
    Mrs J. HAYDEN.
SOLO—FLUTE, Mr. M'CLOSKIE.
SONG—With Guitar and Flute accompaniment.— " When the day with rosy light," .... Newland.
    Miss SEXTON Mr. R. WILSON, and Mr. COWIE.
SOLO—PIANO FORTE—" Barcarole de Oberon," Favarger.
    Mrs. J. SMYTH.
SONG—" Ah per sempre, Io ti perdei"—Puritani, Bellini.
    JOHN C. F. HUNTER, Esq.
TRIO—" Ti Prego," .... Curchsman.
    Mrs. J. M'CLELLAN, Mrs. J. SMYTH, and Mr. GRAY.
SOLO—PIANO FORTE—" Maritana," .... Wallace.
    Miss DAVIDSON.
VALSE—" La Belle Suisse," .... D'Albert.
" Partant Pour la Syrie," and " God Save the Queen."

Doors open at a quarter past Seven. Music to Commence at Eight o'clock precisely.

Tickets—1st Division, 5s; 2d ditto, 2s 6d. Children under 12, Half Price. Tickets to be had of Messrs. HEMPTON.

Carriages to be in Waiting at Twelve o'clock.

(By order,)
    ROBERT WILSON, Secretary.

The Patriotic Fund Concerts in aid of the Crimean War, 1855. (Londonderry Journal, 25 January 1855)

affinity with vocal music, and with choirs and music societies in particular, found fertile ground in Derry.

Presbyterian Precentors and their Music Societies

Presbyterianism had long been a potent force in the city. In 1772, there had been a single Presbyterian congregation; seventy years later there were four, all employing precentors to train their choirs and lead the psalmody in church services. Less that 40 per cent of Presbyterian congregations in Ireland had choirs before 1874, so Derry was unique in having Presbyterian choirs in each congregation, which also sang at Sabbath school soirées, temperance meetings and in music societies. Presbyterians loomed large in Derry's social and political life as well, their voice amplified through their ownership of two of the city's newspapers, the *Sentinel* and the *Standard*. Presbyterian precentors similarly had a major influence on Derry's musical life, their contribution and leadership far outstripping that of other denominations. In particular, First and Third Derry congregations – the largest and wealthiest of the four – led the way in choral music.[23]

First Derry employed a series of Scottish precentors, beginning with William Watson, and followed by James Peterkin in 1853 and William Kerr in 1859. All three brought a passion for choral music to Derry. In the twenty years after 1854, the city had eight choral societies, six of them founded by precentors. By way of comparison, organists were employed in the Anglican and Catholic churches in the 1850s: John Walsh in the Cathedral and James Smyly in the Long Tower church of St Columba. Yet neither was involved in public choral training or choral societies. It was the precentors' commitment to unaccompanied singing which laid the foundations of the city's choral tradition, in which later citizens of Derry have taken so much pride.

Peterkin formed Derry's first choral society, the Londonderry Harmonic Society. Its first concert was in the lecture hall of the church in March 1854, with a programme of psalms and anthems, interspersed with songs by Peterkin. Membership was drawn principally from his church choir, and its repertoire of mainly 'sacred music' was probably an extension of its normal Sunday selection. In the first two years, the society held a few public 'practice meetings' in Corporation Hall, but its role was usually confined to singing at church soirées, temperance meetings and Sunday school events. However, Peterkin had ambitious plans for the society, promising Derry its first 'full' performance of *Messiah* in 1855. Nothing came of this plan, however, and the society did not survive Peterkin's return to Glasgow in 1858.

That same year, Henry Dobson, precentor of Third Derry, started the Londonderry Choral Union, a society similar to Peterkin's in size and repertoire. It numbered forty members 'of both sexes' and met weekly in Corporation Hall to practise 'sacred music'. Notwithstanding the dangers that might have been feared in bringing the sexes together in other circumstances, the Choral Union was lauded by the *Sentinel* in July 1858 for its 'refining and elevating influence on all young persons'.

But in spite of this lively choral activity, there were still complaints made of the poor standard of congregational singing. In February 1858, a correspondent signing himself 'Philharmonic' wrote to the *Standard* complaining of the singing in some congregations, which (he claimed) was 'a perfect mockery'. He recommended that:

> ... some of our Ladies and Gentlemen in Derry should form themselves into an association for the improvement of sacred music. Let all the congregations unite for this purpose and practise in one of the school-rooms, and let them sing on the Sabbath the tunes they have practised during the week.

In short, notwithstanding the efforts of the precentors, at least one Derry Presbyterian thought there was still much to be done to bring singing in church up to an acceptable level.

Musicians from outside Ireland continued to visit the city in a steady trickle, on average about five per year, but more than in the 1830s and '40s, when visits by itinerant musicians had been few and irregular. 'Hybrid concerts' – novelty acts, singing and dancing troupes, and husband and wife duos – featured in public entertainment as in previous decades. In 1850, the Female American Serenaders in April were followed by the Ethiopian Serenaders in November, the highlight of whose performance was 'Juba' dancing (the extravagant form of 'black' dancing popularised by its African-American dancer Master Juba). Both were typical of 'ethnic' or 'blackface' minstrel troupes which toured England and Ireland about this time. The following year, 1851, brought Professor Russell, 'the Real American Magician ... in his Grand Vocal and Instrumental Concert'. He played the piano, accordion and American banjo. He gave six performances in Derry, joined in the last by the military band of the 34th Depot.

Military Bands

Military bands were a familiar sight and sound in Derry in the 1850s. Since 1844, they had played on the walls of the city in the summer months for the benefit of the citizens, and they regularly performed at a wide range of social events in Derry, from the visit of the Lord Lieutenant of Ireland in October 1835, to a dinner celebrating the installation of the Catholic Coadjutor Bishop John McLaughlin in July 1837. Since civilian bands were unknown in Derry before 1850, there was a vacuum in the city's social life that the military bands were well placed to fill. They played at concerts, balls, regattas, flower shows, civic dinners, Apprentice Boys' celebrations, temperance soirées and cricket matches. They had a much appreciated and uncontroversial civic and community-wide role in Derry's musical life.

Derry's first regular outdoor concerts started in May 1849, when the 95th Regiment's brass band played on Wednesday afternoons at Gwyn's Institution. This was a charity school, set up in 1833 in Shipquay Street with a legacy from a wealthy local merchant, John Gwyn; it housed and taught only the Protestant orphan children of Derry. In 1847 it moved to a new building in the grounds of what is today known as Brooke Park.[24] Here, concert-goers could 'have a promenade in the beautiful grounds' and listen to polkas, waltzes, marches, Irish and English airs and operatic melodies. The concerts, however, were not free: admission was by ticket only.

Public performances by military bands were not simply exercises in altruism; band members themselves were responsible for the provision and upkeep of their own instruments and music, and this cost money. In July 1838, for example, the band of the 64th Depot had provided the musical entertainment at a fireworks display in the Linenhall, playing 'several New and Select Airs' throughout the evening. Admission was 'Ladies and Gentlemen 2*s* each, Trades People 1*s*', at least part of which went into the band's coffers. Such money-making events were in addition to the band's 'official' duties of parading for the sovereign's birthday and welcoming dignitaries to the city.

Even when Derry had several of its own civilian bands, military bands continued to give outdoor concerts, often alongside the city bands. However, when it came to the city's most prestigious events, only the military bands played. At the visit of the Channel Fleet in August 1874, military bands alone played at the welcoming reception, the grand ball and the Mayor's Garden Party. In contrast, five local bands led the Apprentice Boys' procession the following week.

From 1861, the bands published their concert programmes in advance. Their repertoires were broad, ranging from operatic melodies by Rossini, Donizetti and Meyerbeer to local favourites, such as 'Derry's Walls' and 'No Surrender'. By 1866, the entire programmes of the band of the Londonderry Light Infantry in Gwyn's Institution were listed in press editorials. Henry Stoll, their conductor, often included his own compositions in the music, like his 'Quick Step' and 'Schottische', in June of that year. Even the music played at Derry's cricket matches was carefully listed in the press, perhaps attributing a level of musical appreciation to the city's sportsmen and their supporters that would seem wildly optimistic today.

The press often praised the military bands and regiments stationed in the city. In 1838, the 35th Regiment was commended for their 'sobriety and propriety of demeanour', and the soldiers of the 15th Depot in 1855 were considered to share that same 'propriety of conduct which contrast[s] sharply with the turbulent spirit of previous regiments'. This was perhaps a dig at members of the locally recruited Londonderry Militia, who were sometimes reported in the press as being involved in street fights and scuffles. In 1855, the Militia numbered 431 men plus 20 officers, and was permanently based at Ebrington Barracks. Notwithstanding its reputation for (occasional) loutish behaviour in the city, the Londonderry Militia Brass Band soon became Derry's 'official' military band. In July and August 1856, its engagements included playing at outdoor concerts at Gwyn's on Wednesdays and Saturdays, two regattas, a Regatta Ball in Buncrana, a Presbyterian Sabbath soirée, and a civic entertainment in the Corporation Hall for visiting representatives of The Honourable The Irish Society of London.

The personnel of military bands made their own contribution to music in the city, with many of the musicians having key roles in music societies, concerts and teaching. Some military musicians offered private music lessons, sold brass instruments and provided band tuition. Henry Klophel was one of the first to do so, in 1833. He lived at 11 Frances Street and taught piano, violin and flute. J.B. Ziegler and Henry Stoll were amongst the last, in the 1860s. All three were born in Germany, arrived in Derry as members of the military, and stayed on in the city after their discharge. Stoll latterly became bandmaster at Foyle College in 1870.[25]

As mentioned earlier, music societies also benefitted: the McCloskie family of wind players were founder members of the LMA, then set up their own 'entertainment' bands which were hired out for soirées and balls. Michael McCloskie taught 'cornopean, bugle, clarinet and flute', and was conductor of the unnamed 'splendid band of teetotallers' in 1846, probably Derry's first amateur band.[26]

The Apprentice Boys

The Apprentice Boys' Clubs, too, depended heavily on military bands, until their own Maiden City Band was formed in 1860. As vividly described in the 1837 *Ordnance Survey Memoir for Londonderry*, during the Apprentice Boys' celebrations the military bands were 'on call' from early morning, 'As early as three o'clock in the morning, parties of youths marched through the streets, preceded by military bands.' The celebrations found the 'houses lined with people ... amid shouts, music and execrations'. The author of the *Memoir* took a dim view of these manifestations, warning that in recent years, 'the perpetuation of such customs ... [has] become a subject of contention' in the city.

However, later in the day, the mood of the celebrations changed: there was an evening of toasts, speeches and communal songs, interspersed with musical interludes by those same bands. Such 'Bottle and Glass' events remained central to the Apprentice Boys' celebrations until the mid-1850s, when they changed to something more in keeping with the changing, stricter moral tone in the city.[27] The Bottle and Glass portion of the festivities was replaced by a respectable soirée in Corporation Hall, to which ladies were invited. The *Sentinel*, once a neutral, if not approving reporter of the uproarious goings-on of the 1830s, commented, 'It is pleasant to find the old system of "Bottle and Glass" has been supplanted by this happier and more intellectual mode of conviviality.'

Local musicians still had their part in the new soirées, as paid performers alongside the usual military brass bands. The 1855 soirée, for example, had music seller

James Hunter on piano alongside Signor Rivelli, an Italian singing teacher. The soirée in the following year had a larger contingent of local musicians, with Logier (on harmonium), church musicians James Peterkin and Robert Stafford, music shop apprentice and singer William Graham, and Hunter once again on piano. There was an unnamed 'chorus' too, though it is unclear if this was an Apprentice Boys' chorus or that of the Londonderry Harmonic Society. The musical items, which came between the speeches and toasts, consisted of 'loyal songs' ('The day our Fathers closed the Gates, a long time ago') and glees ('Glorious Apollo', for four voices, with piano accompaniment). In 1856, piano solos featured for the first time – a form of music not previously associated with Apprentice Boys' gatherings. Welcoming the 'refined' nature of these soirées, the *Sentinel* warmly encouraged attendance at 'this new attempt at social improvement'.

The Piano Wars

By an odd quirk of fate, pianos, usually associated with refinement and polite social intercourse, became the focus of a bitter trade war between rival sellers of the instruments in 1850s Derry. Pianos sales had risen sharply at the beginning of the decade, with two principal sellers leading the market: John Hempton, from his shop (est. 1847) in the Diamond, and the Neills & Minniece partnership at 9/10 Shipquay Street (est. 1855), both, oddly enough, calling themselves the 'London Pianoforte Warehouse'. Alongside them was Andrew Floyd, who had just opened his music shop in the Diamond, and an assortment of part-time traders: music teachers, auctioneers, bookshops and cabinet makers.[28] James Hunter was still selling pianos, but his fortunes were in decline. This was not due to any drop of interest in pianos, but because larger traders had entered the market, with spacious premises and more effective advertising. Hunter moved five times after leaving his second, more prestigious shop at 3 Pump Street, each successive removal to a more down-market location. The market for pianos in Derry had become highly competitive, and in December 1855, the battle was stepped up by rival salesmen via the advertising columns. The opening salvo was a large rectangular notice by Neills & Minniece announcing the opening of their newly extended shop and speaking of 'the disappointment that the Scotch and other inferior pianos have caused to many in this locality'. John Hempton responded two days later by advertising the arrival in his shop of 'new Harmoniums and Pianos that will still more successfully exclude the despised manufacturers from the market here'. No dealer's name was mentioned, nor were particular makes of pianos cited. But the newspaper's readers were left in no doubt about the targets of these comments: pianos imported and sold by Scotsman James Hunter.

The situation was complicated by the fact that Hempton had temporarily employed Hunter – then going through lean times – as a 'buyer' for his pianos. So the

An Edwardian postcard produced by Robert Floyd for his music shop in Pump Street. Note the 'Billiards' room advertised for the first floor. From 1848, three generations of the Floyd family had music shops in Derry, only closing in 1926 when the business moved to Portrush. (Author's collection)

slurs of Neills & Minniece's advertising campaign were as much directed at Hempton as at Hunter. Hempton, for his part, then announced that he would close his shop for the time being so as to go to London and Paris personally to choose pianos 'from the best manufacturers'. In this battle of the piano sellers, it was Hempton who ultimately emerged as the winner, and his became Derry's leading music shop in the latter half of the nineteenth century. The Neills & Minniece partnership was dissolved in 1862. Hunter was declared bankrupt in 1863, but re-emerged as a music trader in 1874.

All this time, piano and sheet music sales continued to grow, fuelled by the middle classes' new passion for amateur music-making. Concerts also flourished during the later 1850s. Economic growth, manifest in the new shirt factories and shipyard works, combined with the introduction of the railway system to Derry, was a major factor in allowing the city to share in an international 'concert boom'. By 1861, Derry's population had reached almost 21,000, small in comparison with most other industrialised cities, but large enough to attract celebrated musicians from the London and European concert platforms. Limerick-born soprano Catherine Hayes, popularly known as the 'Hibernian Nightingale' and the 'Swan of Erin', was the first 'celebrity' musician of this kind to visit Derry, in 1857. At this point she had already completed concert tours of America and Australia.

'The Swan of Erin'

Hayes was the first Irish-born opera singer to achieve international fame and fortune, earning £650 per month at the peak of her career in the early 1850s. Her concerts always aroused intense interest, no doubt heightened by the romantic and often-repeated story of her 'discovery' by Dr Knox, Anglican Bishop of Limerick, who, it was said, had overheard her as a young girl singing by a lakeside, and, impressed by the sweetness of her voice, arranged for her to study singing in Dublin. After further tuition in Milan, Hayes became the first Irish woman to sing at La Scala, in 1846. Her Covent Garden debut followed three years later, when queues a mile long formed to hear her.

Unlike Madame Catalani, who had arrived unheralded in 1829, Hayes' concerts were advertised weeks in advance. Thereafter, the press, as with one voice, built up a fever of excitement, like that which had gripped the city during the 1847 Agricultural Society meeting. The newspapers were filled with advertisements for the concerts – and for appropriate outfits to wear to them: 'Opera Cloaks; Lace Berthas and Jackets; Flowers and Head-dresses' were displayed for weeks beforehand at different draper's shops in the city. Ticket prices were high, at 7s 6d and 5s, but the concerts sold out within two days. Tickets were then offered for sale above their face value by individuals – the first evidence of a black market in concert tickets in Derry. The railway companies became involved for the first time, as sole agents for the gallery seats, available only from their stations at Omagh (for the first concert) and at Coleraine (for the second). Special trains were laid on at reduced fares for ticket-holders.

Hayes' two concerts on 28 and 29 January were the musical highlight of 1857, if not of the decade. For both, Corporation Hall was packed to overflowing 'with every available spot occupied'. The *Sentinel* deemed the concerts 'the most brilliantly successful within our

Celebrated Irish soprano Catherine Hayes (1825-1861), often called as the 'Hibernian Nightingale' in imitation of Jenny Lind, the 'Swedish Nightingale'.

recollection'. It did, however, express some initial disappointment at Hayes' opening aria, 'Softly Sighs the Voice of Evening' from Weber's *Der Freischütz*, 'although rendered with marvellous skill'. This disappointment was soon dispelled when she sang two well-known Irish and Scottish songs, 'The Harp That Once through Tara's Halls' and 'Comin' through the Rye'. The consensus was that Hayes was a 'first rate musician' who 'must be heard'.[29] In her touring party was Limerick-born George Osborne (1806-1893), the noted pianist, composer and friend of Chopin. He delighted Derry audiences with his own compositions, including his own 'Variations on Irish and Scotch Airs', performed on an 'Erard concert-pianoforte'. The reviews were full of praise, describing Osborne as 'one of the first pianists in Europe, if not the first' – an accolade that may not have been so wide of the mark for a man whose advice Berlioz had sought on writing for piano.

Catherine Hayes was only one, albeit easily the most famous, of five visiting musicians or groups of musicians to give concerts in Derry that year. There was a concert party from the London Popular Concerts, led by soprano Miss Magee (in January); three Scottish singers (in May); Henderson's Concert Party from Belfast (in October), and Charles Wood from Armagh Cathedral (in November). When one adds to these the many local musicians' and choral society concerts taking place within the same year, it is clear that, as the decade neared its end, Derry had finally come of age as a concert venue.

Four

'THE GLITTERATI', 1859-1886

The year 1859 was that of 'The Great Revival', when the Protestant population of Ulster was caught up in a spontaneous wave of religious renewal and conversion that spread rapidly across the whole north of Ireland. In Derry too, with its long Presbyterian tradition, its effects were felt in the form of mass open-air meetings in the Victoria Market, special church services, and morning prayer meetings in Corporation Hall so crowded that many were turned away. While the city's religious life was thus in ferment, the profile of music in Derry was raised by four celebrated figures on the European concert circuit. In the space of ten months, Louis Jullien, Henryk Wieniawski, Jenny Lind and Joseph Joachim all performed in Derry. In each case their reputations had preceded them, as they were musicians about whom local newspapers had previously published snippets of gossip culled from London journals.

Louis Jullien and Henryk Wieniawski

Jullien, his thirty-strong orchestra and 'support' musician Wieniawski arrived by train for their concert on 17 January. Advance publicity in the Derry press focused on Jullien himself, on his fame as a composer of light, popular dance music and his reputation for flamboyance. Although it is Wieniawski who is now better remembered as a composer, for his two violin concertos and several programme pieces, including the still popular *Légende*, it was Jullien's extravagances that caught people's attention at the time. One of the first celebrity orchestral conductors, he had his baton brought to him on a silver salver at the beginning of the concert, which he conducted wearing splendid waistcoats and immaculate white gloves.[30] His Derry concert aroused intense local excitement and promised spectacle – and did not disappoint.

Benjamin Roubaud's caricature of the flamboyant conductor Louis Jullien (1812-1860).

'The applause was rapturous and never was applause better deserved.' Thus the *Journal* described the response in Corporation Hall, 'filled from floor to ceiling'. The programme began with Rossini's *William Tell Overture*, followed by the *Pastoral Symphony* and then selections from Weber's *Der Freischütz*.[31] These were interspersed with quadrilles, polkas and marches composed by Jullien himself. Wieniawski was highly praised for his playing of Mendelssohn's *Violin Concerto*, in which, it was said, his 'brilliancy' shone. Listeners marvelled at 'his capacity for making the instrument do anything he pleases'. The press reports leave no doubt that the Derry audience felt that they had got their money's worth, even at the price of 6*s* and 3*s* per ticket. Jullien, in the event, had not long to enjoy his fame: within fourteen months he was dead, his last days spent insane and bankrupt in a Paris jail. By then, Derry had experienced two other celebrity concerts, by Jenny Lind, her husband (and accompanist) Otto Goldschmidt, and Joachim, on 17 and 18 October 1859.

Jenny Lind and Joseph Joachim

Lind was one of the first singers to be marketed as a musical phenomenon. Her ninety-three-concert tour of America in the early 1850s, promoted by the impresario P.T. Barnum, was unprecedented in its use of advertising and produced a reaction in audiences that led to the coining of the term 'Lindmania'. On a more modest scale, her two concerts in Derry were advertised weeks in advance, and notwithstanding – perhaps because of – the unheard of admission charges (15s, 10s and 6s), they attracted 'most crowded audiences'. The railway companies – as they had done for Jullien's concert – played their part in the concerts' success by arranging special trains and reduced rail fares for ticket-holders.

The concerts, one in the evening and one in the afternoon, featured Lind singing operatic arias by Mozart, Bellini and Weber, with other pieces from Moore's Melodies. The Derry newspapers were entranced by her performance and couched their reviews in superlatives. Joachim was accompanied by Goldschmidt on the piano in sonatas by Beethoven and Tartini, as well as in a medley of Irish melodies designed to display his virtuosity on the violin. Here, again, the press reviews were enthusiastic, acclaiming him a 'master of his instrument'.

The significance of these 1859 concerts is that they showed that Derry was able to provide the audiences, and resulting profits, to attract musicians of the highest rank. Other 'glitterati' soon followed; Catherine Hayes made a second visit in 1861 and two years later, pianist Sigismond Thalberg. However the city's first piano recital was by Frederick Eavestaff in September 1859, in the midst of the excitement generated by the Lind concerts.

Swedish soprano Jenny Lind (1820-1887), who appeared in Corporation Hall in 1859.

Derry's First Piano Recital

Eavestaff, son of a London piano manufacturer, arrived in Derry in the summer of 1859 to sell his father's pianos. At first he was merely a salesman, but within a few months he was offering piano tuition as well. Then he announced the first of a series of 'subscription only' piano recitals in Corporation Hall, scheduled for 2 p.m. on 20 September. The recital lasted about an hour and included Beethoven's *Moonlight Sonata*, some of Mendelssohn's *Songs without Words*, an *andante* by Thalberg and a *mazurka elegante* by Eavestaff himself. A brief press report said that the hall was 'filled by a fashionable assembly, mostly ladies'. This was understandable, given the time of day and the fact that admission by subscription ticket would have discouraged all but the well-to-do from attending.

Corporation Hall did not have its own piano; a piano generally being hired from John Hempton's shop and transported the 20 yards or so across the square. For the Lind concerts, a grand piano had been 'brought specially from Belfast'. Eavestaff, however, used one of his own pianos so that the audience could hear its superiority for themselves. After the first recital, there was no further press coverage, other than a brief mention in April 1860 that the recitals were completed 'some time ago'. Nor did Eavestaff's sales benefit as he must have hoped; within five months Neills & Minniece's London Piano Warehouse was selling off his stock at reduced prices. These recitals were the first instance of such brand promotions in Derry, but not the last. Four years later, Thalberg advertised that he was playing on a 'Splendid New Grand Pianoforte' by Messrs Erard & Co. (of Paris), 'expressly Manufactured' for his concerts.

Sigismond Thalberg

Thalberg (1812-1871) was a virtuoso pianist often compared by contemporaries to his friend and rival Franz Liszt. He was phenomenally successful, his concert tours in the early 1860s earning him the equivalent of £1.5 million in today's money. He gave his so-called 'Farewell Concert' – his one and only concert in the city – in Corporation Hall on 26 November 1863. The 'Farewell' may have been to audiences in Ireland in general, as he had performed earlier in Dublin and Belfast, but news of his playing had gone before him and three of Derry's newspapers heralded him as one of the leading pianists of the age. He was, they said, the 'Prince of Pianists', someone who 'must be seen and heard'. The exception was the *Standard*, which wondered about Thalberg's ability to retain the audience's attention for a full two hours. Afterwards, the paper had to confess that its doubts had been totally misplaced.

Thalberg played ten pieces, including six of his own compositions, designed to show off the virtuoso side of his piano-playing.[32] He also performed works by Beethoven, Chopin and Mendelssohn. Here was yet another celebrity concert that drew a huge Derry audience attracted by the reputation of the performer. But a factor in its success may have been the popularity of the piano itself, by now well established as the instrument *par excellence* of the Victorian home.

John Hempton

As noted earlier, John Hempton's London Pianoforte Warehouse had emerged as the clear winner in the piano-sales wars, and by late 1863 it was Derry's leading music shop. Hempton himself came from a family of booksellers, but trained as an attorney before turning to the book and music trade.[33] His interest in music seems to have been exclusively commercial. He neither sang (so far as we know) nor was he a member of any music society or band, and his involvement in concerts seems to have been limited to hiring out pianos to Corporation Hall and selling tickets for performances. His evidence to the 1869 Parliamentary Commission of Inquiry into street riots in Derry reveals an indifference to, or affected ignorance of, matters musical.[34] Questioned about band music played on two occasions when he was within earshot, Hempton replied that the first time he could not remember what the band

The London Pianoforte Warehouse in the Diamond established by John Hempton (1800-1873) in the later 1840s. (By kind permission of the National Library of Ireland)

had played, and that on the second occasion, he did not know the names of the tunes played. His music shop thrived on the sales of band music and instruments, so his plea of ignorance is hard to take seriously. Other witnesses had no difficulty in recalling the music played and hinted at a possible explanation for Hempton's lapse of memory, describing him as a 'habitual drinker'.

Hempton cut something of a controversial figure in Derry politics. He was an alderman for two years and often took the lead in local disputes, such as the 1862 'pew' disturbances in St Columb's Cathedral, when the Apprentice Boys protested against places being allocated to 'outsiders' from the Waterside. Hempton was a leading member of the organisation and provided uniforms and instruments for its Maiden City Band. He was also, for a time, a member of the Orange Order. But, ever quarrelsome, he fell out with both groups, and responded, so it was said, by demanding that the band members hand back their instruments and uniforms.

For whatever reason, he made many enemies. He was assaulted by the son of the caretaker of Corporation Hall, and his shop windows were put in by a mob chanting abuse. No other music retailer in Derry excited this degree of antagonism or seems to have been so cordially disliked. Hempton died unmarried, without heirs or descendants. He was perhaps too good at picking quarrels to settle comfortably into family life. The *Sentinel*'s obituary notice was dry and caustic, a more literate version of the name-calling he had provoked in life. The magistrate at the Parliamentary Inquiry, picking up on other witnesses' hostility towards Hempton, suggested to one of them that he might care to burn Hempton's effigy instead of Lundy's, only to be told, 'He is not worth wasting a match upon.'

Hempton died a wealthy man, but volatile and unpredictable to the last, he amended his will several times.[35] His music shop and business was eventually left to his faithful and long-time assistant William Graham. There is, however, one revealing bequest that hints at a side of Hempton otherwise unexpected: a sum of £200, not a small amount at the time, to 'John Donnelly, farmer, of Ballintoy, in token of gratitude for hospitality to a stranger'. What this refers to is anyone's guess, but it points to a more complex and perhaps more sympathetic personality than the uncompromising, combative character he appeared to most of his contemporaries.[36] He is buried in a grave outside the West Door of St Columb's Cathedral, with which he had once been at odds. He is probably now best remembered as the author of *The Siege of Londonderry*, published in 1861. What is beyond doubt is that he was a shrewd businessman; the first locally born music retailer in Derry, whose commercial operations paved the way for the development of music in the city and the surrounding area.

'The Glitterati', 1859-1886

The Queen's Theatre

While domestic music-making increased among the middle classes, theatre-going in Derry continued to decline. By the early 1860s, Derry had acquired another theatre, the Queen's Theatre, but its location in Chamberlain Place, close to shirt factories, shipbuilding works and stone yards, was off-putting for many.[37] We first learn about it from an advert placed by its proprietor Edward Heffernon in *The Era*, the journal of the theatre profession, in November 1862, seeking a 'leading lady and a singing chambermaid'.[38] Two weeks later, Phillips and Webb, 'Pantomimists, Swordsmen and Character Artistes with their wonderful Performing Dogs, Hector and Carlo', entertained the theatre's patrons for twelve nights. No doubt Heffernon's audience of shipyard and factory employees enjoyed the novelty of these performances and were attracted generally by action-packed programmes, pantomimes, burlesques, and melodramas with stunning visual effects and 'mechanical devices'. But the well-to-do, who had provided the audience for theatre in earlier decades and who had more sophisticated tastes, were not likely to be drawn back to theatre-going by shows like these.

Like its predecessor, the Queen's Theatre was situated outside the city walls, but near the Bogside. The industrial workers who lived there were able to afford the cheap admission prices of 1*s*, 6*d*, 4*d* and 3*d*, which were halved ('Second Prices', as they were known) after 9 p.m. The theatre was rectangular and flanked on one side by a coach factory; it had a small interior, with access through a narrow alleyway. Press advertisements described it in flattering terms as having 'Centre Boxes, Side Boxes' and the usual gallery and pit. Its bearing the Queen's name meant nothing, as that did not require official permission. The theatre probably held a large number, given that people then were physically smaller and prepared to make room for additional ticket-holders. Those in the gallery and pit in particular were used to cramped conditions.

Heffernon (1812-1876) was the first Derry-born actor to own a theatre in the city, and he became something of an impresario, running theatre seasons in Sligo, Strabane, Magherafelt and Enniskillen, as well as in Derry. In Derry he put on mainly pantomime, burlesque and melodramas of a type popular with mid-Victorian audiences who enjoyed – and demanded – thrills and spectacle. Indeed the programming was probably planned with industrial workers in mind and tailored to their demands. Pantomime was provided all year round and not just at Easter-time. 'Music hall' made its first appearance there too, its variety and earthy character appealing to those looking for entertainment after a hard day's work in Derry's factories and shipyards.

Heffernon's theatre broke new ground in being the first Derry theatre to have its own resident repertory company. This is clear from his advertising for 'Leading Gents and Leading Ladies' to 'make up [his] Company for the season'.[39] Other advertisements give us some idea of his requirements. In 1864 he wanted 'A Gentleman to Combine Second Heavies and Old Men' and 'Two good Nigger Singers and Dancers'.

QUEEN'S THEATRE,

CHAMBERLAIN-PLACE.
LAST NIGHT OF THE PANTOMIME.

THIS Evening, SATURDAY, JANUARY 6, the Performance will commence with the renowned historical Drama, "WALLACE, THE HERO OF SCOTLAND."

Wallace,.............................Mr. W. CROSBY.
Lady Helen Marr,....................Miss R. WARNER.

Song, Mr. B. STEWART. Concluding with (for the last time) the original Pantomime, "KATE KEARNEY."

On MONDAY Evening, JANUARY 8, will be presented (first time in Derry) the thrilling, nautical, sensation Drama, "THE WIZARD OF THE WAVE; or, THE SHIP OF THE AVENGER," with Scenic and Mechanical decorations and embellishments on a scale unequalled at this Theatre.

☞ The main feature in the Plot of this most extraordinary Drama is founded on fact.

Captain Falkner, (on Secret Service,) Mr. W. CROSBY.
Timothy Treacle,....................Mr. HEFFERNON, jun.
Henry Belford, (first Lieutenant.)....Miss ROSE WARNER.
Isabinda,...........................Miss MILLWARD.

(Chief of the unknown Schooner, termed "El Malachor," the Evil One.

ABRIDGEMENT OF SCENERY.

ACT 1—Main Deck of the "Wizard of the Wave," illuminated for a fancy ball.
ACT 2—Interior of a Spanish Posada.
ACT 3—The open Sea—the Sea Chase—after-deck of the unknown Schooner—distant view of the "Wizard of the Wave"—destruction of the Pirate—imposing Tableaux.

Doors open at Seven o'clock; performance to commence at Half-past Seven.

ADMISSION—Centre Boxes, 1s; Side Boxes, 6d; Pit, 4d; Gallery, 8d.

No Smoking permitted.

The Queen's Theatre advertises its fare in 1866: historical drama and pantomime, all with special effects 'on a scale unequalled at this theatre'. (Londonderry Journal, 6 January 1866)

The following year he required 'Stars and First-Class Novelties' and 'A clown and a Columbine who must dance well'. Eight years later he was looking for 'A Harlequin ... and a good Marionette entertainment'. But regardless of their particular talents, advertisements made it clear that players were required to 'double up' as general stagehands. In November 1864, for example, Heffernon specifically advertised for a 'quick scene painter to act'.

Presumably no such demands were made of the celebrated Irish actor Gustavus Brooke, who, putting his earlier bad experiences at the Theatre Royal behind him, returned to Derry in 1864 to perform in the Queen's Theatre 'with great success'. Brooke combined his theatre performances with Shakespearean readings in Corporation Hall aimed at a more middle-class audience.

Like its predecessor, the Queen's Theatre did not advertise its performances in the Derry newspapers, probably because its target clientele were neither newspaper buyers nor readers. In return, reviews of performances were rare, brief and give only scanty information about productions. The attitude of the press was generally condescending, exemplified in the *Sentinel*'s description of the Queen's Theatre as 'a miserable wooden structure ... mainly supported by third and fourth-class actors and the lower cream [*sic*] of the community'.

A letter in *The Era* in the early 1870s must have confirmed such prejudices. It complained about an absconding Derry actor who 'received his salary on Saturday morning, left the city, leaving a scene half-painted, no one to play his part at night, his lodgings 23*s* in debt ... and [taking] likewise the paintbrushes bought for use by him to do his work'.

Heffernon's advertisements for actors are often revealing of underlying problems, in their insistence that 'None but sober parties need apply' and that 'Respectability and Sobriety [are] Indispensable'. Respectability, if that was what was wanted, was more likely to be found in concerts by local musicians and choral societies, now held regularly in Corporation Hall.

Music in the 1860s

Complete opera performances were popular in Derry's theatres before 1833, but gradually they were replaced by drama, farce and comedy. Thereafter, operatic arias and overtures could be heard at concerts by Madame D'Alberti, Regondi, Jenny Lind and military bands, all of which included music by one or more of Verdi, Rossini, Bellini, Donizetti, Balfe and Offenbach. Simplified piano arrangements of opera tunes were available also from Hempton's music shop. So, although full opera had vanished from Derry's stages, its melodies were familiar to many through concerts, drawing-room recitals, and being sung or played in private homes.

Derry's first proper stage performances of opera for twenty-seven years were mounted by the London-based Anglo-Italian Opera Company in February 1860. It took over Corporation Hall for three nights, with Verdi's *Il Trovatore* and *La Traviata*, and William Vincent Wallace's *Maritana*. The company brought nine soloists from the Drury Lane and Covent Garden theatres, including Augustus Braham, the celebrated English tenor. But in audience terms the venture was a flop. Local newspapers reported 'miserable audiences' and apathy in the city generally. As a result, it was another thirteen years before the experiment was repeated.

By 1860, Derry had a nucleus of around twenty-five talented local musicians: organists and precentors, military musicians, and instrumental and singing teachers. Stimulated perhaps by the visits of celebrity musicians and the excitement they generated, they organised their own annual concerts. Whereas in 1857 there were no concerts by local musicians, in 1866 there were seven, including four organised by Presbyterian precentors. This 'music circle' was, however, a fairly loose grouping which relied upon a core of professional musicians for leadership, and the assistance of church choirs and amateurs to perform choral works. William Kerr, the new Glasgow-born precentor of First Derry, was the first to give an annual concert, in 1860. In fact, he held two concerts that year, followed by a third in 1862. Initially his concerts were showcases for his choir and music pupils, but they soon included performances by Derry's professional musicians. Other annual concerts followed, including many by newcomers: Waldemar Malmene; Mr Syme, precentor of Third Derry, and William Stafford, the 'First Singer' in the Cathedral Choir. The musical content of the concerts was broadly similar: choral works, Irish and Scottish songs, instrumental items by amateur performers to show off their talents, and more difficult pieces by the professional musicians. These concerts were small in scale and literally parochial in some cases, but they did play a key role in building up local audiences for music.

William Kerr (1829-1872) was a central figure in the 'music circle', but his influence on Derry's musical life was more wide ranging. He trained two of the earliest bands: the Gwyn's Institution Band and the Maiden City Band, both formed in 1860. He also set up the Harmonia Sacra Society, the city's third choral group. At first they performed at church events and temperance meetings, rather than at concerts or 'public rehearsals' (the name given to music society concerts at this time). But soon the group began to spread its wings. At Kerr's April 1862 concert, the Harmonia Sacra Society sang pieces by 'Mozart, Bishop, Calcott, Webbe and Smith' – a fairly broad repertoire. Kerr's premature death robbed the city of a talented and enterprising musician who seemed destined to play a crucial role in the development of its musical life.

Apprentice Boys' Entertainments

In February 1862, the Apprentice Boys, in addition to their usual August and December celebrations, held a 'Ball and Soirée' in Corporation Hall at which over 400 people were present. The following February, over 300 attended and there was 'Mazy Dancing' until the early hours to the music of a 'select band of brass and stringed instruments'. Two years later they resorted to the usual expedient of those wanting to attract young ladies to their entertainments: tickets were sold at 3s for a 'Joint ticket for Gentleman and Lady', but at 1s each for single ladies.

For some time, Apprentice Boys' entertainments had provided welcome additional income for the city's musicians, many of whom had poorly paid part-time posts in churches and schools. But the formation of the Apprentice Boys' own band, the Maiden City Band, in 1860 put an end to this. When the Britannia Band was formed in 1866, it too became an 'official' band for the Apprentice Boys. They led the parades in August and December and played at the clubs' soirees and balls. Around this time, the *Sentinel* began to list the music played at the Apprentice Boys' religious services in the Cathedral. In August 1866, St Columb's organist John Horan played a voluntary based on Handel's 'Hallelujah Chorus', and the Cathedral bell-ringers kept up this mood of celebration throughout the day with their 'joyous' renditions of 'party tunes'.

Waldemar Malmene

The dominant figure in Derry's musical life in the later 1860s was the multi-talented and energetic – but controversial – German musician Waldemar Malmene. He arrived in the city in 1865 and took lodgings in Clarendon Street, close to Third Derry, where he had been appointed precentor. His appointment was something of a coup for the congregation, given Malmene's nationality and outstanding music qualifications (he had a Mus. Bac. from Cambridge and had studied at the Royal Institute for Music in Berlin and Conservatoire Impérial de Musique in Paris). He lost no time in making his presence felt in the city.

Almost immediately, he advertised his services in all four local newspapers, offering to teach piano, organ, harmonium, guitar, violin, viola, singing, harmony and thorough bass. Much was made in these advertisements of his origins (he was born in Berlin) and his professional qualifications. In addition, Malmene held public classes in vocal music for adults, Saturday singing classes for children and German language classes – as he claimed, 'without dialect': presumably the purest *Hochdeutsch*.

He promoted concerts. Between September 1864 and March 1868, he organised three separate series of subscription concerts, a step change in the regularity and frequency of concerts unprecedented in Derry's history, although it would have been

> **CONCERT IN STRABANE.**
> **HERR MALMENE**
> BEGS to announce that he will give a GRAND POPULAR CONCERT in the TOWN HALL, STRABANE, on MONDAY Evening, DECEMBER 16th, assisted by
> **Miss M. SHERRAN,**
> Principal Soprano from the Glasgow and Manchester Concerts.
> **Mr. A. DIXIE,**
> The renowned and highly popular Comic Vocalist from the London, Birmingham, and Manchester Concerts.
> MASTER GRIGGS, ...Pianoforte and Clarionet Solo.
> Mr. T. MURPHY,............Cornet Solo.
> Tickets and Programmes to be had at Mr. GRAY's, Bookseller, Strabane.
>
> **CONCERT IN DERRY.**
> **HERR MALMENE**
> BEGS to announce that, in compliance with numerous requests, he will give his FOURTH POPULAR CONCERT, in the CORPORATION-HALL, DERRY, on TUESDAY Evening, DECEMBER 17th, assisted by
> **Miss M. SHERRAN,**
> Principal Soprano from the Glasgow and Manchester Concerts;
> **Mr. A. DIXIE,**
> The renowned and highly-popular Comic Vocalist from the London, Birmingham, and Manchester Concerts.
> The Members of the Derry Philharmonic Association will assist.
> Tickets and Programmes to be had at the Booksellers.

Concerts by Derry's first impresario Waldemar Malmene (1836-1906). (Londonderry Journal, 14 December 1867)

unremarkable in Belfast and other cities by the mid-1850s. Malmene introduced fashionable neologisms such as 'Soirée Musicale' and so-called 'Popular Concerts', for which he brought in sopranos and instrumentalists from elsewhere. In November 1866, he engaged Miss Emma Jenkins from the 'London, Aberdeen and Glasgow Concerts' and Mr Lee from the 'Belfast Concerts'. For his October 1867 concert, he had 'Miss Emily Spiller R.A.M.' from the 'Monday Popular Concerts' at St James's Hall, London. He also pioneered tiered pricing to attract new audiences, effectively lowering admission prices. Previously, tickets to local concerts had been at a single set price, around 3s, whereas at 3s, 2s and 1s, concert-going became more affordable.

He started music societies. He briefly revived the LMA in 1865, and two years later set up the Londonderry Philharmonic Society, with John Horan, the Dublin-born organist of St Columb's Cathedral. He held concerts in Coleraine and Strabane, using musicians brought from Derry. He himself was a frequent performer at the city's factory soirees and literary society meetings, and the Apprentice Boys' Bottle and Glass parties. In the midst of all this frenetic activity he went off to Europe for four months in summer 1865 and again in 1867, when he gave a piano recital at the Paris Exposition. And he somehow found time to compose music – an eclectic mix of pieces with titles such as 'Adieu to Berlin', 'The Belfast Quadrilles', and 'Long Life to the Queen'.

Despite Malmene's versatility as a musician, his qualifications and connections with the wider musical world, and the sheer energy with which he threw himself into his musical activities in Derry, he seems not to have been universally welcomed in the city. His concerts, which were in the main well attended, became the target of a disorderly and vociferous minority. Malmene himself was jeered, booed and heckled, missiles were thrown from the gallery and performances were disrupted. In February 1865, a newspaper reported that one concert had to be abandoned altogether because 'the gods *en masse*' had 'selected Herr Malmene as an object for expressions of dislike'. What made this the more regrettable was that, 'We are not aware that he has done anything to warrant such a display.' The editor appealed for more 'courtesy towards this comparative stranger in our midst'.

One can only guess at the reasons for Malmene's unpopularity. It may be that there was resentment among some members of the Derry public at Malmene's immodest (and possibly considered 'un-Irish'?) use of advertising to publicise his various projects and activities. The tone of his public pronouncements could be insensitive, as in January 1865, when he placed a notice in the *Sentinel* complaining that he had had to cancel a singing practice because it clashed with a prayer meeting. He was prone to complain in the press about poor attendance at his concerts, and once threatened to cancel his remaining concerts because a previous two 'had not been attended as they ought' to have been. Audiences, whether in Derry or elsewhere, do not generally care to be talked down to in this way.

Matters came to a head at a concert in February 1867, when Malmene's solo from Gounod's *Faust* was greeted with 'mingled hissing and applause' while other performers were given a rapturous reception. Within the year, Malmene announced (yet again in the press!) that he was emigrating to the United States, and after a 'Farewell Concert' in Corporation Hall in March 1868, he and his young family sailed for America. He was appointed music professor at Washington University in St Louis, Missouri, in 1869, and enjoyed a long and productive career as composer, church organist and teacher. His compositions included both secular and church music, and he was the author of a work still in print, *The Masonic Hymnbook*. Malmene died in St Louis and his obituary was published in *The New York Times*, an indication of the reputation he had established in his new homeland. There was no mention of his years in Derry.

By the late 1860s, Edward Heffernon had given up the unequal struggle to build up a permanent audience for theatre in Derry and retired to Drogheda to lick his wounds. His theatre was leased out to a succession of managers who put on short seasons of melodramas and variety shows, but it closed for the last time in the mid-1870s. The vacuum left by its closure was filled by touring companies, notably Joseph Warden's Theatre Royal Company.

Return of Respectability: J.F. Warden's Visits

On their first visit to Derry in 1869, Warden's company gave eleven performances in Corporation Hall over two weeks, with the promise that, if well supported, this short season would be 'the forerunner to future ones on a more extended scale'. The works staged were varied: comedies, dramas, melodramas, 'operatic farces' and Shakespeare plays. The 'liberal patronage' he was looking for was forthcoming, the company playing to packed houses every night, and he kept his word by returning in January 1870 for three weeks and again in November for two more weeks. Thereafter, Warden's company gave twice yearly visits until September 1876, attracting fashionable audiences happy to attend drama and opera again in the familiar surroundings of Corporation Hall.

From the outset, Warden's press reviews were uniformly complimentary. The manager, actors, musicians and singers were all praised to the skies, in sharp contrast to the way the press had ignored the entertainments in the Queen's Theatre. In 1870, the *Journal* singled out Warden's orchestra for its 'especial excellence', 'independently of the dramatic performance, the band accompanying the entertainment would, to lovers of classic music, be a sufficient inducement to visit the Hall'. The *Sentinel* gave its approval too, albeit in its own staid terms, describing Warden's

Joseph Frederick Warden (1836-1898), actor, manager and owner of Derry and Belfast's Opera Houses. (PRONI, T1129/274: by kind permission of the Deputy Keeper of the Public Record Office of Northern Ireland)

company in 1872 as 'first-class in style, free from the coarseness and vulgarity associated with itinerant theatricals'. It recommended the performances to 'all who desire an evening of harmless amusement'.

By the time Warden's company had got round to bringing opera to Derry (his 1876 staging of Bellini's *La Sonnambula* with Jenny Bellair, Warden's wife, in the lead role), opera had already regained much of its former popularity with audiences there. Indeed, after a succession of performances by Irish, English and Italian touring opera companies, in the years following 1873, one local newspaper spoke about the 'immense success of opera in Derry' – a comment that would have been unthinkable only a few years before.

The visits to Corporation Hall by Henry Walsham's National Opera Company were testament to this sudden turnaround. The company had two separate runs of fifteen performances in May and December 1874, and then returned two years later for what was originally scheduled to be a single week of opera. But by 'popular demand' this was extended to two weeks (ten performances), with two extra nights in Strabane. A wide repertoire was presented, with a different opera each evening by Balfe, Wallace, Verdi, Gounod, Bellini, Auber and Flotow. Wallace's *Maritana* uniquely was performed twice, the second time as a 'grand finale of the season' on the closing night. The press reported 'packed houses nightly ... with continued suc-

The Fisk Jubilee Singers who gave concerts in Derry in 1873 whilst on tour to raise funds for Fisk University, Nashville, Tennessee. They pioneered the singing of Negro spirituals for a public audience. (London Illustrated News, *July 1873*)

cess'. Once more, Derry's middle and upper classes were turning out in numbers to watch drama and opera. Warden's company in particular had a social cachet among the well-to-do that earlier touring companies had lacked. For the time being he could enjoy his success, but it seems likely he was already weighing up this revival of interest in drama and opera in the city, and pondering the viability of tapping into it.

An event of a quite different character was the visit of the Jubilee Singers. These all-black vocalists (seven women and four men) from the United States were touring Great Britain to raise money for their home college, Fisk University in Tennessee. They gave a 'service of song' in First Derry on Friday 6 September 1873, where they performed the 'negro spirituals' with which they were particularly associated, and by request they repeated the performance the following Monday evening. Their 'natural and untrammelled manner' and the gravity, sweetness and 'pious ardour' of their singing of 'Steal Away to Jesus' and other songs, made a deep impression on all who heard them.

Derry's First Amateur Drama Club

The performances by Warden's company in the 1870s provided the example and inspiration for what was – if we exclude the performances put on by members of the garrison in the 1830s – Derry's first amateur dramatics society. The City of Derry Dramatic Club was started by several young men who rehearsed three nights a week at their 'Clubrooms on the Middle Quay'. They were from well-known Derry families: Bob Philson; John and George Ferguson, sons of the architect John Guy Ferguson; Tom Goodman; J.P. Coyle, and the Trimble brothers. One member later described the others and himself as 'merely stage-struck lads'. Their first performance was in February 1870. Billed as a 'Dramatic and Christy Minstrel Entertainment', it began with Hazlewood's domestic drama *The Harvest Storm* followed by musical entertainments, presumably by members blacked-up for the occasion.[40] Over the next two years they performed other dramas, songs, musical interludes and sketches, mainly for the amusement of families and friends.

Their performances involved a lot of 'physical combat and sword fighting', which the participants engaged in with gusto. A cast member later recalled the delight they took in playing a scene from Home's tragedy *Douglas*, 'We were great in combats with broadswords, from which the sparks were made to fly, and the villain was eventually dispatched by a final thrust (under the armpit) and the hero, with his foot planted on his antagonist's dead body, wiped his gory blade as the curtain slowly descended.' If, as sometimes happened, the curtain failed to descend properly, the young actors were forced to 'slink off' the stage in full view of the audience.

As numbers grew, the scope of the club's activities widened. By the mid-1870s, it was renting a rehearsal room in London Street and later it took over a derelict skating rink on Strand Road for rehearsals of longer plays. They accepted their first engagements for performances outside Derry in Strabane and Limavady. More ambitious still, in 1875 they booked Corporation Hall for two plays, *Still Waters Run Deep* and *The Ticket-of-Leave Man*, the latter a staple of Warden's Company. The City of Derry Dramatic Club was still going strong in the early 1880s, by which time the 'stage-struck lads' had given Derry its first decade of amateur drama.

Moving Towards *Messiah*

Amateur music-making was by now well established in the city. As mentioned earlier, John Horan, the organist in Derry Cathedral, had been co-founder with Waldemar Malmene of the city's first (and short-lived) Philharmonic Society, an instrumental and choral group. He formed his own Londonderry Choral Society in 1869, followed a year later by St Columb's Choral Union. Over the years, leadership in matters choral had passed from the singing clerks and Presbyterian precentors to the 'newer' church organists employed by Derry's different religious denominations. Nevertheless, there was also a strong tradition in the city of co-operation between the different churches, with church musicians frequently playing for each other's societies, as when Patrick Mulholland, the newly appointed organist of St Eugene's Cathedral, played the harmonium at St Columb's Choral Union concerts in 1874 and 1876.

For the first time, 'regular' concerts of the city's music societies began to feature outside performers as their soloists. In October 1875, for example, Mrs Muncey of the Crystal Palace Opera Company was brought from London by the St Columb's Choral Union for their 'operatic recital' of *Der Freischütz*.[41] A Mr Houseley of the Nottingham Choral Union was engaged to play the harmonium on the same occasion. Derry's amateur musicians were clearly adopting a more 'professional' approach to music-making.

Surprisingly, considering that Derry is a Cathedral city, its first full oratorio performance was not until March 1875, when Root's *Belshazzar's Feast* was performed by the St Andrew's Choral Union.[42] But then oratorio performances followed in quick succession. St Columb's Choral Union gave a full performance of Handel's *Messiah* in February 1876, albeit with only keyboard accompaniment. The following year there was Mendelssohn's *St Paul*, by the same society. Other oratorios followed by Handel, Mendelssohn, Root, Romberg and Sterndale Bennett. By the mid-1880s, the city had four or five different oratorio performances per year, usually clustered around Christmas time.

This heightened musical activity was made possible by the arrival of a new generation of church musicians who took over from those who had died (Kerr and Logier) or moved elsewhere (Malmene and Horan). They were as committed to mounting concerts as their predecessors but seemed more commercially minded. Church musicians in Derry had always sold, tuned and repaired instruments, so some involvement with the music trade was nothing new.[43] What was different was the extent of the new arrivals' involvement. They lent their names to local press advertisements for mechanical organs such as Davis's American Hamlin organs and harmoniums, providing endorsements and personal testimonials. One can hardly object to Derry's musicians using their public and professional status to their own financial advantage in this way, but, ironically, each of the three organists concerned (Mulholland from St Eugene's, Turpin from St Columb's and Palmer from All Saints', Clooney) played a pipe organ in his own church. The only organist actually to play a mechanical Hamlin organ (in the Methodist church on Carlisle Road) took no part in promoting their sale.

To these new church musicians we must add several female musicians, music teachers for the most part, who played a major role in the city's musical activities. Some were the daughters of Derry's long-standing male musicians: the Misses Walsh, Logier, Minniece, MacDonald and Smyly. A Mrs Persee came to Derry from Montreal. Others, such as the German-born Fräulein Hauffe and a Mrs Bauer, arrived in the city from Europe. Male musicians who arrived by the same route were Mr Micheljohn and the German music teacher at Foyle College Frederick Liebich, who provided Derry's first regular piano recitals.

Patrick Mulholland and the Birth of Catholic Music-Making

One of Liebich's colleagues at Foyle College was Patrick Mulholland, organist at St Eugene's Cathedral, who had been appointed to that post in May 1873. Over the following fifteen years, Mulholland carved out a unique position for himself as the musical leader of Derry's Catholics, providing them with a 'voice' for the first time in its musical conversations.[44]

Derry's Catholics were late starters among the city's music-makers, initially because of the Penal Laws, but later on because of the reluctance of their organists to join with others in public musical activity.[45] Although they formed the majority of the population of Derry by 1871, they lacked the leadership of an experienced musician to make an impact on its musical life.

Mulholland brought to Derry an awareness of a wider musical world. He had previously been organist at St Malachy's church in Belfast, and had played at the 'Monday Evening Popular Concerts' in the Ulster Hall. He had even performed in Derry, in two concerts in Corporation Hall in April 1863, with a party of four singers from the 'London, Dublin and Belfast Concerts'. In terms of experience, then, Mulholland was similar to Derry's other, Presbyterian and Church of Ireland, musicians, and, like them, he quickly became involved in its concerts, band tuition and music societies.

Mulholland's tenure as Cathedral organist was inaugurated by a musical performance of distinction: the opening consecration ceremony in May 1873, including Henry G. Farmer's (sung) Mass and music by Haydn and Rossini.[46] Mulholland trained the new Cathedral choir himself. It had twenty-one singers – seven sopranos, six contraltos, three tenors and five basses – and for this opening service it was joined by three Belfast soloists, Mrs Ling, and Mr and Mrs Schroder. It was a relatively large choir; bigger than that of St Columb's Cathedral, which had a mere sixteen members, three of whom were girls. The *Journal*'s account of the service paid tribute to Mulholland's contribution, acknowledging him as a 'talented and accomplished organist'.

His first public concert was in November 1873, and featured the same three Belfast soloists and the Donegal Militia Band. Thereafter, each of his annual concerts combined his own band and local amateurs: the McTaggart, McCloskey, Doherty and McChrystal families (members of his choir), and the St Columb's Total Abstinence Association Band. In recruiting and training his musicians, Mulholland encouraged them to participate in activities hitherto dominated by the other two main denominations in Derry. The *Journal* acknowledged as much, referring to Mulholland's protégées as 'principally youthful tyros, whose nerves [have] never been tried before'.

Mulholland was also the key musical figure in the Catholic Literary Association, formed in 1868. It had its own rooms in Diamond Square, where members met socially for entertainments that were 'greatly appreciated by the Catholic young men' of the city. Within ten months of Mulholland's arrival, however, the association was hosting musical entertainments to which women were invited. From spring 1876, there were fortnightly concerts and literary evenings, drawing in large audiences. But unlike their Presbyterian and Church of Ireland brethren, Derry's Catholics did not form themselves into a music society as such. The Literary Association was the nearest equivalent, but it remained essentially a hybrid body including drama, music, lectures and recitations in its round of public entertainments.

What was distinctive about the music of Derry's Catholics was its Irish character. Derry's other music societies conformed to an established 'English' pattern in performing oratorios and cantatas by composers such as Handel, Mendelssohn and Romberg. In contrast, Mulholland's concerts favoured music by Irish composers: songs, duets and choruses by John William Glover and popular Irish songs and ballads like Moore's Melodies.[47] A Mulholland concert in January 1876 had as its centrepiece Glover's cantata *St Patrick at Tara*, composed only the year before to commemorate the centenary of the birth of Daniel O'Connell. The audience in Corporation Hall greeted the cantata – 'Its First time in the Provinces' – with 'rapturous applause' and demanded numerous encores.

Although Mulholland's concerts regularly included musicians from the city's other denominations, they were essentially a platform for his own Cathedral choir. Their skills were keenly tested in the premiere of Mulholland's *Brian Boru* cantata in April 1877 – the first full-scale composition by a musician in Derry.

> **CORPORATION HALL, LONDONDERRY.**
>
> **THURSDAY EVENING, APRIL 19, and FRIDAY EVENING, APRIL 20, 1877.**
>
> THE NEW CANTATA,
>
> **"BRIAN BORU,"**
>
> AND
>
> **MISCELLANEOUS SELECTION OF MUSIC.**
>
> Doors Open at 7.30; Concert to commence at 8 p.m.
>
> Tickets—Front Seats, 2s 6d; Body of Hall, 1s 6d; Gallery, 1s.
>
> Books of Words will be ready on Wednesday.

*The premiere of Patrick Mulholland's Brian Boru cantata in Corporation Hall in 1877, the beginning of choral singing by Derry's Catholics. (*Londonderry Journal*, 18 April 1877)*

The subject of Mulholland's cantata was the Battle of Clontarf, fought on Good Friday 1014 between the Irish, led by Brian Boru, and an occupying Danish army. The battle was won by the Irish but resulted in Boru's death. Calling it a cantata, with all the religious overtones of that term, rather than an opera or operetta, lent the piece a certain solemnity, while the theme of martyrdom in the cause of Irish freedom would have appealed to Derry's Catholic concert-goers. The work had twenty sections: an overture, eight choruses, ten solos and a trio, and was performed by a twenty-five-strong choir. The St Columb's Temperance Brass Band provided the orchestral accompaniment. The librettist used the pseudonym 'N.D. Ariel', which the *Journal* noted coyly was 'more anagrammatic than baptismal'. Local people presumably knew who it was.

The *Journal* described the cantata's reception as 'euphoric', with Corporation Hall packed for both performances. Encores were called for throughout both evenings. The band was singled out as being 'exceptionally effective in the battle scenes' and 'attaining an excellence second to few in Ireland'. The work was judged 'the production of a masterhand'. Against the background of tenants' right protests and the rise of Charles Stewart Parnell, the cantata's theme of Irish resistance to foreign occupation carried a message that would not have been lost upon the audience or the

Journal's readership.[48] Perhaps for that very reason, the performance of the cantata was ignored by the other three Derry newspapers.

If the appeal of *Brian Boru* was largely for the Catholic, Nationalist population of the city, in general, Derry's church musicians co-operated well together. Two weeks after *Brian Boru*, Mulholland was again in Corporation Hall, this time accompanying St Columb's Choral Union in Mendelssohn's oratorio *St Paul*. And in the later 1870s, when Mulholland was joined in Derry by Dr Daniel Jones (1856-1911), newly arrived from Lichfield to be organist at St Columb's Cathedral, he and Jones developed a particularly close working relationship through concert-giving and music society events.

Public Demands

Up to this point, Derry's concerts and opera stagings were all in Corporation Hall, once its premier civic building but now generally reckoned inadequate for 'grand performances'. There had been calls for a new venue as early as 1859, when the *Sentinel* criticised the hall as ill suited to 'extensive musical display' and appealed to 'gentlemen in the city to come forward' and provide a new music hall. All four newspapers pressed – albeit at different times and with differing degrees of persistence – for a new venue for Derry's rapidly increasing population, which by 1871 had reached 31,000. There was acute awareness, perhaps even a little envy, of Belfast and its Ulster Hall, which was completed in 1862 and was capable of holding 1,600 people; not to mention the older Music Hall in May Street.

Criticism surfaced again in 1872, when a 78th Highlanders and Londonderry Light Infantry Band concert 'attracted an attendance more numerous than the Hall could, with any regard to comfort, accommodate'. Similar complaints appeared regularly in the press, usually after operas and concerts which exposed the hall's shortcomings. In October 1876, after a visit by Walter Newport's Italian Opera Company, the *Standard* attributed the paucity of visiting musicians and inadequacies in the city's musical life to its poor concert facilities. It stressed that the citizens were not to blame, there being 'no want of appreciation' amongst them.

The Apprentice Boys, who had traditionally held their soirées and balls in Corporation Hall, had ideas for an impressive new building of their own in Society Street. The foundation stone was laid on 12 August 1873, amid much band-playing and general rejoicing. After a few more years of fundraising, through concerts, recitations and entertainments of all kinds held in their band practice rooms in London Street, the new Apprentice Boys' building, incorporating a stage and hall, finally opened in August 1877. It was designed in Scots Baronial style by city architect and President of the Apprentice Boys' Clubs, John Guy Ferguson, father of two of the 'stage-struck lads' who had formed Derry's first amateur drama club.

As for the building that was to replace the existing Corporation Hall, and answer Derry's need for an appropriate and worthy venue for concert and opera, the solution, when it came, owed nothing to local initiative and everything to the entrepreneurial drive of J.F. Warden. In January 1877, Warden began building work on a new theatre on a vacant site on Carlisle Road. The location was well chosen. It was close to the Carlisle Bridge (opened in 1863) and the railway stations, and so ideally placed for theatre patrons from outside Derry to catch late trains to Buncrana, Strabane and Omagh. It was close to the quays, which made it convenient for travelling theatre companies. There were boarding houses in nearby streets, with landladies eager to accommodate visiting actors and musicians. Within seven months – the building time for theatres in the 1870s was astonishingly short – Warden was able to welcome his first audience to the opening of Derry's New Royal Opera House.

The New Royal Opera House

'No man devotes exertion, time, money and experience without the hope of profit. I certainly would not.' This was Warden's message to the packed auditorium on the opening night of his New Royal Opera House on Friday 10 August 1877. It was the first Opera House in Ulster and only the second in Ireland, and it had cost Warden £5,000. There were no shareholders for this theatre, such as there would be for his Belfast Grand Opera House eighteen years later. So Warden was letting his audience know from the start that, although he wanted the theatre to succeed in its own terms, for him the bottom line was whether it was a success financially.

The opening night was, by all accounts, a splendid occasion. The Opera House orchestra began the evening with an (unnamed) overture. The orchestra comprised violins, piano, clarinet, flutes, trombone, double bass and percussion, and was led by 'Musical Director' Charles Davis, a London-born bandleader. He had lived in Derry since 1871 and owned a music shop on the Mall Wall, from where he hired out his own 'string band' for dances, parties and concerts. The *Journal* described the ensemble as 'admirable, and well in keeping with the high-class character of the Opera House itself'.

The overture was followed by a play: Lord Lytton's five-act romantic melodrama *Lady of Lyons*, written in 1838. This went down well with the Derry audience. Edward Bulwer-Lytton was a well-known playwright and novelist whose works had then a wide popular appeal.[49] At the conclusion of the evening, after loud cheers and ovations, Warden came to the front of the stage to deliver the customary manager's speech, outlining his plans for the theatre and the coming season. He announced that nine firm bookings had been made, including two opera and four drama companies; more 'Engagements [were] pending with other Celebrated Artistes'.

NEW ROYAL OPERA HOUSE,
CARLISLE-ROAD, LONDONDERRY.

Proprietor and Manager;........Mr. J. F. WARDEN.

Mr. WARDEN begs to announce that the OPENING of the above Establishment will take place on

FRIDAY Evening, AUGUST 10th.

This magnificent Building, Second to None in the Three Kingdoms, has been Erected at a Cost of several Thousand Pounds, by the well-known firm of M'CLELLAND & Co., of Londonderry. The elaborate Decorations designed and executed by the famous London Decorative Artist, Mr. EDWARD BELL, and a large staff of the best Workmen of London, Paris, and Edinburgh. The Gas Work has been executed by Mr. AARON BAXTER, of Londonderry. The Upholstery by Messrs. CAMPBELL, Bishop-st., Londonderry. The Chairs of Balcony Stalls manufactured by Messrs. N. A. CAMPBELL & Co., Belfast. The extensive New Scenery and Act Drop by Mr. THOMAS GILMORE, of Belfast, and numerous Assistants. The whole of the Works have been designed and executed under the personal superintendence of CHAS. J. PHIPPS, Esq., F.S.A., of London, special Architect of Gaiety, Queen's, Vaudevill, and Variety Theatres, London; The Gaiety, Dublin; Theatre Royal, Cork; Her Majesty's Opera House, Aberdeen; Theatres Royal, Bath and Bristol; Theatre Royal, Nottingham; and some Twelve others in various parts of England.

THE First Season will be inaugurated on FRIDAY Evening, AUGUST 10th, 1877, Mr. and Mrs. J. F. WARDEN and their Famous COMPANY.

On FRIDAY, AUGUST 10th, Lord LYTTON's great Play of the LADY OF LYONS; after which Mr. J. F. WARDEN will deliver an INAUGURAL ADDRESS.

On SATURDAY EVENING, AUGUST 11th, SHAKESPEARE's ROMEO and JULIET. To conclude each Evening with STAGE STRUCK—Sally Scraggs, Mrs. J. F. WARDEN.

On MONDAY, AUGUST 13, production of CLANCARTY.

Mr. WARDEN begs to announce having already made arrangements with the following Novelties:—Mr. H. LORRAINE, Mr. G. W. ANSON; Miss HEATH and Famous London Company; Miss F. HARRISON's Opera Bouffe Company; Italian Opera Concert; Mr. CLAYTON; Miss ROSE LECLERCQ; Messs. PITT and HAMILTON's Comedy Company; and Mr. BARRY SULLIVAN. Engagements pending with other Celebrated Artistes.

Doors Open each Evening at Seven, Curtain to rise at Half-past Seven.

Private Boxes, 30s and 20s; Balcony Stalls (Reserved and Numbered), 4s; Upper Circle, 2s; Pit, 1s; Gallery, 6d. No Second Price. Pass Out Checks not Transferable. No Smoking allowed in any part of the Building on any pretence whatever.

Private Boxes and Seats for Balcony Stalls can be secured from 10 till 3 o'clock Daily at Box Office of Opera House.

Business Manager and Box Book-keeper, Mr. M. BODEN; Musical Director, Mr. C. B. DAVIS; Stage Manager, Mr. S. JOHNSON. (26 R)

*The opening night at Derry's new Royal Opera House on Friday 10 August 1877. (*Londonderry Journal*, 6 August 1877)*

Joseph Frederick Warden

Warden was a well-respected figure in Derry and he was generally given the credit for turning around the fortunes of theatre in the city. He was also a successful businessman, owner of both the new Derry Opera House and Belfast's Theatre Royal, home of his repertory company. It was a family affair: his wife was his principal actress and singer, and his son Fred was also an actor. Warden himself had considerable experience as actor, manager and theatre proprietor. Born in Hull in 1836, he first appeared as an eighteen year old on stage in Scarborough, then, like other young actors embarking on a stage career, he travelled about, playing in theatres in Scotland and in Ireland (in the latter mainly in Dublin and Belfast). His whole life had been devoted to the theatre, first as an actor, then as owner of a theatre company and, from the early 1860s, as manager of theatres in Belfast.

However, he was careful to keep up his contacts with other actors and managers by touring in England, and he was never far away from the centre of theatrical life. Many of the leading actors of the day were personal friends, including Henry Irving, Herbert Beerbohm Tree and Frank Benson. No doubt this explains Warden's success in persuading famous names to come to his Irish theatres. He was also well acquainted with the two leading theatre architects of the day: Frank Matcham[50] and Charles J. Phipps. Indeed, according to Warden, it was Phipps who designed the Opera House in Derry, a claim repeated in *The Irish Builder*, although his absence on the theatre's opening night raises a question about the extent of his involvement in the project. It may be that Phipps merely provided rough drawings and designs, and that the detailed execution of the project was carried out by the 'resident clerk of works', named in the local press as Robert Jeffries.

Phipps had a reputation for providing 'good value for money' and for producing 'the greatest accommodation in a limited space at a low cost'. The new Opera House certainly fitted this description: it was built on a small rectangular site but had a large capacity. It could hold 1,600 people altogether, in four private boxes, balcony stalls, upper circle, pit and gallery, the majority being squeezed together in the pit and gallery. The cavernous pit could take around 600 people in twenty-two rows of backless benches, while the gallery (the gods) held another 700 in fourteen rows. The gallery and pit had their own entrances so that their occupants were kept apart from those in the more expensive seats. The gallery was reached by a steep set of stone steps, while entrance to the pit was through a doorway at the lower side of the facade. The theatre manager (always in a dress suit) stood at the main entrance to greet the ladies and gentlemen of the boxes, circle and balcony stalls, grandly attired in their evening gowns and dress suits – *de rigueur* for those in the better seats for an evening at the theatre.

The Opera House was typically Victorian in its ornate interior, elaborately decorated ceiling, carved elephants' heads and plush upholstered seats. The *Belfast*

Newsletter described it, aptly enough, as 'an elaborate temple dedicated solely to thespian pursuits'. No expense had been spared on its interior décor. Warden appreciated that if theatre was not to seem tawdry, it must be housed in a setting that was suitably grand and imposing. Another difference from Derry's earlier theatres was that the new Opera House had a large stage, 30ft deep by 40ft wide, with a proscenium arch 24ft across. There was gas lighting. At the rear of the building there was a tradesmen's entrance on John Street, through which scenery and props could be loaded and unloaded, convenient for the Glasgow steamship or the Belfast train.

It must have seemed to those who were there on the opening night, or who had campaigned for Derry to have a suitable 'house' for theatre and music, that their dreams had finally been realised.

'Canter and Ranter': Revd Craig

Not everyone in the city was delighted. On the Sunday following the opening of the Opera House, Revd S. Runsie Craig preached a lengthy sermon in Third Derry based on 'First Thessalonians', verse 22 ('Abstain from all appearance of evil'), that was a bitter tirade against theatre-going in general and Derry's new theatre in particular. Those who missed the service were able to read the full text of the sermon in Monday's edition of the *Sentinel*. Craig didn't mince his words:

> You know it to be a fact that many in the audience are the very scum and off-scourings of the community – thieves and drunkards, spendthrifts and profligates – designing men and lost women. How few are the pure and good in comparison with the unclean and reprobate who crowd the doorways and fill the pit and galleries.

'Would you,' he asked his listeners (and the readers of the *Sentinel*), 'look upon a ballet dancer as a desirable visiting acquaintance or allow a low comedian to share the innocent joys of your domestic circle?'

His views did not go unchallenged, even in the *Sentinel*. In the paper's next edition there was an angry letter from 'A Citizen' saying that Warden was 'not only guiltless, but beyond suspicion'. The writer claimed to speak for 'nine-tenths of the citizens of Londonderry' in defending the theatre manager. More predictably, *The Era*, the 'house magazine' of the theatrical profession, picked up on the story a few weeks later and called Craig 'a canter and a ranter', describing his sermon as 'the ravings of a sectarian bigot'. Warden himself was well aware of anti-theatre attitudes in Derry. Indeed he had alluded to them in his speech on the opening night, when he spoke of the need to win over those who 'now stand aloof' from theatre. How successful he would be in doing so remained to be seen.

Straightaway Warden introduced some changes. 'Second Prices' were abolished and smoking was prohibited 'in any part of the building on any pretence whatsoever'. Tickets to the balcony stalls and upper circle were expensive, at 4*s* and 2*s* respectively, but Warden kept entry to the pit and gallery – where the poorer people went – at rates they could afford, 1*s* and 6*d*. Because of his Belfast commitments, he delegated the day-to-day management of the theatre to a series of local managers: initially a Mr Boden, then Mr J. Savile in summer 1878, and finally George Sadleir, an auctioneer in Castle Street, was appointed business manager on a long-term basis. Warden's own Belfast theatre company, on their regular visits to Derry, provided the kernel of the performances given in the Opera House, and Warden himself was known occasionally to act, sing and give recitations. His first appearance on his new Derry stage was in August 1877, when he took the title role in Lytton's historical drama *Richelieu*. The company was back again for four nights in February 1878, with two Shakespeare plays, *As You Like It* and *The Merchant of Venice*, and a selection of other melodramas, comedies and songs. Their annual pantomime was the highlight of the spring season.

The longer-term significance of Derry's Opera House was that it brought regular theatre seasons for the first time in decades. Audiences eagerly anticipated Warden's manager's speech every August, where he announced the highlights of the coming season, when shows ran six nights a week. In the years that followed, a succession of actors, opera singers, dancers, musicians, circus troupes, cyclists, music hall artistes, blackface minstrels, all-female singing and dancing groups, wizards and ventriloquists played to Derry audiences. The acts usually came from Warden's Theatre Royal in Belfast and allowed the Derry public to share in Belfast's cultural life in a way they had been unable to do since the 1830s.

Programmes and Performers

Derry's drama club and music societies took full advantage of the new stage, forsaking Corporation Hall for the glamour and greater opportunities offered by the New Royal Opera House. By 1879, the theatre's name was generally shortened to 'The Opera House', but the glamour remained, and when local amateur performers took to its stage, they invariably advertised with the 'Royal' reinstated.

The City of Derry Dramatic Club and the Londonderry Musical Union were among the first to try out the new venue. The latter was the most recent of the music societies, being organised and led by musicians of the three largest religious denominations. In December 1878, they gave a landmark performance of Handel's *Messiah*, the first full-length performance in Derry to have a complete orchestral accompaniment. The musicians were seated in the 'new-fangled orchestra pit'. Daniel Jones was on harmonium with Minnie Franks (organist of Christ Church) on piano; Patrick Mulholland was leader of the orchestra.[51] The conductor was William Drysdale,

> [THIS EVENING.]
> LONDONDERRY MUSICAL UNION.
> CONCERT
> IN THE OPERA HOUSE,
> On *TUESDAY, 17th DECEMBER,*
> At EIGHT o'clock,
> In aid of the Funds of the City and County Infirmary.
> HANDEL's "MESSIAH,"
> WITH ORCHESTRAL ACCOMPANIMENTS.
> Pianoforte .... Mrs. FRANKS.
> Harmonium .... Mr. D. JONES, F.C.O.
> Leader of Orchestra........... Mr. P. MULHOLLAND.
> Conductor .... Mr. W. DRYSDALE.
>
> Boxes, 14s and 20s ; Balcony Stalls (Reserved), 8s ; Upper Circle, 2s ; Pit, 1s.
>
> Doors open at 7.30 p.m.
>
> Plan of the Opera House may be seen, and Tickets secured, at Mr. W. GRAHAM's, Diamond.
> 830   R. N. GORDON, Secretary.

The first complete performance of Handel's Messiah *in Derry with 'orchestral accompaniments', given by church musicians of all denominations.* (Londonderry Sentinel, *17 December 1878)*

precentor of First Derry, which had a certain appropriateness, as it was one of his predecessors, James Peterkin, who had promised Derry its first *Messiah* twenty-three years earlier. The concert had an 'enthusiastic' audience which would have more than filled Corporation Hall, but the *Journal* had misgivings. It complained of cold and draughts in the Opera House, and suggested that the music society might have been better advised to sing 'something simpler [which] would be more readily appreciated by an average audience'.

Warden was generous to local groups, often providing the theatre free for charitable events. In April 1883, the City of Derry Dramatic Club staged 'Two Grand Fashionable Dramatic and Operatic Performances' in aid of the County Infirmary.

Amateur shows of this type were generally well supported, although probably more out of personal loyalty or curiosity than for their artistic qualities.

Warden's seasons featured concerts, operas and music hall artistes. An early highlight was a concert in January 1880 by Barton McGuckin and William Ludwig, both 'ranked at the very head of the operatic and concert profession'. It was a 'sell-out' – a rare opportunity for Derry audiences to hear these two leading Irish tenors. They sang operatic arias and songs from the ever-popular Moore's Melodies: 'The Minstrel Boy', 'Oft in the Stilly Night' and 'Silent, O Moyle'.

Opera drew large crowds too, particularly as Warden brought highly regarded London opera companies directly from his Belfast theatre. Starting in the early 1880s, the D'Oyly Carte Opera Company made annual visits with their Gilbert and Sullivan operettas. In a three-day run in February 1882, the company staged *HMS Pinafore*, *The Pirates of Penzance* and the lesser known *On the Sulks* to full houses. Derry audiences got good value for their money, hearing two operettas per night and calling for – even insisting upon – many encores. D'Oyly Carte brought new productions every year: *Iolanthe* and *Patience* in February 1885, and *The Mikado* and *The Yeomen of the Guard* in December 1889 (the latter within fourteen months of its London premiere). Visits by the Carl Rosa Opera Company were also eagerly awaited for their contrasting repertoire of Italian, French and German operas.

Warden's way of working was to bring the companies or individual performers first to Belfast – usually for a one-week run – and then send them on to Derry for a further few days. This was the case with English actor Barry Sullivan (1821-1891) and Scottish music hall entertainer Arthur Lloyd (1839-1904), both of whom came to Derry several times. Sullivan, famous for his Shakespearean roles, almost guaranteed full houses. He played at the Opera House three times: in November 1878, January 1881 and finally in January 1887. Lloyd played in Derry on more than five occasions, beginning in October 1879.[52] He was a versatile performer, especially good at putting across his own songs and recitations, but twice he brought his own drama company to Derry to perform his Irish-based play *Ballyvogan*.

These, however, were the highlights. In the main, those performing in Derry were lesser-known musicians, concert groups and opera companies, such as the forty-two-strong Horace Lingard Comic Opera Company, the Belfast-based Walter Newport Company, and Dublin's Moody-Manners Opera Company, each of whom returned to the Opera House many times. What made their visits possible – complete with bulky sets, costumes and musical instruments – was the ease and availability of cheaper rail travel to and from Derry.

Drama was close to Warden's heart and he brought many drama companies to the Opera House, including, of course, his own. Most of these companies were minor stock companies which toured throughout Britain and Ireland at this time, like Charles Sullivan's Hibernian Drama Company, Miss Alleyn's Theatre Company, and Edward Compton's Comedy Company. All staged a variety of dramas, farces, melodramas and comedies, and were remarkable more for their range of productions (changing productions nightly) than for their artistic excellence.

When the Opera House was not being used, Warden occasionally leased out the building to local speakers for political lectures, talks and 'orations'. In December 1883, for example, Mr J. Darling, editor of the *Sentinel*, delivered a lecture on 'Eloquence'. However, the most famous speaker at the Opera House came a couple of weeks later, when Oscar Wilde delivered two lectures to an 'eminently select' audience, mainly seated 'in the more expensive parts of the house'.

Oscar Wilde

Wilde appeared in Derry in 1884, speaking on 'The House Beautiful' and 'Personal Impressions of America', the latter based on his recent ten-month trip across the United States. The local press declared itself surprised at his appearance. Instead of the 'fantastically dressed, intense young man [who] spent his time in the meditation of lilies' they had been led to expect, they found 'nothing uncommon ... a fine figure' and 'his tone rather monotonous'. Nevertheless, Wilde's lectures provoked lively follow-up letters in the press, debating his 'style ideas'. Unfortunately one of his lectures clashed with a concert organised by the two Cathedral organists in Corporation Hall, with the result that the turn-out for the latter was miserably low.

While in Derry, Wilde visited Corporation Hall, which had undergone renovation as the Government School of Art. He was impressed neither by the building nor its facilities. Instead he told the Opera House audience that the 'accommodation there was anything but creditable to the citizens' of Derry, in terms of lighting and space for the art students. He hoped

Oscar Wilde's lectures at Derry's Opera House in January 1884. (Londonderry Journal, *31 December 1883)*

> [THIS EVENING.]
> **OPERA HOUSE,**
> *LONDONDERRY.*
> MR. OSCAR WILDE'S LECTURES,
> THURSDAY and FRIDAY,
> JANUARY 3 and 4, 1884.
>
> MR. J. F. WARDEN has the honour to announce that Mr. OSCAR WILDE will Deliver TWO LECTURES at the OPERA HOUSE, DERRY, on THURSDAY and FRIDAY, JANUARY 3 and 4.,
> On THURSDAY Evening, JANUARY 3—" THE HOUSE BEAUTIFUL." The True Principles of Decorative Art as applied to the Exterior and Interior Decoration of the Homes of the People.
> Doors open at 7.30. Lecture at Eight o'clock. Carriages at 9.15.
> On FRIDAY Evening, JAN. 4—" PERSONAL IMPRESSIONS OF AMERICA." An Address upon Topics suggested by a Year's Travel in the United States and Canada.
> Doors open at 7.30. Lecture at Eight o'clock. Carriages at 9.15.
> Prices of Admission :—Balcony Stalls, 4s ; Upper Circle, 2s ; Pit, 1s ; Gallery, 6d. Children under Twelve—Balcony Stalls, 2s ; Upper Circle, 1s ; Pit, 6d. No Half-price to Gallery. Private Boxes, to hold Six, £1 4s ; to hold Four, 16s.
> Balcony Stalls and Private Boxes can be secured Daily, from 10 till 3 o'clock, at Box Office, under the direction of Mr. SADLEIR, Business Manager. 470

Oscar Wilde (1854-1900), the epitome of the fashionable man-about-town and celebrated wit, raconteur and aesthete. (Author's collection)

that, were he to return to Derry, he would find a more appropriate art school. Wilde never did return to the city. Eleven years later, following his trial and imprisonment for indecency, the local newspapers went into lurid detail on the affair, but forbore to mention his earlier visit to Derry.

Although serving as an art school, Corporation Hall was still occasionally used for concerts. The Irish songwriter Percy French (1854-1920) gave a 'Grand Miscellaneous Concert' there in March 1883, playing the banjo, singing his own comic songs and telling humorous stories. This was the first of French's many trips back to the town where he had been a schoolboy (at Foyle College in the 1860s). He was one of the few artists to appear in all three city venues: Corporation Hall in 1883, the Opera House in 1891 and the Guildhall in 1899. His Derry concerts gave him opportunities to visit Donegal, and Falcarragh in particular, where he spent long hours painting the watercolours for which he is now also remembered.

In common with Derry's earlier theatres, the Opera House often staged novelty acts like 'Madame Cicely Nott's Company of Thirty Ladies' with 'Full Orchestra' in August 1884, and eight months later, 'Lotto and Lilo – Infant Bicycle Phenomena', billed, improbably, as 'The Greatest Show on Earth'. In at least one such case, the audience's reaction caused a problem for the management. In January 1882, Herr Dobler, 'The Wizard of the World', arrived in Derry for a five-night run of an act involving 'Flying Bird Cages' and 'Dark Séances'. But the gallery had to be closed off after the first night, as some in the gods refused to leave at the end of the show, insisting on staying on, without paying, for a further semi-private séance by Dobler. This was probably just high spirits (if one can forgive the pun) on the part of the gallery occupants, but more serious disturbances did occur as the 1880s progressed.

The 1885 Riot

The 1880s in Ireland were the 'Parnell decade', when the demands for Home Rule by the Nationalist leader Charles Stewart Parnell led to heightened political and religious tensions throughout the island. These tensions were felt in Derry and were often played out in the theatre. There was another factor peculiar to Derry, namely that the 1871 census had, for the first time, shown Catholics in a majority in the city; this served to further inflame feelings between them and the Protestants. In Belfast there was an informal agreement between Catholics and Protestants to attend the theatre on different nights. Derry, with a much smaller population, reached its own local accommodation, with Protestants in the pit and Catholics in the gallery.

In 1884, in a portent of things to come, there were minor disruptions during performances in the Opera House. On one occasion the 'pitties' and upper circle (mainly Protestants) hissed at stage representations of a Midnight Mass and the 'Crypt of the Holy Sepulchre'. A few months later, Catholics reacted to the playing of the national anthem by groaning and hooting from the gallery. This, however, was small beer compared with the events of April 1885, which the *Sentinel* claimed were carefully pre-planned 'with murderous intent by the denizens of the Bogside'.

A visit to Derry by the Prince of Wales and a performance of Warden's pantomime *Aladdin* were the occasion for a riot which was reported in detail in many English newspapers and was the subject of questions in the House of Commons. Even before the Prince arrived there was resentment, in what was becoming increasingly a 'Catholic' city, at the lavish arrangements planned for his reception. On his arrival at the Northern Railway Station on the morning of Monday 27 April, he was greeted by rows of civic dignitaries and entertained by the splendidly named Henry Purcell Dixon's 300-strong choir. Prince and dignitaries then went in procession to the Court House on Bishop Street, setting off a day of loyalist flag-waving and celebrations. The riot in the Opera House that same evening was perhaps a delayed reaction on the part of Derry's Catholics to the way in which their protests at the Prince's visit had been ignored.

Trouble began when the Catholics in the gallery started to shout out their objections to a scene in the pantomime which seemed to them to make fun of Parnell. The Protestants in the pit responded by singing the national anthem *con amore*, knowing that this would be a loyalist red rag to a Nationalist bull. Sensing trouble, the actors decided to abandon the performance. They quickly left the stage and the footlights were extinguished. A hail of missiles (including, it was later claimed, two open knives) was fired from the gallery, accompanied by 'loud groans, hooting, vile language and cat-calls'. Next, a heavy wooden bench was thrown down into the pit, causing general panic and a stampede for the doors. Inside the theatre the stand-off lasted for about an hour. Outside it was mayhem, with the two sides spilling out into the Carlisle Road and joining in fights and scuffles that continued for hours.

The *Sentinel* put the blame for the riot squarely on the Catholics, and held the 'Bogsiders' in particular responsible. *The Journal*, while condemning the rioters, 'repeat[ed] emphatically ... that there was cause', claiming that the scene in the pantomime and the singing of the national anthem had been provocative. News of the riot soon spread beyond Derry, and it was reported in newspapers as distant as the *London Daily News*, *Chester Observer* and *Aberdeen Weekly Journal*. The *Huddersfield Chronicle and West Yorkshire Advertiser* claimed to have information that 'many respectable Protestants were beaten' but didn't identify its source. *The Era*, as was perhaps to be expected, saw the whole event in dramatic terms, and reported it under the headline, 'Exciting Scene in an Opera House'. Warden, for his part, responded forcefully, issuing a statement through the press saying he wasn't prepared to have his theatre used as a battleground and closed the Opera House for the time being.

The affair blew over quite quickly; within a week or so the Opera House had reopened and cultural life in Derry returned to normal. By late 1885, Derry had a well-established round of concerts – on average two per week – performed by its own musicians, music societies and religious and educational organisations, an impressive level of musical activity for a city of 33,000 people. The next step for this prosperous city would be the building of a new civic hall.

Five

CALM SEA AND PROSPEROUS VOYAGE, 1887-1914

In the later 1880s, Derry's cultural life was enriched by several new venues for the arts. The first was begun on 1 November 1887 when the Mayor of Derry and several aldermen gathered in Shipquay Place to lay the foundation stone for the city's new major civic building. It was then named the Victoria Hall in honour of the Queen's Golden Jubilee that year. When it was completed in 1890, it was renamed the Guildhall, and the main assembly room upstairs became Derry's premier venue for gala and music society concerts, music and drama competitions, drama performances and grand balls. Here, the Feis Ceoil and Londonderry Philharmonic Society found a home, and Henry B. Phillips – still an apprentice piano tuner in 1887 – started his career as an impresario.

The second new building, St Columb's Hall, was originally built as a temperance hall for Derry's Catholics, but soon it was hosting concerts, plays, bazaars, variety shows and the new 'moving pictures'. After 1889, it was in almost constant use and attended by all sections of the city. The Union Hall (in lower Shipquay Street), the Victoria Hall and the Craig Memorial Hall were other new venues. Meanwhile, the Opera House continued to attract respectable audiences – in both senses of that term – to dramas, concerts, opera and novelty entertainments brought by Warden. Corporation Hall remained open too, although no longer a first or even second choice for cultural events. It mainly held smaller local charity functions, like the 'Musical and Dramatic Entertainment' put on in January 1887 in aid of St Columb's Court Cricket Club, in which the Misses Alexander, daughters of the Bishop of Derry and his hymn-writing wife Cecil Frances Alexander, took part.

In the later Victorian and Edwardian ages, then, Derry had come to full maturity as a city, with its Opera House, new Guildhall, Government School of Art in Corporation Hall, and numerous other venues. By 1891, the population had reached 33,200, with plentiful employment in Derry's shirt factories and shipyards. In these years before the First World War the city was flourishing economically and culturally, although the growing demands for Home Rule and deepening political unrest within Ireland as a whole were to have a crucial effect on its future prospects.

The Opera House

Business at the Opera House was still brisk, with a second staircase added to the gallery in 1887, partly for safety reasons (in case of fire), partly to ease movement upstairs when the customers for the gods arrived for the evening. Queuing was unheard of at this time, and few in the gods and pit were prepared to pay 6*d* extra for the 'early doors' to secure a good seat. A gallery devotee later described the entire scramble for admission as being like a rugby scrum; he reckoned himself lucky if he reached his place with his ribcage intact and with only a few buttons lost from his shirt.

Barry Sullivan's final visit to the Opera House, in January 1887, provoked just such a scramble for the gallery. The press reported that special trains laid on for theatre-goers from outside the city meant that many local people were turned away. This was in spite of gallery prices being doubled to cover 'the very great expense' of bringing Sullivan to Derry. Sullivan was then sixty-six years old, but according to the Derry press, his 'genius [was] still undimmed'. His thin, wiry frame allowed him still to play convincingly the roles of a much younger man, such as the King in Shakespeare's *Richard III*. The audience rose to applaud him and refused to leave the theatre until he gave in to their demands to come before the curtain several times.

Plays of a more controversial nature also came to the Opera House. In September 1888, the 'celebrated Irish Comedians' Mr and Mrs Hugh O'Grady, and their 'powerful' Irish Company, came for five nights with some of O'Grady's own plays based on Irish history. They included the drama *Eviction*, a four-act 'modern drama' *Famine*, and the 'celebrated Irish Comedy-Drama' *Emigration*. These plays had a sharper political edge than Warden's usual offerings, but had already drawn 'large and enthusiastic crowds' to the Theatre Royal in Belfast the week before. Large audiences came to see them in Derry too, but members of the local garrison were expressly forbidden to attend by their superior officers, concerned that their presence at plays with such highly charged subject matter might spark trouble. This drew criticism from the *Bristol Mercury and Daily Post*, which, measuring Irish political sensitivities by the calm beat of its own pulse, denounced the iniquity of such an order.

A year later, Warden's theatre came in for criticism after a visit by soloists of the (usually) much loved Carl Rosa Opera Company. Eleven singers gave 'A Grand Operatic and Ballad Concert' on 18 September 1889, featuring excerpts from the operas *Mignon*, *Maritana* and *Faust*. Admission prices had been raised by 50 per cent for most areas of the theatre for this concert, but by 100 per cent for the gallery, to

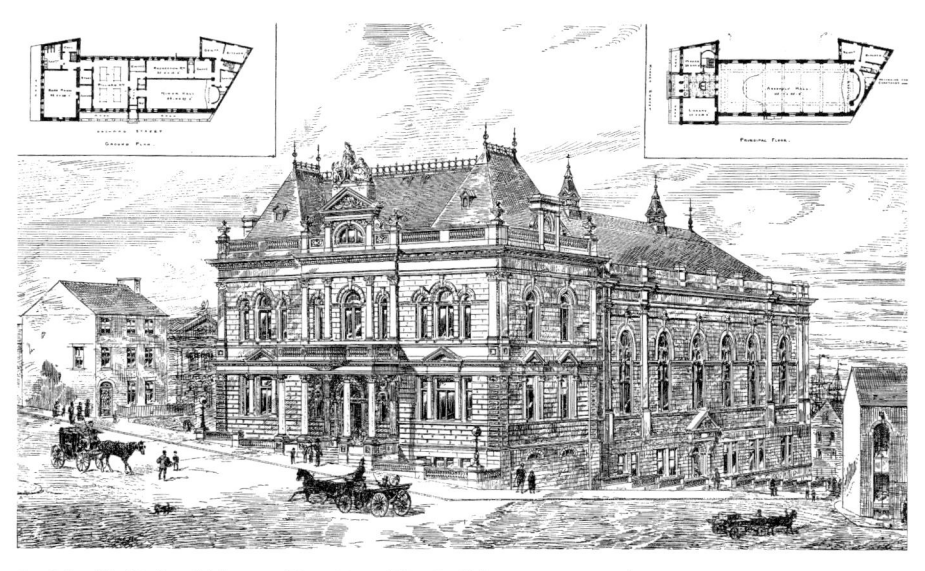

St Columb's Hall, which opened in 1887. (The Building News, 1 July 1887)

1s. Already chafing at this – and ever the defender of the gods (the Catholics) – the *Journal* was in the mood to find fault. It complained that 'the operatic character of the concert [was] nowhere observable' and that 'there was no dramatic continuity or dramatic effect'.

However, Warden soon won back his audience's good opinion by lending the theatre for charitable events. This generally happened about three times per season when the Opera House hosted a concert or drama in aid of a local disaster or needy family. Outside entrepreneurs were welcomed too, such as William Houston Collisson, already a frequent visitor to Derry with concert parties. In spring 1888, Collisson, who had been running 'Popular Concerts' in Dublin for some time, decided to try something similar in Derry. To test the market he put on three 'trial' concerts: there were operatic solos, 'popular' songs and some instrumental pieces in the first half, and the third and fifth acts of Gounod's *Faust* in the second half. The audience response was favourable, and Collisson launched his first series of 'Popular Concerts' in the Opera House in autumn 1888.

But by this time, the Opera House had a new rival, St Columb's Hall.

St Columb's Hall

St Columb's Hall opened in November 1888 and held its first 'Grand Evening Concert' three months later, in aid of the St Vincent de Paul Society. Previously these concerts had been in the Opera House, but they were now held in St Columb's Hall, with its larger 2,000 capacity. This was the first indication that the Opera House might lose its monopoly on elite concerts. The concert on 5 February was a gala event, with the St Columb's Temperance Society Band and the combined choirs of St Eugene's Cathedral and the Long Tower church. All were conducted by George Mulholland (1866-1902), who had succeeded his father as organist in 1888. The programme consisted of Irish songs, comic sketches, recitations, choral items and band interludes. The *Journal* noted an 'enormous audience', and praised the 'admirable suitability' of the hall and the 'excellence of the music'.

St Columb's Hall was designed by local architects Crome and Toye in 'a mixture of Italianate and Gothic styles'. The building still occupies a sloping site straddling Orchard and Newmarket/Richmond Streets adjacent to the East Wall. The facade remains largely unchanged, although streets and buildings nearby have been extensively remodelled in recent years. It has a main upstairs auditorium, largely unchanged from its original layout, and a smaller hall below on Orchard Street. The hall came to have a vital role in nurturing Catholic music-making. From 1889 it had its own bands, drama and music societies, and choirs, many of whom rehearsed in the smaller hall and then gave concerts in the main hall upstairs.

However, the hall was used by all sections of the population. From 1889, the precentor of First Derry, another Scotsman, John Ferguson, held his 'Tonic Solfa Association' classes in its library, drawing huge numbers of enthusiastic singers keen to learn to sing using this simplified notation. They held their 'Annual Grand Concerts' in the upper hall with visiting artists, during which all sang 'glees, choruses and Part Songs'. The usual accompanist (on piano or harmonium) was Edward Conaghan, once a young violinist at the Queen's Theatre but organist at the Long Tower church since 1882. Conaghan became the first Derry-born musician to play a major part in shaping the musical heritage of his city.

Conaghan's musical career spanned almost fifty years and most areas of Derry's musical life. He was not only a church and theatre musician, but also band conductor, concert organiser, accompanist and frequent soloist at concerts. Conaghan and his Scottish-born wife Catherine lived in Orchard Street, from where he taught piano and brass and wind instruments. He was conductor, too, of the Opera House orchestra (since 1883) and lead violinist in the Londonderry Musical Union. As the *Journal* later said in his eulogy, his was 'a crowded life'. In December 1889, Conaghan had started the Londonderry Orchestral Society, the only purely orchestral society in the history of the city. Its orchestra was thirty strong, including twelve strings, two clarinets and two cornets, bassoon, flute, piccolo, drum and harmonium. The press described its first concert in Corporation Hall in March 1890 as 'rather ambitious': there were selections from Rossini's *William Tell* and Flotow's opera *Martha*, and then some solos to showcase the talents of individual instrumentalists. Attendance was, gratifyingly, 'very large'.

The Guildhall and H.B. Phillips

Derry's new Guildhall took three years to complete. It was paid for by The Honourable The Irish Society, which also provided Londonderry Corporation with the site in Shipquay Place free of charge. It was named 'The Guildhall' after the parent hall of its London funders. The building was designed by John Guy Ferguson in 'loose Tudoresque Gothic' style in red sandstone. Its primary function was as the main civic building of Londonderry Corporation, which carried on its official business in the elaborate Council Chamber, directly modelled on the Guildhall Chamber in London. From the start, the Londonderry Musical Union held its weekly practices in this Council Chamber, but it was a 'Grand Subscription Concert' organised by Henry B. Phillips (1866-1950) that gave the Guildhall its 'musical baptism'.

Henry Bettesworth Phillips, or H.B. as he was known, was born in Athy, County Kildare, the son of a station master. After his father's death in 1879, the family moved to Derry, where H.B. had been awarded a scholarship as a chorister in St Columb's Cathedral. Here, and at Foyle College, Phillips received his early musical education. He trained for a time as a piano tuner in London before returning to Derry in the later 1880s to open his first music warehouse in Marlborough Street. Four years later, he moved into more central premises at the lower end of Shipquay Street, from where he sold sheet music, pianos, harmoniums, organs and early gramophones. However, by this time, his restless entrepreneurial spirit had led him into new ventures, in particular concert promotion, for which he proved to have decided flair.

Phillips' concert on 8 October 1891 was the first in Derry not organised by a professional musician, and marked the beginning of his career as an impresario. From the first, he made a shrewd use of older practices: the concert was held 'Under the Distinguished Patronage of Their Graces the Duke and Duchess of Abercorn, Lord Frederick Hamilton and Colonel Perry and the Officers of the Garrison.' The performers included a number of noted musicians, chief among them Hungarian violinist Tivadar Nachéz (1859-1930) and Irish tenor William Ludwig (1847-1923). The programme consisted of operatic melodies and solos by Nachéz, including Paganini's *Variations on the G String*, then Ludwig as soloist in Mrs Alexander's hymn 'There is a Green Hill Far Away' – no doubt a gesture to the local audience – and Irish songs, mainly 'those in which his admirers in Derry most desired to hear him'. Songs from the all-female Queen's Vocal Quartette completed the concert. The evening was deemed 'eminently successful' and 'highly creditable' to Phillips, the *Sentinel* claiming that 'no audience more brilliant or appreciative' had yet been to the building. The *Journal*, also warmly appreciative, commented on another change, 'During the singing and playing the profound silence which reigned in the crowded hall was not a little remarkable, and even the "gallery gods" seemed captivated.' Here was something new: the beginnings of more respectful and attentive behaviour at concerts, which we now take for granted.

The Guildhall was used for musical events other than Phillips' concerts. Local musicians like Daniel Jones, Ann Eliza MacDonald and Fred Day moved their annual concerts from the Opera House to the new building. The Londonderry Musical Union did likewise, and in March 1892 it performed Handel's *Judas Maccabaeus*, bringing together all the church musicians of the city. However, the *Journal* added a sour note, claiming that the *Sentinel* had, 'as usual', deliberately omitted the name of the leading Catholic soloist (Miss MacDonald) in its review of the performance. Here – in the allegation itself as much as in the truth of what was alleged – was a symptom of growing sectarian tensions in Derry. The political uncertainty of the 1890s, following the failure of the first Home Rule Bill, had begun to take its toll on relations between Catholics and Protestants.

The Diva: Madame Albani

Phillips' second concert season began with his most celebrated performer to date, the Canadian soprano Madame Emma Albani (1847-1930), whose reputation at that time rivalled those of Jenny Lind and Catherine Hayes thirty years before. As with those famous sopranos, there were excited editorials in local newspapers and advertisements for appropriate outfits to wear to the concert. The *Sentinel* hailed Albani as 'the most distinguished vocalist who has ever sung in our midst', describing her Derry concert as 'an opportunity ... which in all probability can never occur again'. For the benefit of its mainly Unionist readership, it dwelt on her 'personal friendship' with Queen Victoria and on Albani's ownership of property close to Balmoral.

Phillips provided a wide range of tickets: subscribers' tickets for the entire three-con-

Canadian soprano Madame Emma Albani (1847-1930), who gave a concert in the Guildhall in October 1892. A leading singer of the age, Albani was brought to Derry by H.B. Phillips in the second year of his concerts. (Illustrated London News, 1884)

cert season (from 5s to 1 guinea) and single tickets for 'The Albani Festival Concert' from 3s to 12s 6d. (The two other concerts featured Nachéz in December and 'dramatic soprano' Madamoiselle Rosina Isidor in February 1893.) It made financial sense, provided you could afford it, to buy a season ticket.

Albani's concert was advertised for 13 October, her fellow musicians being the pianist Chevalier Emil Bach (a direct descendant of J.S. Bach and 'Court Pianist to the German Emperor') and Mr Ben Davis, 'the great English tenor'. (In the event, Chevalier Bach did not appear 'due to illness'.) The event was a sell-out. The Duke and Duchess of Abercorn were among the notables present, adding to the glamour of the occasion. The atmosphere at the start was electric, with 'everyone on tiptoe to hear the prima donna'. When Albani began to sing an aria from Verdi's *La Traviata*, 'a pin could be heard to drop [sic]'. She followed this with arias from Gounod's *Faust* and then Moore's 'The Last Rose of Summer'. However, it was her singing of Henry Bishop's 'Home, Sweet Home' which received the 'heartiest applause' from the audience. Afterwards Albani dined with Bishop Alexander and his wife, and stayed overnight at the palace.

Twelve days after the Albani concert, the new Guildhall organ, an elaborate four-manual instrument by Conacher's of Huddersfield, was inaugurated in the presence of the Duke and Duchess of Abercorn.[53] The purchase of the organ had been made possible or, as the *Journal* put it, brought from 'distant hope ... to possibility, and lastly [to] realisation' by Sir William Miller, the Mayor, giving his salary for 1888 to the organ fund. At the opening ceremony, Daniel Jones, organist at St Columb's Cathedral, gave a recital to show off the new instrument. But in case organ music on its own was not enough for the distinguished guests, a soprano from 'The Newcastle and Yorkshire Popular Concerts' and Belfast tenor R. Patterson were also engaged to perform some songs.

The Londonderry Musical Union was greatly taken with the new organ and advertised its first *Messiah* with 'organ accompaniment' for later that year. The *Journal* expressed delight, too, suggesting that it would be of 'vast advantage [to the society] in the production of classic music in the best style'. But the Union was not alone in performing oratorio at the Guildhall. The Carlisle Choir, conducted by George Anderson, precentor of Fourth Derry, performed Handel's *Samson* in December 1892, confirming the Guildhall – with its superb new organ – as the premier city venue for music society concerts.

'Smoking Concerts' – smoking was then considered the healthy alternative to alcohol – were popular entertainments by the early 1890s. They were held weekly in the Recreation Rooms in London Street for just 6d, and in the People's Hall in Bishop Street there were Saturday concerts for 'Working men and their families', also for 6d admission. The message in both was abstinence: the songs and recitations of the first part of the concerts were always followed by communal hymn-singing and sermons on the evils of alcohol.

The St Columb's Hall Bazaar

Although St Columb's Hall itself was originally planned as a temperance hall, its role in fundraising meant it came to be used for other purposes. In April 1895, it hosted 'The Long Tower Bazaar': four days of music and entertainments in aid of church renovations and new Catholic schools. The bazaar was open daily for eight and a half hours and featured the St Columb's Brass and Reed Band, a chorus of over 'one hundred voices', and an 'orchestral band' conducted by Conaghan. Interesting new inventions were on display, including 'Edison's Latest Phonograph [and] the telephone'. They could be seen and heard alongside an older type of novelty in the person of 'Guma Sahib – The Great Indian Juggler'. Daily tickets were 6*d*, with season tickets for the indefatigable at 2*s* 6*d*. Bazaars of this kind were one favoured method of raising funds for parish needs, especially for the completion of St Eugene's Cathedral.[54] To the same end, drama societies, choirs, music societies and bands of the two churches competed in a frenzy of activity, organising concerts, play performances and musical entertainments. New groups were started specifically to stage events for this purpose, such as various 'guilds' named after particular saints, which vied with each other in fundraising.

In the mid-1890s, St Columb's Hall had its own amateur drama society, the first city drama society since the 'young lads' of twenty years before. But this new Star Dramatic Company had members of all ages. It practised in the smaller St Columb's Hall, where it also staged well-advertised public performances. Like the music of the Catholic bands, choirs and singers, its plays were predominantly Irish in character. One of its early productions, in September 1895, was the 1831 play *Pyke O'Callaghan, or The Irish Patriot* (also called *Oonagh's Lament*) by London actor Wybert Reeve. The plot came with a complete set of Irish stereotypes of the period – Sir James Blackadder (an English Lord), Neil O'Connor (a patriot), Red Rufus (an informer) and Pyke himself (an Irish boy) – which allowed the audience to boo, hiss and cheer *ad libitum*. Plays of a similar character followed, no doubt appealing to grass-roots nationalism in Derry. The foundation of a local branch of the Gaelic League in October 1899 was another expression of growing Nationalist feeling in Derry, promoting the Irish language and traditional music through its classes and social events.

Warden Bows Out

Warden had continued to bring a wide range of performing artists and companies from Belfast to his Derry Opera House. As well as the usual drama, comedy and opera companies, there were variety and novelty acts. In August 1891, Professor Crocker and his troupe of 'marvellously educated horses, ponies, donkeys and mules' opened the season with a six-night run, advertised as 'never witnessed before in this city'. The theatre had been closed that summer for redecoration of the interior, with the walls, ceilings and entrances repainted and regilded. Luckily – or perhaps by design – work on cleaning and renovating the stage area was put off till after Crocker's 'marvellously educated', but perhaps imperfectly continent, troupe of equines had moved on to pastures new.

Old favourites returned too: Arthur Lloyd with his *Ballyvogan* play for four nights in September 1891 and Horace Lingard's Comic Opera for five nights in January 1892. Kennedy Miller's Dublin-based drama company followed that autumn. Their double bill of Irish playwright Dion Boucicault's *The Colleen Bawn* and *The Shaughraun* brought packed houses, as they would do in future decades. Derry welcomed other companies for the first time, such as the Dublin-based Moody-Manners Opera Company in late January 1895. The next week, Frank Benson's Shakespearean Company took to the stage with four nights of Shakespeare: *Hamlet*, *Romeo and Juliet*, *Richard III* and *The Taming of the Shrew*.

A more unusual performance, two weeks earlier, was a 'thought reading' display by a Mr Stuart Cumberland and Miss Phyllis Bentley. At this event, a group of local dignitaries, the High Sheriff of the city (John Cooke) and other 'well-known local gentlemen', were invited onto the Opera House stage and seated near to the performers, to observe at close quarters. Their role was to vouch for the demonstrations of their peculiar skills being genuine and 'without any mechanical or other assistance' – in other words, to reassure an otherwise sceptical audience that everything was above board. Predictably, the observers found nothing untoward, enabling the gods and 'pitties' to go home happy and amazed at the performers' 'remarkable skills'.

The Opera House hosted lectures too, as in May 1895 when the strikingly named Mrs Longshore-Potts, a doctor from the Women's Medical College of Philadelphia, gave five daily talks at 3 p.m. on 'Health and Disease' and 'Maternity'. Each lecture, for 'women only', was illustrated by 'two hundred Limelight Views'.

By 1896, Warden owned three theatres: the Derry Opera House, Belfast's Theatre Royal and its Grand Opera House, the last of these having opened in December 1895. He had owned the Derry theatre for almost twenty years, but it was often closed for long periods when Warden was preoccupied with his Belfast enterprises. The pressure of running three theatres – and perhaps failing health – may have persuaded Warden to put the Opera House up for sale.[55]

H.B. Phillips' Early Years

In October 1896, a syndicate led by Phillips bought the theatre. The transfer of ownership occurred imperceptibly: there was no public announcement of the change, except for an Opera House advertisement on 24 October in which Phillips' name replaced that of Warden as proprietor. Phillips had been business manager for the previous two years, running the box office from his music shop, so it is likely that negotiations had been ongoing for some time. The Opera House was a huge undertaking for any new proprietor, and particularly for Phillips, who had no experience in theatre. He was barely thirty years old, and already had a demanding concert business and music shop. So, for the rest of the 1896/7 season, there was no change in programming. It is probable that Phillips had agreed to honour bookings made by Warden, most of which were for companies coming directly from his Belfast theatres. Phillips then closed the Opera House during summer 1897 for redecoration, in preparation for his first full season as proprietor.

Plays continued to be popular, with regular visits by English and Irish drama companies. Benson's Shakespearean Company, Kennedy Miller's Irish Theatre Company, Fred Jarman's Drama Company and Mark Melford's London Comedy Sketch and Variety Company were among those which came to the Opera House over the next few years. Phillips regularly advertised in *The Era*, seeking drama companies and individual acts for the theatre, which he now claimed held 1,760 people. This enlarged capacity – it was always quoted as 1,600 in Warden's time – was probably achieved by extending the pit area by shifting the barrier backwards and removing some seating from the stalls.

Tyrone Power (1869-1931), father of the future Hollywood film actor of the same name and a celebrated actor in his own right, appeared three years running (in September 1899, January 1901 and January 1902) with the Kennedy Miller Company. On each visit, Power took lead roles in the mainly Irish plays presented: *The Colleen Bawn*, *The Shaughraun*, *The Irishman*, *Rory O'More* and *Lord Edward, or '98*. Oscar Wilde's plays were also popular, *The Importance of Being Earnest* running for six consecutive nights in January 1900. For this production by Miss Elsie Laueham's Company, press advertisements described the play as 'the celebrated Society Drama' without mentioning the name of its author. (By then Wilde was living out the final months of his life in self-imposed exile in Paris.) Frank Benson's Company returned to Derry for one week in February 1901, performing four Shakespeare plays and Sheridan's *School for Scandal*.

As in Warden's time, visits by opera companies drew large audiences, attracted by the dramatic spectacle and costumes, one suspects, as much as the music. The Royal Carl Rosa Opera Company came in September 1899 with a different opera each night (*Faust*, *Maritana*, *Tannhäuser* and *The Bohemian Girl*), a working schedule and repertoire at which any modern opera company would blanch. It was billed as 'The Event of the Season' and the theatre was advertised for the occasion as 'The Royal Opera House'. (It reverted to its everyday name the following week.) Phillips also hired out opera glasses for 3*d*, an innovation in Derry, although they had been obtainable in Belfast theatres for several years. There were other changes. In January 1899, Herr Hahn was appointed conductor of the Opera House orchestra with the grand title of *Chef d'Orchestre* and Conaghan relegated to first violin. Then, in September 1903, the twenty-two-year-old Derry violinist Mr M.P. Duddy, former leader of Belfast's Empire Theatre Orchestra, took over as bandleader.

Pantomime was one constant in Opera House seasons, always guaranteeing full houses and a healthy profit for the owner. Phillips' annual pantomime was at Easter time (as was the tradition during the era), but unlike Warden, he did not always bring it from Belfast; his 1897 pantomime *Jack and the Beanstalk* came from Newcastle-Upon-Tyne.

But while Phillips' Opera House featured drama, opera, pantomimes, variety shows and performances by local amateur groups, he reserved the Guildhall for his prestigious subscription concerts and for his lecture series. In spring 1898, he brought four speakers there, including the African traveller Mary Kingsley and early Zionist writer Israel Zangwill; admission was by subscription ticket only, a hefty 10*s* for the series.

1898 and All That

The music in St Columb's Hall – and of Derry's Catholics – continued to be led by their organists, George Mulholland and Edward Conaghan. They were not just organists and choirmasters, but also music teachers, bandmasters and concert promoters. Their choir members formed the nucleus of their newly formed music society, the St Cecilia's Society (1896), and their band, the St Columb's Temperance Brass and Reed Band. Conaghan was also a gifted composer. For the centenary of the Long Tower in June 1897, he composed the 'Hymn to St Columba', sung annually in the church for many decades thereafter. This was followed by his much loved '98 *Cantata*.

From early 1898, the *Journal* ran editorials canvassing ideas for marking the centenary.[56] In April it finally announced that a new cantata would be performed, with music by Edward Conaghan and libretto by Thomas Francis Mullan, a local teacher. The 1798 theme was not a new one: Whitbread had written ten plays on the Rebellion and Boucicault had used it as backdrop to his 1864 play *Arrah-na-Pogue*. Conaghan's '98 *Cantata* was performed twice in St Columb's Hall in May 1898, with a 'Powerful Chorus of 100 voices and full orchestra of 25 performers'. The soloists included Conaghan's wife, Catherine (who sang with 'marked taste and intelligence') and John Hemingway, principal bass in St Columb's Cathedral (who sang with 'much skill and success'). Immediately after the premiere, the *Journal* accorded it a lengthy and highly appreciative review, urging concert-goers to attend the second night, when they would be assured of an 'exceedingly pleasurable' performance.

The cantata was repeated in January 1900 by the same chorus and orchestra, but this time in the Opera House. Again, the *Journal* acclaimed it 'a masterpiece', and the cantata remains a work which Derry's Catholics have cherished down the years.

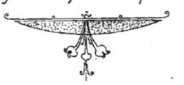

The title page of the final song and chorus of Edward Conaghan's '98 Cantata: Home of My Heart, Holy Ireland. The cantata has been performed many times since its premiere in May 1898: once in 1900, three times in the later 1940s and again in 1998. (By kind permission of Denis Mullan)

There were other centenary celebrations in Derry that year, including performances by William Ludwig, part of his all-Ireland tour of "98 Concerts'. Ludwig, who had adopted a German name in place of his actual name (Ledwidge), was a Dublin-based baritone much loved by Irish audiences. (He is mentioned in James Joyce's *Ulysses*.) Ludwig's concerts on 28 February and 1 March featured many patriotic Irish songs and other 'songs of love and war, keenes and lullabies'. The *Journal*, favourable to all things Irish, hailed them as 'The Concerts of the Season'.

Alexandrina McCausland Stewart

That same year, a newly married young couple, the McCausland Stewarts, arrived in Derry. The bride was Alexandrina, the daughter of German cellist Wilhelm Elsner, a former teacher at the Dublin Academy of Music. Already, in February 1887, as a twenty-two-year-old contralto, she had been a soloist in Derry at a St Columb's Choral Union concert conducted by Daniel Jones. The concert had featured Barnett's cantata *The Building of the Ship* and some part-songs and 'duetts [*sic*]'. The *Sentinel* gave it a glowing review, particularly Alexandrina, who, it said, sang with the 'most delightful freshness and grace', her solo of Gluck's 'Che Faro' being 'her greatest success'. By the time of her second concert, in October 1889, she was already 'quite a favourite with Derry audiences'. Her return to Derry, through her marriage to Abraham McCausland Stewart, was to bring a new influence to bear on the musical life of her adopted city.[57]

Shortly after their fashionable Dublin wedding, the McCausland Stewarts moved into a three-storey house at 9 Crawford Square, Derry. Abraham was Derry's new harbour engineer, and on her marriage, Alexandrina (or Alex as she was generally known) gave up her career as a full-time singer. However, she quickly became involved in local musical matters, renewing her acquaintance with Daniel Jones and forging a new friendship with H.B. Phillips, whose music shop was close to her husband's surveying business. Within a few months, Alex invited a representative from the Dublin Feis Ceoil to advise on the establishment of a similar Feis in Derry. By autumn 1899 there was an organising committee, including Alex Stewart, Daniel Jones, Eva Chadwick (wife of the new Bishop of Derry) and Captain Jack Herdman, and the Guildhall was booked for 7 April 1900. Derry's Feis Ceoil was only the second in Ireland, before Sligo in 1903 and Belfast in 1908. For the next century, its music, elocution and dancing classes was to draw competitors from all over Ireland, and from further afield.[58]

The Feis Ceoil and the Londonderry Philharmonic Society

Early in 1900, the first Feis Ceoil was advertised with its six competitions: four were choral, for church, factory, school and juvenile choirs; one was for drum and fife bands, and one was for solo singing. The Derry Branch of the Gaelic League presented a gold medal for the 'best rendering of a song in Irish' and the McCausland Stewarts presented the prize of a 'conductor's baton' for the winning church choir. City dignitaries, businessmen and the Feis committee donated other awards. In its early years, the Feis Ceoil was true to its name ('Festival of Music') and had only music competitions. It was an immediate stimulus to choral singing, with employees at three shirt factories (Tillie & Henderson, Welch & Margetson & Co., and Hogg & Mitchell) starting choirs specifically to take part in the Feis. Rivalry at that year's competition was intense, with each choir vying to achieve the highest marks and praise from the adjudicator, a Professor Rogers. At the close, the Mayor described the Feis as 'one of the brightest things we have yet witnessed in the city of Derry'. Alex Stewart was Honorary Secretary of the Feis, responsible for publication of the syllabus, selecting adjudicators, receiving entries and day-to-day administration. In the three years after 1900, despite having three children in quick succession, she still managed to run the Feis and have time left over for what would become the city's largest music society, the Philharmonic, which she and Daniel Jones had started in 1899.[59]

The new Philharmonic Society had two aims, 'the practice of choral and instrumental music and the promotion of a taste therefor'. It was an immediate success, lasted for forty-one years, and became Derry's longest-existing choral society. During this time it presented eighty oratorios and cantatas in twice-yearly concerts, including Handel's *Messiah* thirteen times. Its first concert was, of course, *Messiah*, performed by a chorus of 100 voices and a nineteen-strong orchestra conducted by Daniel Jones – the society firmly establishing itself as part of 'the annual outbreak of Messiahtide'. Its next concert, in spring 1900, featured Mozart's *Twelfth Mass*, with *Messiah* repeated at Christmas.

In December 1901, there was yet another *Messiah*, with Alex Stewart sharing the platform with soloists from the Moody-Manners Opera Company. Daniel Jones, at the organ, was now in his thirteenth year in Derry, the second of five successive English-born organists at St Columb's Cathedral.[60] (A pattern was beginning to emerge – similar to the Presbyterians' employment of mainly Scottish precentors – of Derry's Anglican churches employing English-born musicians.) The conductor was a newcomer to the city, Englishman Albert J. Cunningham (1870-1935), a former bandmaster with the Royal Artillery. He had first come to Derry as bandmaster to the Royal Irish Rifles, but then married Joan Gibson, daughter of the proprietor of the Northern Counties Hotel, where they both set up home. Given his army rather than church background, Cunningham was an unusual choice for the post and his appointment was something of a departure for Derry's choral societies.

Advertisement for the first Londonderry Feis Ceoil, later the Londonderry Musical Festival. (Derry Journal, *4 February 1900*)

PUBLIC MUSICAL COMPETITION

IN THE

GUILDHALL, LONDONDERRY,

ON

SATURDAY, 7th APRIL, 1900,

HOURS OF COMPETITION:

10 a.m.—Miscellaneous Choirs.
11 a.m.—Church Choirs.
12 Noon—Irish Solo Singing.
2 p.m. till 4 p.m.—School Choirs.
4 p.m. till 6.30 p.m.—Factory Choirs.
7 p.m.—Fife-and-Drum Competition.

Admission to Public, 1s and 6d.

☞ Last Day when Entries can be made—1st APRIL, 1900.

HON. SECRETARIES:

MRS. ALEX. STEWART,
9, Crawford-square, Derry.

MISS EVA CHADWICK,
The Palace, Londonderry.

The Londonderry Philharmonic Society's Messiah *in December 1901, with Alex Stewart as contralto soloist. Her Dublin friends Fanny Moody and Charles Manners were fellow soloists.* (Author's collection)

⁂ LONDONDERRY PHILHARMONIC SOCIETY ⁂

THIRD SEASON, 1901-2.

The First Concert of the Season,

⁂ GUILDHALL ⁂

WEDNESDAY EVENING, 18th DECEMBER, 1901,
AT EIGHT O'CLOCK.

HANDEL'S "MESSIAH"

Artistes:		
MADAME FANNY MOODY,	-	Soprano.
MRS. ABRAHAM M'C. STEWART,	-	Contralto.
MR. JOHN CHILD,	-	Tenor.
MR. CHARLES MANNERS,	-	Bass.
MR. A. J. CUNNINGHAM,	-	Conductor.
MR. D. C. JONES, Mus. Doc.,	-	Organist.

Chorus and Orchestra about 180 Performers.

Phillips: The Beginnings of Empire

In 1899, Phillips moved to more spacious premises at 30 Shipquay Street, and, as the building had been a private house, he employed local architect John Guy Ferguson to completely redesign the first two floors. The new shop had a street frontage of 27ft and a large plate-glass window (13ft by 12ft) to 'admit a flood of light' into his 800ft^2 piano showroom on the ground floor. Here he had pianos for hire, for sale and available on hire purchase. The shop specialised in keyboard instruments of all kinds, the upstairs showroom being for organs, pianos and harmoniums. It was around this time that the catchphrase 'Phillip's Perfect Pianos' was coined, a strapline that the business continued to use over the next forty years. Every available space was utilised. The back of the premises had a teaching studio which was rented out to piano teachers – something none of Phillips' predecessors had thought of doing and which sums up his 'try anything' mentality. His only centrally located competition was William Graham's shop (formerly Hempton's), but in 1905 it moved to Strand Road, leaving Phillips as the major city centre music shop. Two years later, in another innovation, Phillips' shop was one of the first city businesses to have a telephone (Derry 127).

Phillips' brother George, ten years his junior, became his business partner and ran the shop on a day-to-day basis, leaving H.B. free to pursue his concert projects. In 1899, in the same year as he opened his new music shop, Phillips began putting on concerts in Belfast. Thereafter his career as an impresario was meteoric. He set up parallel concert series, 'Phillips' Subscription Concerts' and 'Phillips' Dublin, Belfast and Irish Provincial Concerts', for venues in eighteen different Irish towns.

By 1902, the Opera House was used by amateur groups too. In February, some local people staged Gilbert and Sullivan's *Trial by Jury*, followed by Martin Becher's one-act farce *Painless Dentistry*. They were not a music or drama society as such, but merely a group of townspeople who came together from time to time to perform for charitable causes, on this occasion for the St Eugene's Cathedral Bazaar. The conductor was H.P. Dixon, with the Opera House Band once again under Conaghan. On both evenings, the Opera House was 'crowded from floor to ceiling', with many sitting in the aisles and passageways. The Mayor, solicitor Francis Miller, and his wife attended on the second night, lending lustre to the occasion. At this time, fundraising to erect the Cathedral spire had reached fever pitch in the city, different groups competing with one another to raise the money required. And this was not restricted to Catholics; there were genuine 'cross-community' groups involved. The City of Derry Dramatic Company presented H.P. Grattan's domestic drama *The Fairy Circle* and *The Shaughraun*, in February and April 1902, for the spire fund. Dixon's group returned with the same Gilbert and Sullivan operetta in April, this time billed as a 'dramatic cantata', with the aim of raising funds for crews from the City of Derry Boating Club to attend the Cork International Regatta. Again, the Opera House was packed, and the evening ended 'amid great applause'.

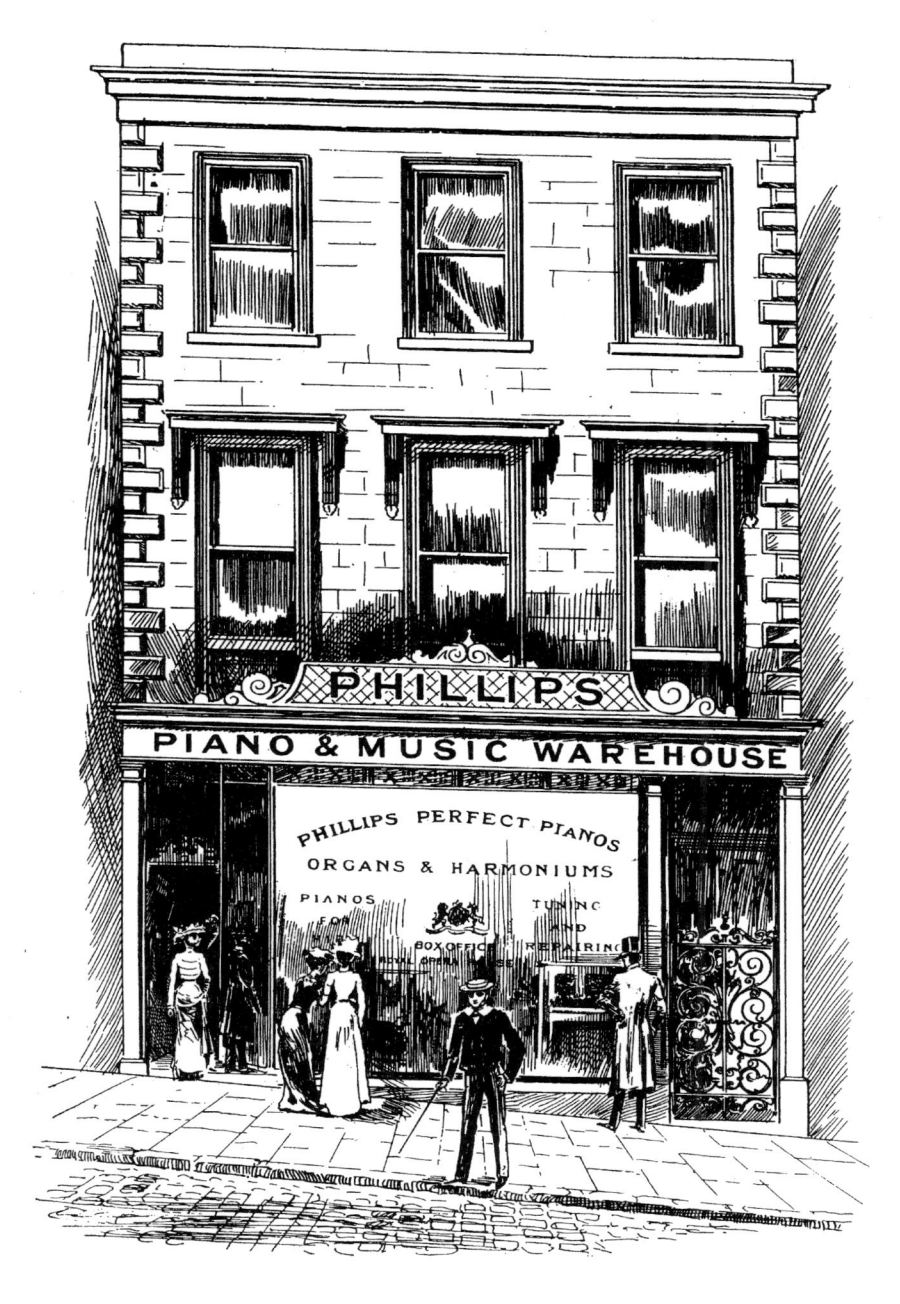

An artist's impression of Phillips' Beethoven House in Shipquay Street around 1900. The site is now marked with an Ulster History Circle plaque. (PRONI, D/3497/3: by kind permission of the Deputy Keeper of the Public Record Office of Northern Ireland)

The following year, the Opera House was leased to Harry Foxwell, then sold in 1904 to W. Payne Seddon. These successive changes in management suggest that Phillips no longer had time to give to the Opera House, or perhaps had lost interest in it as his concert business grew. In 1903, he had married Nettie, daughter of Henry Prior, who owned a chemist's shop in Ferryquay Street.[61] Nettie was already a skilled pianist, having studied at the London's Royal College of Music. In the early years of their marriage she was a professional asset to H.B., often playing at his concerts in Derry and Belfast. Phillips' concert empire was expanding year by year, but he was still rooted in Derry and did not neglect the Guildhall, where it had all begun, providing four concert in his 1903/4 season.

Payne Seddon and The Hippodrome

The new Opera House owner, William Payne Seddon (1877-1924), was the second Englishman to own the theatre. He was born in Cheshire but had acted throughout Ireland, eventually owning his own theatre company. So he was neither new to drama nor to the financial risks of owning a theatre. He later said that when he was deliberating over buying the Opera House, English friends had advised against it, saying, 'the country is so unsettled you never know what will happen over there'. From his travels around Ireland, Seddon knew that the island was in a state of ferment, as pressure for Home Rule increased and political agitation spread. But he was confident of his audience and reckoned he could revive the Opera House's flagging fortunes. Besides which, Derry had not up to this date been a major focus of political unrest.

Seddon made a number of changes at the Opera House. In 1905, he introduced twice-nightly performances instead of the single lengthy show, with 'Smoking allowed in all Parts'. He lowered admission to 'popular prices', reducing the pit from 1s to 6d and the gallery from 6d to 4d. He started mid-week matinees, and negotiated with railway companies for special excursion tickets and late trains for those travelling from outlying towns like Strabane, Limavady and Buncrana. To begin with, live drama was the cornerstone of Seddon's programming, with companies from previous years returning with the usual popular Irish plays of Boucicault, Whitfield and Wilde. The Victorian melodrama *East Lynne*, based on the novel by Mrs Henry Wood, which had appeared occasionally before 1900, now became one of the theatre's 'bankers', its harrowing storyline and shameless appeal to the emotions of its audience the guarantee of good returns at the box office.[62]

However, theatres everywhere were facing up to change, and Seddon realised that Derry audiences were also demanding more of the variety shows, revues and silent films available elsewhere. Gradually he brought in more of these, alongside the older types of entertainment – the melodramas, comedies and farces. And in summer 1906, to get rid of any stuffiness attached to the name 'Opera House', he changed

A painting of First Derry Presbyterian church as it was before 1850. A small building behind the church housed the Singing Boys of the Blue School', Derry's first school of music in the eighteenth century. Here Scottish-born precentors laid the foundations of choral singing in the city. (By kind permission of First Derry Presbyterian church)

Postcard of Corporation Hall as seen from Hempton's music shop. The hall hosted concerts from 1826 onwards, including those by Louis Jullien, Henryk Wieniawski, Jenny Lind and Joseph Joachim in 1859. It became the Government School of Art in the later 1870s and was finally demolished in 1909. (Author's collection)

W. Houston Collisson's best-known composition, 'The Mountains of Mourne', with lyrics by his stage partner, Percy French (pictured). Collisson, later an Anglican clergyman, first ran 'Popular Concerts' in Derry's Opera House in 1888. (Author's collection)

'Old Chap', a song made popular by Margaret Cooper, pianist and 'salon-type' singer (pictured), who gave one of H.B. Phillips' concerts in St Columb's Hall in 1911. (Author's collection)

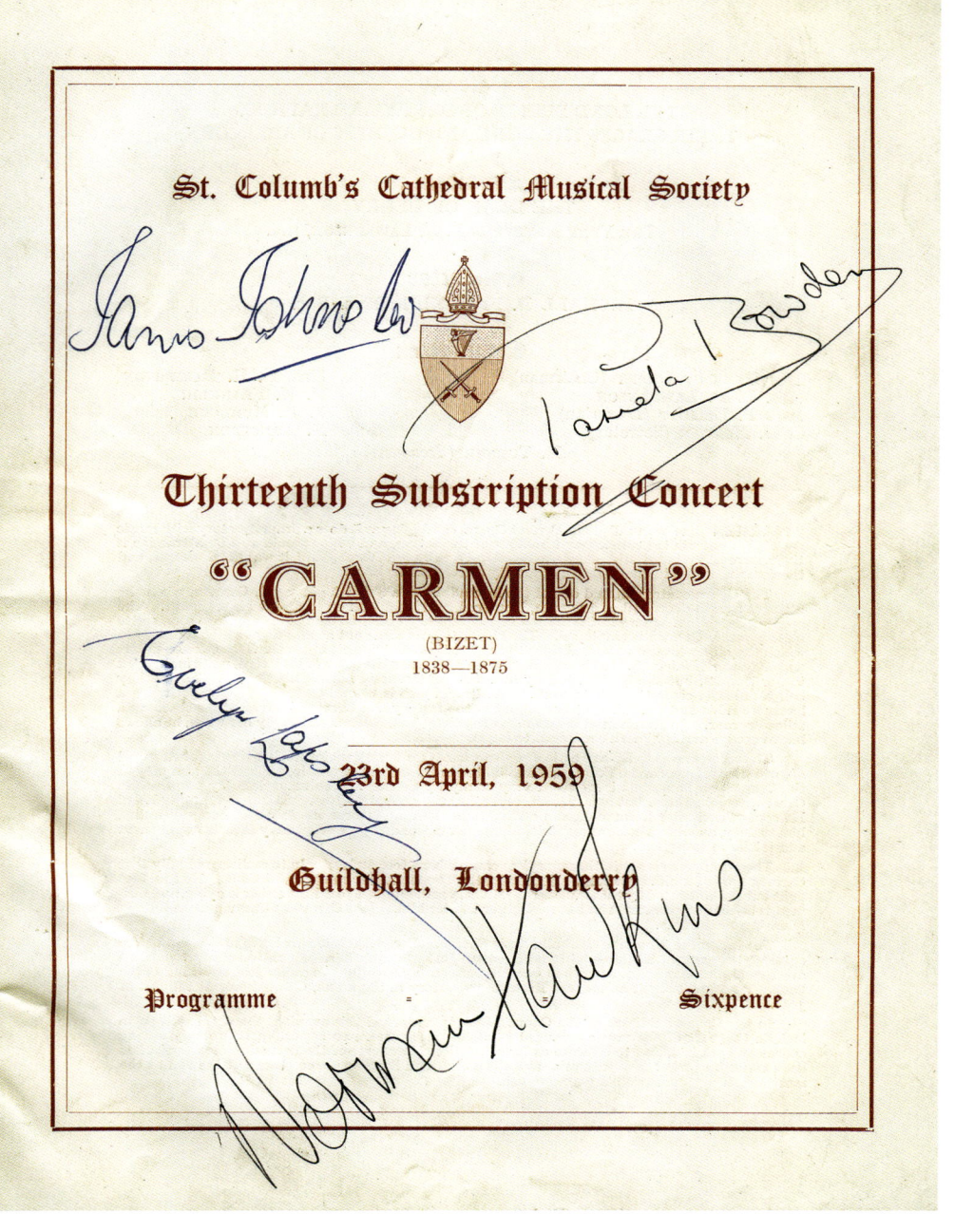

Programme for the spring 1959 concert by the St Columb's Cathedral Musical Society. It is autographed by James Johnston, who took the role of Don José in Bizet's Carmen. *(Author's collection)*

A return to their roots: Londonderry Amateur Operatic Society's seventeenth production, The Mikado, *in March 1982, directed by Scott Marshall. Cover design by Tim Webster. (By kind permission of Tim Webster)*

Leading musicians of the 1960s and '70s: first left, James MacCafferty (1915-1995), second left, Phil Coulter (b. 1942) and second right Josef Locke (1918-1999). (By kind permission of the MacCafferty family)

Octoberfest '92: A bench in the Guildhall seated three renowned writers of the modern age: (from left) Brian Friel, Seamus Heaney and Ted Hughes, the Derry Journal, *17 October 1992. (By kind permission of the* Derry Journal*)*

Harry Christophers and The Sixteen, frequent performers at the Two Cathedrals' Festivals in the later 1990s. (By kind permission of Harry Christophers)

The Opera House, Carlisle Road; built by Joseph Warden in 1877, owned by H.B. Phillips Ltd between 1896 and 1904, and thereafter by W. Payne Seddon and then a series of Dublin proprietors. (The Bigger McDonald Collection: by kind permission of Derry Central Library)

it to 'The Hippodrome', just as two years earlier Belfast's Grand Opera House had become 'The Palace of Varieties'. The following year, in another innovation, Seddon had the theatre perfumed with 'Prior's Lavender Water' from the chemist's shop in Pump Street. Though at first glance a step backward into an earlier era, it may have been that most modern of commercial arrangements: a sponsorship deal with Henry Prior's shop.

The Battle of the Bands

The Feis continued to expand, and in these early years the classes for brass bands in particular were highly contested. There was lengthy practising in advance, close secrecy regarding the 'free' work chosen as the second piece, and intense rivalry on the day itself. The 1905 competition was between three bands: the eighteen-strong Britannia Band, the forty-two-member St Columb's Band, and a band from Omagh. It was won by the St Columb's Band, much to the chagrin of the 'Brits'.

In the 1906 Feis there were two entrants: the now twenty-two-strong Britannia Band and the St Columb's Band. The set piece was an 'Irish Medley' followed by the bands' own free choice. For this, the Britannia chose *Coonland*, 'a combination of nigger songs, songs, whistling, and clog-dancing imitations' calculated to entertain both audience and players. The competition, it was said, 'created more feeling than any election', and 'being [of] different religion, excitement was keen' – so much so that the adjudicator was required to listen to the bands from behind a screen to avoid any hint of bias. The Brits won by a margin of three marks – their first victory at the Feis – and were overjoyed. On leaving the hall, they were surrounded by their jubilant supporters and, perhaps deliberately, rubbed salt in the wounds of the losers by giving an impromptu rendition of 'Derry's Walls'. Not everyone was convinced that their victory had been fairly won, 'Talk was freely used afterwards by certain sections that the adjudicator, being military, was biased against St Columb's…' Sour grapes perhaps, but even musical competitions were not immune to suggestions of political and religious bias that were affecting other aspects of the city's life.

The largely middle-class world of the Philharmonic Society remained relatively untouched by these tensions. Since its inception, the society had spread its musical wings, singing thirteen different oratorios and cantatas since 1899. These included the more popular works by Handel (three *Messiah*s), Mendelssohn (two *Elijah*s and one *St Paul*), and also Mozart, Weber, Rossini, Haydn and Coleridge Taylor. Their conductor, Cunningham, had brought more intensive training to the Philharmonic orchestra and it became a regular – and often the only – entrant in the orchestral class at the Feis. Their choice of Beethoven's *Symphony No.1* as a Feis competition piece suggests that they were, if not an accomplished ensemble, at least one that set its sights high.

Alex Stewart remained central to the Philharmonic as a committee member and frequent soloist at their concerts. She also formed her own Derry Ladies' Choir, which competed at both the Derry and Dublin Feisanna in 1904, winning prizes at each. At the Philharmonic concerts, Alex usually sang alongside soloists brought from London and Dublin, often booked by H.B. Phillips at specially negotiated rates.

The Guildhall Fire

The burning of the Guildhall on Easter Sunday, 19 April 1908, was described in the press as 'the greatest fire ever witnessed in Derry'. Even in bright sunshine it could be seen clearly from 3 miles away by church-goers taking their early afternoon stroll on the heights above the Waterside. In the space of two hours, the flames consumed the upper part of the building, destroying the Assembly Hall and bringing down the roof in a shower of sparks and burning embers. In the heart of the fire, the final moments of the great organ, the 'king of instruments', seemed to an imaginative onlooker like those of a living thing, 'As the flames gained upon it, deep sighs were heard coming from its pipes, and these developed into a sort of low moan as the flames gradu-

Aftermath of the blaze: the Guildhall smouldering on Easter Sunday, 1908. (Author's collection)

ally enveloped it ... a dirge of agony was fated to be the last tune to come from the organ.' What remained of the building after the fire had burned itself out – the ground floor, outer walls and tower – was sealed off, awaiting reconstruction of the damaged areas, and corporation business transferred elsewhere. It would be four years before rebuilding was completed and the Guildhall open to the public again.

The loss of the Guildhall meant new opportunities for St Columb's Hall, the only other venue available for the Feis, the Philharmonic and Phillips' concerts. The Opera House, now The Hippodrome, was out of the question. Under Seddon it now had a well-established programme of variety shows, occasional dramas and silent films, offered to the public at prices as low as 2*d*, and he was not going to sacrifice these more popular and profitable entertainments in order to stage music competitions and concerts.

So the Feis moved to St Columb's Hall, adding more competitions, cups and awards every year. In 1910, a 'Children's Day' was started on the Wednesday of Feis Week, with 'lunch and tea' provided free to all competitors aged between eight and fifteen. It quickly established itself as the most popular day of the Feis, both for its free meals and for the 'Action Song' competition. Several children's choirs travelled from Belfast on the early morning train to compete and then returned by the Great Northern Railway's midnight mail train!

By this time, Phillips had opened a new music shop on the corner of Bedford Street and Donegall Square, Belfast. Like its Derry counterpart, it was in a prominent city centre site and close to the Ulster Hall, home of 'Phillips' Belfast Concerts'. Both city shops now traded under the name of 'Beethoven House'. There was even a Beethoven House Orchestra, conducted by Edgar Haines, which Phillips hired out for concerts,

PHILLIPS'
DUBLIN, BELFAST, AND IRISH PROVINCIAL
CONCERTS.

ST. COLUMB'S HALL,
LONDONDERRY,
THURSDAY, 14th OCTOBER, 1909, at EIGHT.

FAREWELL APPEARANCE OF IRELAND'S
GREAT TENOR,

Mr. John M'Cormack,

Prior to his Departure for America.

Mr. M'Cormack will be heard in several of the Songs with which his Name is associated, including :—
"She is far from the Land ;"
"I hear you calling Me ;"
"The Snowy Breasted Pearl," &c. ;

And will be supported by
MISS JESSIE SHERRARD,
The new Soprano.
MISS VIOLET ELLIOTT,
The well-known Contralto.
MISS ELLEN BOYD,
The distinguised Young Irish Violinist.
MR. ALFRED KAUFMANN,
The famous Basso.

At the Piano—Mrs. H. B. Phillips.
Prices—Reserved Seats, 5s ; Second Seats, 3s ; Admission, 1s 6d.
Tickets and Plan at Beethoven House.
Ticketholders admitted by early Door, 7.15.
Doors open 7.30.

The first of John McCormack's three concerts in Derry; the others were in 1932 and 1935. (Londonderry Sentinel, 5 October 1909.)

seaside entertainments and social functions. By 1909, Phillips was living in Belfast, which had become the centre of his concert business and the main beneficiary of his activities as an impresario. In the years before 1914, he brought the most sought-after musicians of the Edwardian era to the Ulster Hall: Fritz Kreisler, Hans Richter, Enrico Caruso, Thomas Beecham, Percy Grainger, John McCormack and Edward Sousa. And for all these concerts, Phillips organised special late trains for Derry concert-goers. Yet he brought only two of these musicians to Derry: John McCormack and Edward Sousa. The first was Irish tenor John McCormack in 1909.

McCormack appeared in Derry a few weeks before his well-publicised first tour of America. Phillips' advertisements for the concert had one of the first photographs to appear in the Derry press, with a handsome, rather portly McCormack pictured looking solemn above details of the concert. His concert programme was a combination of operatic arias by Gounod and Verdi, several of Moore's Melodies and, of course, the popular ballads for which he is often remembered. At this time McCormack was still performing in opera, which he later abandoned for a more popular repertoire. The capacity audience in St Columb's Hall was thrilled to hear the famous tenor and they demanded encore after encore, unwilling to let him go. He was accompanied on piano by H.B. Phillips' wife Nettie, sitting in for his usual accompanist, Vincent O'Brien.[63] The concert over, Derry's wealthier concert-goers could keep their memories of McCormack alive by playing records of his singing on the new gramophones; both records and gramophones being available for sale, of course, at Phillips' music shop.

Seddon's Hippodrome

By 1909, The Hippodrome had largely gone over to screening silent films, with a change of programme three times a week. Seddon was a pragmatist and could see that the new 'Living Pictures' were gaining ground with the public at large, at the expense of live drama. Derry's population had by now reached 39,000, so provided he could tempt enough of them into his theatre, even with tickets priced as low as 2*d*, he stood to make a reasonable profit.

However, The Hippodrome was not just an early cinema; it still presented plays, revues, music hall sketches, comedies and musical shows. In his first three years at the Opera House, Seddon had given music hall a respectable home in the city and he continued to do so. For his twice-nightly shows in summer 1909 – advertised simply as 'Varieties' – he brought over 'Refined Artists from the Leading Hippodromes in the United Kingdom'. These figures from the English music halls sang the popular songs of the day, danced, acted comedy sketches, told jokes and practised ventriloquism – and attracted huge, enthusiastic crowds twice a night to fill the gallery benches and better seats, with people even standing the aisles. So far, had Seddon made good his early promise to 'do my best to add to the happiness of this grey old city'.

OPERA HOUSE & HIPPODROME,
DERRY.

Monday, October 17th, 1910
And During the Week.
7 AND 9—TWICE NIGHTLY—7 AND 9
Matinee on Saturday at 2-30.

JOHN H. TOMKINSON'S
—— NO. 1 ——

ROYAL GIPSY CO.

An Amazing Federation of Amusement Novelties.

The Acme of Sensationalism, Smartness, Effectiveness and Refinement — THE

AERIALS

In a Daring Gymnastic Display

Miss OLIVE HAYDEN, Soprano Vocalist | **Miss AMY WOOD** Contralto Vocalist.

GEORGE KEITH, Baritone and Descriptive Vocalist | **Arthur Walker,** Comedian

Elsie Rubina
The Beautiful Princess of Equipoise

Miss NELLIE PORTER Flute and Piccolo Soloist | **Miss Pamela Chandler** Solo Violinist

Miss LETTY CONOLLY Cornet Soloist. | **Miss Mabel Lewis** In Up-to-Date Illustrated Songs

TOMKINSON'S QUARTETTE PARTY, Refined Vocalists. | **George Russell** Laughing Comedian

Wee Winnie
Vocalist and Dancer. Without doubt the Smartest Juvenile Artiste now before the public

☛ DIAMOND AND HART,
Britain's Best Burlesque Boys,

Sisters Lesmere Charming Duettists and Dancers. | New Series of Up-to-Date Subjects on the American **BIOSCOPE**

ERIC & NORA
In their Bright and Brisk Musical Act.

The whole up to the high standard of excellence which has made the name of "Tomkinson" a household word throughout the Empire. For Prices, etc., see other bills

WILLSONS', PRINTERS, LEICESTER.

Opera House and Hippodrome playbill from October 1910, showing the typical 'music hall' fare on offer. (Author's collection)

Alongside music hall and the new attractions of 'animated [moving] photography', Seddon still presented the occasional stage play. The September 1909 productions of *Charley's Aunt* and *The Face at the Window* drew crowds described in the press as 'the largest ever recorded' in the city, with the theatre 'packed from stalls to gallery'. The *Journal* welcomed the return of live drama to the city, contrasting it with what it called 'the [recent] light and laughable form of entertainment'. It commended the manager on his 'latest departure and enterprise'. A similar note of condescension crept into its reviewer's remarks in January 1912. The occasion was a one-week run of Irish plays by the Chalmers Mackey Drama Company, during which it staged two now forgotten plays: the comedy *Rollicking Rory* and the musical drama *The Wearing of the Green*. In the course of its favourable review, the *Journal* commented that the audience 'seemed glad, and rightly so, at having presented [to them] a play free from vulgarity... There is none of that straining after comedy and smartness which is so distasteful a feature of modern nondescript productions.' The review went on to deplore 'the existence of a decadent taste among Derry theatregoers', clearly a swipe at the popularity of 'Music Hall Varieties' which had been playing regularly to packed houses.

Seddon was not to be swayed in his programming by the carping of the press. On the contrary, he took the view that a theatre manager who ignores public taste does so at his peril. In one of his annual speeches to his audience, he quoted the advice of the great actor–manager Herbert Beerbohm Tree, 'Don't give the public what they want, give them what you want them to want, and in time they will want it.' Seddon begged to differ, 'That may be all very well for Sir Herbert, who has the population of London to draw upon ... but if [he] had the population of Derry to draw upon he would find that he would have to give his pit and gallery what they want.'

He was happy enough to think up new ways of pleasing his patrons, and in 1913 he was first to introduce the 'continuous' film show to Derry, with films running nightly at The Hippodrome from 7 p.m. until 11 p.m. He suggested in his annual manager's address that this would appeal particularly to young, time-pressed married couples, 'I know what a strain it is to a busy man to get home to his meal and to be at the theatre at a fixed time and the ladies often experience the same difficulties.' This went down well, especially when he added, 'We married men will never be punctual as long as the ladies will insist upon having their dresses made to do up all the way down the back.'

Sousa strikes up the Band

In 1911, the second of Phillips' celebrity musicians was Edward Sousa (1854-1932), the American composer and bandmaster. He was then at the height of his popularity; a household name in the United States and in Great Britain for his military-style band and his own compositions, in particular marches like 'Stars and Stripes' and 'Washington Post'. Sousa's band gave two concerts in Derry, one a matinee and one on the evening of 11 February. Tickets, at 4*s* and 2*s* 6*d*, sold out quickly. The local press declared his concerts 'the musical event of the decade', their enthusiasm reflected in the huge turnout for the evening concert, when apparently there were 'two hundred turned away at the door'. 'Spellbound' was how the *Journal* described the audience at both concerts. 'People sat still through piece after piece on the programme, while inwardly – one can be sure – they were stirred and swayed by feelings more varied than common words can express.'

Sousa played popular favourites like 'The Last Rose of Summer', 'Let Erin Remember' and 'Men of Harlech', and two longer works: Tchaikovsky's *1812 Overture* and Strauss's *Till Eulenspiegel*. The press commented on Sousa's sparing use of the 'big bass drum … so beloved by many Ulster Bands'. It barely received a dozen strokes throughout the afternoon matinee. This might, they thought, be the 'modern' approach to drum-playing, but added (with local bands in mind) that, 'ingrained customs are notoriously hard to shake off'. The audiences for Sousa's concerts probably included many members of the city's ten bands. The concern with detail in the local reviews of Sousa's concerts probably reflected the keen interest in band music in Derry at this time, albeit fiercely competitive and linked as much to the marking out of territory by the different bands as to enjoyment of the music.

Just over a month after the Sousa concerts, Phillips brought the London entertainer Miss Margaret Cooper and her 'brilliant concert party' to St Columb's Hall for a concert on 27 March. Cooper was a glamorous and elegant singer – a blend of 'salon-type' and polite music hall – who sang witty songs while accompanying herself on piano. Her performance delighted a large audience, keen to see this well-known Edwardian singer of whom it was said, 'almost every girl who could play the piano and sing (as well as quite a number who could not) wanted to be known as the Margaret Cooper of her own little town, village or suburb'.

The Guildhall reopened in 1912. Rebuilding work cost £26,000, borne jointly by insurance compensation and The Irish Society. Perhaps as a token of appreciation to the latter, the restoration incorporated a visual celebration of Derry's links with London, in the form of new stained-glass windows illustrating the different London companies which had undertaken the Plantation of north-west Ulster in 1609 and the building of Derry's walls. Henceforward, competitors at the Feis and the singers of the Philharmonic would pass in front of those elaborately decorated windows as they came up the ornate, wooden staircase to the main assembly room. At the time, symbolising those links in the new building was not controversial. It would become more so when changed political circumstances, the creation of a border between north and south, and gerrymandering within Londonderry Corporation, whose offices the Guildhall housed, would make Derry's Catholics more sensitive to its significance.

Phillips' DUBLIN, BELFAST & IRISH PROVINCIAL Concerts

FAREWELL VISIT of SOUSA AND HIS BAND

———— SIXTY PERFORMERS ————

(By arrangement with the Quinlan International Musical Agency)

IN

CORK	*February 13th, at 3 and 8 o'clock*
LIMERICK	*February 14th, at 3 and 8 o'clock*
DUBLIN	*February 15th, at 3 and 8 o'clock*
BELFAST	*February 16th, at 3 and 8 o'clock*
LONDONDERRY	*February 17th, at 3 and 8 o'clock*

Conductor: JOHN PHILIP SOUSA.

Assisted by

Miss VIRGINIA ROOT (Soprano)

Miss NICHOLINE ZEDELER (Violinist)

and

Mr. HERBERT L. CLARKE (Solo Cornet)

The Last Opportunity of hearing this famous Band

Edward Sousa's celebrated military-style band which delighted St Columb's Hall audiences in February 1911.
(Derry Journal, *13 February 1911*)

The first Feis in the restored Guildhall was in 1913, when Londonderry Corporation agreed to hire the building to the Feis Committee at half the usual charges. That year there were fifty competitions with 350 entrants, and a special Feis office was opened at Waterloo Place to deal with administration. The Feis syllabus was sold in Phillips' music shops in Belfast and Derry and posted to competitors throughout Ireland. The reputation of the Feis regularly attracted competitors from Scotland and England, and also drew large numbers of visitors to Derry. During its competitions an air of excitement permeated the city, with streets around the Guildhall thronged with young competitors, their anxious mothers and the perhaps equally nervous adjudicators. There was a constant flow of people between lower Shipquay Street (where competitors could have a last rehearsal in Phillips' practice rooms) and the two halls in the Guildhall used for singing and instrumental classes.

Alex Stewart continued to use her Dublin contacts to enhance the Feis. In 1913 she arranged for the introduction of the Denis O'Sullivan Memorial Medal for solo Irish singing, its first award outside Dublin. It soon became the most hotly contested competition of the Derry Feis. The local press reported verbatim the remarks, favourable and critical, of the adjudicators, giving columns of space to detailed descriptions of the competitions. When one adjudicator, Mr Booth (of the Hallé Orchestra), urged Miss Boyd, the leader of the Philharmonic Orchestra, to 'take the others in hand now and again' to improve their ensemble playing, it raised 'laughter and applause' among the audience, who perhaps had their own ideas about what 'taking in hand' might mean.

In 1914, a new organ was installed in the Guildhall to replace that destroyed in the fire. Again, it was a magnificent instrument: a three-manual organ with thirty-nine speaking stops designed by William Hill & Son of London. It occupied the entire width of the upstairs hall and was housed inside an ornate, carved oak case designed and built locally.

Cinema Days

In his annual manager's speech in March 1913, Seddon claimed to have turned The Hippodrome into a paying proposition again, as in J.F. Warden's time. He described how his predecessor (H.B. Phillips), 'after several years' struggle, threw up the sponge', leaving the theatre 'on the rocks'. Seddon, however, had brought a different style of management and programming, and reversed the theatre's decline. He now interspersed his films, stage plays and revues with novelties of various kinds. An 'evening at the cinema' still included musical interludes, short sketches and songs between the films. In April 1914, he presented Derry's first beauty competition, in which the audience voted for 'the prettiest child in Derry'. Then, for Good Friday, the following week, he screened 'Splendid Religious Pictures', a

Photograph of the interior of the Opera House/Hippodrome/Empire, showing the huge gallery and upper circle. (Author's collection)

series of films on biblical themes. The theatre was clearly making money, as the year before Seddon had turned enough of a profit to buy his second business in Derry, the Picture Palace in Shipquay Street.[64]

Nevertheless, Seddon told his audience, 'The Drama was my first love', and, like Warden before him, he kept up his links with the wider world of play-acting. He was well respected in local drama circles, being chosen as drama adjudicator at the Feis in March 1914. He still had his own touring theatre company, the Hippodrome Players, which came to Derry that same month to present 'the beautiful, romantic Costume Dramatic Sketch in 5 Scenes, *A Fight for a Kingdom*'. However, as an indication of the compromises he was prepared to make, the play was staged alongside 'The Usual All-Star Programme of Pictures'. By then, admission prices had dropped to just 1*s*, 9*d*, 6*d*, 4*d* and 2*d*.

In March 1913, St Columb's Hall was leased to the London Motion Picture Company, which started showing 'Moving Pictures' twice per night, four nights a week, plus a Saturday matinee. Within days, the *Journal* recorded 'one of the largest audiences of juveniles ever seen in that spacious building' – a portent of the future, when cinema-going would eclipse theatre and concert attendance. That same week, Seddon's Picture Palace was showing 'a drama of intense interest, entitled *On the Steps of the Throne*'. In spring 1914, Seddon's press advertisements again referred to the theatre as the 'Opera House', but with large, bold print under-

LONDONDERRY FEIS.

(FIFTEENTH SEASON).

Morning and Afternoon Sessions—GUILDHALL. Admission, 1/

Evening Sessions — ST. COLUMB'S HALL. Admission, 1/- and 6d.

TO-MORROW,
TUESDAY, 3RD MARCH.

GUILDHALL : —
Morning and Afternoon — Soprano and Contralto Solos, Senior Violin, Instrumental Trio, and Intermediate Piano.

ST. COLUMB'S HALL :—
7.30 p.m.—Grand Orchestral Concert (Third of Series of Subscription Concerts).

SPECIAL ENGAGEMENT by Mr. H. B. Phillips of the

Celebrated Hallé Band

(AND)

HERR MICHAEL BALLING.

VOCALIST (who has kindly consented to sing)—
Mrs. ABRAHAM STEWART.

N.B.—Feis Season Tickets do not admit to this Concert.

Cheap Tickets to Derry by all Railways.

Special LATE TRAINS to Limavady and Buncrana and Intermediate Stations.   O

Advertisement for the 'Hallé Band' (orchestra) concert in March 1914. (Derry Journal, 2 March 1914)

neath stating that it was 'The Home of Exclusive Pictures', an acknowledgment that the future lay with silent films. Concerts, by contrast, were invariably held in either the Guildhall or St Columb's Hall.

The Hallé Orchestra

Phillips' last major concert in Derry took place in St Columb's Hall on 3 March 1914, and probably owed as much to Alex Stewart as to Phillips himself. The Hallé Orchestra from Manchester was appearing at one of Phillips' Belfast subscription concerts and by 'special arrangement' – probably through pressure from Alex Stewart, who saw how great a coup this would be for her beloved Feis – their tour was expanded to include Derry. The concert was widely advertised in advance, with 'Special Late Trains' laid on to Limavady and Buncrana. On the night, the Hall was filled to capacity and the press reported that the Hallé Orchestra 'stirred the audience to such a pitch of enthusiasm as is rarely witnessed at orchestral recitals'. But it was the local favourite who received the loudest applause, when Alex Stewart, accompanied by the full orchestra, sang a Saint-Saëns aria. The *Journal* reported that she sang 'with that admirable enunciation, technical accuracy and soulful interpretation which have placed her in the front rank of Irish vocalists'. Then, amid 'repeated rounds of applause', she was presented with two bouquets, one by H.B. Phillips, the other by Captain Herdman on behalf of the Feis Committee. It was the greatest triumph of her career, her swan song, and the highpoint of the Feis in the pre-war years.

Since 1911, H.B. Phillips had been living in London and working in opera management with Thomas Beecham's Opera Company. Although he continued to mount celebrated concerts in Belfast, including one by virtuoso pianist Ferruccio Busoni in 1913, there was – with the exception of the Hallé Orchestra concert in St Columb's Hall – a distinct falling away in the quality of his concerts in Derry.

With the advent of the First World War, Phillips' concerts in Derry stopped altogether. His Derry music shop remained open, run by his younger brother, but the Belfast Beethoven House shop had closed for good. The era of the prestigious Phillips' concerts had ended in Derry and the troubled years after 1914 would bring irrevocable change to the city whose musical life he had done so much to enrich.

Six

WARS AND DIVISIONS, 1914-1945

In autumn 1914, at the outbreak of the First World War, Derry's Hamilton Flute Band, it is said, joined the 10th Inniskilling Fusiliers 'to a man' and became its regimental band. Such group volunteering was common in English towns and villages, but less so in Ulster. It says a lot about the Derry bandsmen's view of themselves as loyal subjects of the Crown, responding to its call in an hour of need. Although by 1914 the city's role as a garrison town had diminished, the tradition of military service was still strong. A similar patriotic response was reflected in the many concerts and entertainments organised in aid of the war effort, beginning that autumn with weekly wartime concerts in the Guildhall.

In Ireland in particular, the First World War marked the end of one era and the beginning of another. The Third Home Rule Bill had received Royal Assent in September 1914, although it was suspended for the duration of the war and with the future political status of Ulster still to be determined. Eight years later, after a bitter civil war, Ireland was partitioned between an Irish Free State in the south and Northern Ireland, incorporating six counties of Ulster, including Derry. The city was thus dealt a double blow, caught up in political turmoil and in economic decline as its once thriving industries contracted after the war. As its prosperity waned amid increasing political and religious acrimony, Derry's cultural life, too, became increasingly divided along political and religious lines. No longer did the city's musicians and actors share concerts, stages and facilities irrespective of religion and political allegiance. Instead, Nationalists and Unionists drew apart, developing different and separate cultural lives and identities, with one group looking to the Irish Free State to define itself and the other looking to Great Britain.

Another important social change was that cinema took over from live drama and music as the main source of entertainment in Derry. Both the Opera House and St Columb's Hall bowed to the inevitable and showed silent films, followed in the early 1930s by the 'talkies'. The Guildhall remained a concert venue, although it was increasingly used for public dances. It was the venue for the first Feis Dhoire in 1922, a festival of Irish song and dance, but a challenge also to the existing Feis, seen by many as 'the festival of the garrison'. The older institutions, the Feis and Philharmonic, struggled to maintain support. The Philharmonic had its counterpart in O'Brien's Choir and Amateur Operatic Society, but there was not the mixing between members of the different groups that there had been in previous decades. Overall, the years between the wars, while showing some notable musical and dramatic highs, lacked the vitality and buzz of the previous era.

Wartime Entertainments

Concerts in support of the war effort were held in the Guildhall throughout the war by amateur singers, musicians and actors from the city's middle classes. Members of the Gilliland, Colquhoun and Darcus families were joined onstage by locally based military personnel in 'concert parties', individual 'acts' and military bands. Distinctions of military rank were set aside, with officers, sergeants, bombardiers and privates singing, acting and reciting together in a spirit of camaraderie. There were musical items, songs, recitations and comic acts, and even organ recitals by members of the military. Soldiers and sailors were admitted free of charge, while civilians paid 3*d*, 6*d* or 1*s*, with all profits going to wartime charities. Special transport was laid on at the close of the concerts, with a 'late ferry' from the Guildhall to the Waterside for servicemen returning to the barracks.

Derry's two long-standing musical institutions, the Feis and the Philharmonic, continued throughout the war, but, as the local press was at pains to stress, with their profits donated to 'War Relief Funds'.[65] The number of Feis entries fell slightly, but choirs like the 'Little Whales' still travelled from Belfast for Children's Day, undeterred by wartime stringencies. The winning choir in the Action Song competition in March 1917 caught the popular mood with their rendering of Stanley Kirby's 'Somewhere in France, Dear Mother', its combination of jaunty rhythms, cheerful jingoism and sentimentality going down well with the Guildhall audience. Any bruised feelings in other contestants were soothed when Mrs Whale announced to the hall that she was providing prizes for all of them in recognition of the huge efforts involved in preparation, travelling and performance.

The Philharmonic continued to hold twice-yearly concerts. Handel's *Messiah* was performed at three of their Christmas wartime concerts, probably because, at a time of paper shortage, the singers already had scores and knew the work. But the Philharmonic's springtime concerts broke new ground, while appealing to people's sense of patriotism, by featuring shorter choral works by Elgar such as 'England Expects' and 'Banner of St George' (1916), and 'For the Fallen' (1917); the last

SOMEWHERE IN FRANCE, DEAR MOTHER (2).

Somewhere in France, dear mother, somewhere—but I can't tell,
In the midst of the fray, I'm writing to say that I'm still alive and well;
There's some fine big boys from Tipperary, somewhere in France with me,
So cheer up, dear, the next time you hear, I'll be somewhere in Germany.

The winning song in the Action Song competition at the 1917 Feis, 'Somewhere in France, Dear Mother'. (Author's collection)

The Londonderry Philharmonic Society concert in February 1917, which appropriately – in view of the Ulster Division's losses at the Battle of the Somme – featured Elgar's oratorio For the Fallen. *(Author's collection)*

Londonderry Philharmonic Society.
(Eighteenth Season.)

PRESIDENT:
HER GRACE THE DUCHESS OF ABERCORN.

SECOND GRAND

Subscription Concert,

"For the Fallen," *Elgar.*
A Choral Fantasia on "Mignon," *Thomas.*
AND
MISCELLANEOUS,
Guildhall, Derry,

Thursday, 22nd February, 1917,
At 8 p.m.

Artistes:
Miss PERCEVAL ALLEN ... ... (Soprano).
Mr. SPENCER THOMAS ... ... (Tenor).
(Invalided out of the Army after fourteen months' service abroad.)
Mr. LAWRENCE M^cCANN, B.E. ... (Violinist)
and Leader of Orchestra.
Mr. H. COLEMAN, F.R.C.O. ... ... (Organist).
Miss TAAFFE, A.R.C.M. ... ... (Pianist).

Conductor:
Mr. A. J. CUNNINGHAM.

(*Net Proceeds in aid of Local War Hospital Supply Depôt and Sphagnum Moss Department*).

was repeated in 1918 with 'The Fourth of August' and 'To Women'. Alexandrina Stewart, as always, sang the contralto solos in these concerts. The 1919 spring concert featured another Elgar piece, *King Olaf*. But in the post-war years, Elgar's music had fallen out of favour with audiences, or perhaps the Philharmonic chorus had had their fill of him, and he was dropped from their repertoire in favour of works by Mendelssohn, Handel, Gounod and Coleridge Taylor. The Philharmonic chorus and orchestra were still under the baton of Albert Cunningham, one of Derry's most active musicians in the inter-war years, as choirmaster and bandleader.

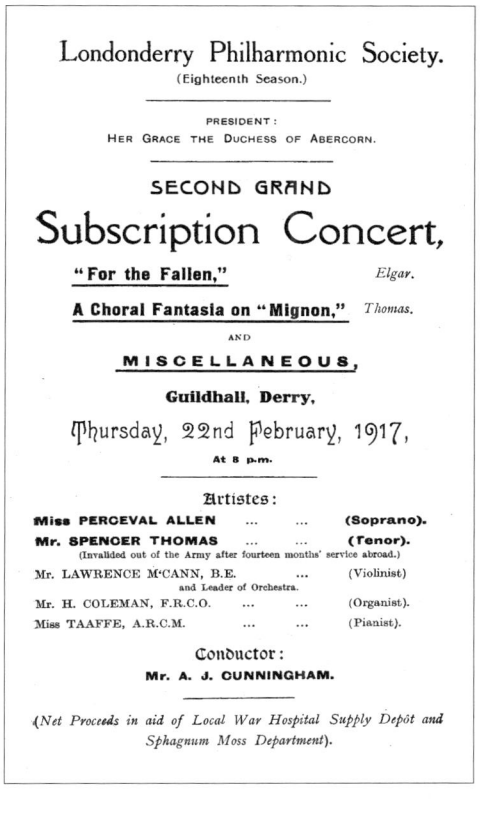

At the beginning of the war, Seddon was quick to respond to the popular mood in the city by lending the Opera House to local groups raising war funds. In October 1914, Raymond Brown-Lecky's 'Amateurs' took over the theatre for a matinee performance of Palgrave Simpson's *Time and the Hour*. Its being a charity performance probably reconciled audiences to paying the higher prices for admission. But all prices at the Opera House were soon increased by the new entertainment tax levied in the war years, with the gallery rising to 4*d* and the pit to 7*d*. Initially, perhaps, this was not felt to be onerous, as Derry's wartime economy was booming, with almost full employment. The city's shirt factories and shipyards were drawn into the war effort, with full order books for army uniforms, munitions and ships. (Derry then had forty shirt factories, employing 18,000 factory hands and 80,000 outworkers.) As a result, Seddon's pantomimes, Irish plays and variety shows drew large audiences, as did his screenings of silent films. For those who were not able to go on holiday, Seddon opened his August 1916 season with a Pierrot show, normally a seaside entertainment. That same season, an older tradition was honoured in Derry for the last time, when a 'Grand Complimentary Benefit' was held for theatre manager Gerald James in February 1917.

The Philharmonic Orchestra pictured in the 1930s. Their long-term conductor Albert J. Cunningham is middle of back row. (The Bigger McDonald Collection: by kind permission of Derry Central Library)

When films were shown in theatres and cinemas, it was usually alongside live acts, managers apparently feeling that films on their own weren't enough. In the Opera House, for example, a showing of two films, *Eve's Daughter* and *Roped with Scandal*, was coupled with Pat White ('Irish Comedian, Singer and Dancer'), 'Gotto' (the Japanese Juggler) and the 'De Vere Performing Dogs'.

One side-effect of the new silent films was that musicians were in demand to accompany the action on screen and to provide musical interludes during the evening. This was particularly important when the reels were being changed, as gallery and pit audiences could become restive and start to quarrel among themselves. In larger English cities, the cinema organ filled this role, forerunner of the 'Mighty Wurlitzer' of the 1930s. But neither the Opera House nor any Derry cinema had an organ console. Instead, Derry's church organists filled in on piano, their secular improvisations on weekdays a welcome contrast, perhaps, to their standard Sunday repertoire.

Yorkshireman Richard Tolson was the first Opera House pianist. He arrived in Derry in 1914 as organist of First Derry, and combined his church duties with accompanying silent films in the evenings. The elders of the church did not take kindly to their organist's extra-mural activities, and after many bitter arguments they parted company. He then moved to the Methodist church on Carlisle Road, which (by chance?) was next door to the Opera House. The Catholic Church was more easy-going: Joseph O'Brien, organist at St Eugene's Cathedral, was pianist in the Palace Cinema at the foot of Shipquay Place until he formed his own orchestra to accompany 'the silents' in St Columb's Hall.

Joseph O'Brien

O'Brien came from a family of organists, and when he arrived in Derry in 1912 he was already an experienced musician. His musical activities in Derry were all-embracing: he taught piano and singing in the studios in Beethoven House – conveniently close to the Palace Cinema – and in 'the College', as St Columb's was known locally. Shortly after he arrived he started his own choir, drawn mainly from his Cathedral singers, and for the next seventeen years they presented annual operas and oratorios, in effect continuing the work started by Patrick Mulholland in giving a musical 'voice' to Derry's Catholics. Within a few years, the O'Brien Choir's cantatas and oratorios rivalled those of the Philharmonic. In November 1915, they sang Arthur Sullivan's *The Prodigal Son* in the Guildhall, accompanied by full orchestra.

The following year, O'Brien's Amateur Operatic Society booked the Opera House for a week for Wallace's *Maritana* and Balfe's *The Lady of Killarney*. This, the first operatic society in Derry, had the same personnel as the O'Brien Choir, but greater ambitions. O'Brien promised 'Professional Principals, Chorus of 60 and Full Orchestra' for these 1916 productions, guaranteed to rival those of professional companies. His amateur chorus was joined by four professional Dublin soloists, including the well-known baritone Walter McNally. After packed houses every night – 'with standing room at a premium' – the *Journal* declared it 'a week of great triumph' during which the company 'piled success on top of success'. It added, 'Too much praise could scarcely be bestowed upon the conductor.' The chorus, which sang with 'great precision and spirit', contained many names that would later figure prominently in Derry's musical life: MacCafferty, Gallagher, Durnin, Carlin, O'Doherty and McCloskey.[66]

In 1915, O'Brien's society was joined by the Londonderry Amateur Operatic Society, founded by English-born Henry Coleman, organist at St Columb's Cathedral.[67] This new society also used the Opera House for its annual operas, invariably to great (and perhaps undiscriminating) acclaim by local audiences and the press.

It is noticeable that around this time, local music reviews in the *Sentinel* lose the critical edge they once had and all amateur performances are hailed in uniformly glowing terms. The review of Gilbert and Sullivan's *The Yeoman of the Guard* in March 1917 was no exception. At the end of the last performance, 'an epidemic of bouquets and chocolate' arrived on stage, such that 'some of the chorus went off fully laden', the 'toothsome offerings' in particular being prized amid the deprivations of wartime.

Alongside the operetta, a short newsreel film was shown entitled, *The Battle of the Ancre*, which depicted the 'Advance of the Tanks and the Irish Brigade in Action' – scenes from the Battle of the Somme, the previous November. As all profits from the operetta were donated to the Wounded Soldiers' and Sailors' Fund, the film no doubt served to encourage members of the audience to give generously.

There were other fundraising events, such as 'War teas' (a blend of musical entertainments and tea-drinking), 'Bridge and Music' in Thornhill ('In Aid of Our Boys in Mesopotamia'), and Boys' Brigade Concerts in the YMCA Hall. Brooke Park hosted summer concerts by military bands playing patriotic songs and marches, assisted by 'military singers, clowns and dancers', to which soldiers and sailors in uniform were admitted half price.

The end of the war in 1918 was a time of significant change. Seddon sold the Opera House to Barney Armstrong for £5,500, so as to concentrate on his growing empire of theatres, cinemas and music halls in England.[68] He had already been living in London for six years, in order, as he explained to his Derry audience, to be 'pulling the strings at the other end in the centre of theatre and kinematograph land'. Yet he continued to express great affection for Derry, where, he said, he had 'spent some of the happiest years of his life' and had 'invested all [his] savings' to buy his first theatre and cinema. The owners and managers who followed Seddon had a hard act to follow. First to try his hand was Armstrong, a veteran actor, and owner of Dublin and Belfast's Empire Theatres.[69]

Struggling To Survive: Barney Armstrong

Although the signing of the Armistice was followed in Ireland by political unrest that culminated in civil war, Armstrong's early publicity for the Opera House suggested that audiences were booming. He claimed that 2,500 people attended films at the theatre on Saturday 5 April 1919, and 'as many people more were turned away unable to obtain admission'. One wonders how credible these figures were; they would have represented a significant percentage of the city's 42,000 population and came within a month of a resurgence of Spanish 'Flu that had led to troops being prohibited from entering local places of amusement.

Like all new owners, Armstrong made changes. In September 1919, the theatre was renamed The Empire, in line with his other theatres, and two new staff were added: Vincent Potter as general manager and Jack Mathers as resident manager. There was even a rechristening of the seating; the darkly evocative term 'pit' being replaced by the anodyne 'front stalls'. Armstrong kept the two staples, music hall and silent films, during the winter months, with twice-nightly performances. Admission was 4*d* for the gods and 5*d* for the stalls, with the (now unpopular) wartime entertainment tax incorporated in the price.

Music hall continued to have its devotees among Derry's lower orders. But it was not the vulgarities of music hall that in December 1919 brought public opprobrium on the Opera House, but its hitherto blameless Christmas pantomime. All three Derry newspapers expressed outrage at 'smut' and 'alleged jokes' in the script that were offensive to women, with the *Journal* leading the charge in its 'agitation for a clean stage'. The Opera House management promptly cut the offending material from the pantomime, but, in the newspaper's view, showed their true colours by petulantly cancelling their advertising with the *Journal*. The affair blew over but left a residue of ill-feeling.

There were deeper political problems in the city itself that tended to reduce theatre audiences. Derry, with its overwhelmingly Catholic and Nationalist population, had expected to be part of the new Irish Free State. Anger and disappointment at its inclusion in Northern Ireland exploded in the early 1920s, resulting in widespread sectarian rioting, violence and killings. Running battles became commonplace on Derry's streets, reaching a peak in June 1920, when shops and businesses were forced to close for several days and a curfew was imposed. Attendances at the Opera House fell away sharply, and the theatre faced the double challenge of attracting audiences from a divided and now financially strapped city. Armstrong's Dublin and Belfast theatres had already closed because of the unrest. His Derry theatre alone remained open but incurred a loss of over £250 between April and September 1921. To make matters worse, English and Scottish actors and singers – hitherto main attractions on the Opera House stage – refused to come to Ireland because of the political trouble.

Armstrong's sudden death towards the end of 1921 brought to light debts of over £10,000 and consequently the deeds of the Derry Empire were lodged as surety for his loans with the Munster and Leinster Bank. Lengthy court proceedings followed, during which the bank administered the theatre through a succession of managers. Nonetheless, the theatre – or the Opera House, as it was once again renamed on 23 October 1922 – struggled on with few outward signs of change. Music hall revues, variety acts and silent films were its staple fare, as in Seddon's later years.

St Columb's Hall remained the Opera House's main competitor, with its 'continuous' films, Irish plays, dances and concerts at roughly comparable prices. In October 1921 it announced 'The Biggest Attraction ever put before a Derry audience' in 'The Famous American Southern Syncopated Orchestra', a ragtime and jazz band. This was Derry audiences' first opportunity to experience this latest fashion in music. Other events in St Columb's Hall were the locally organised Boxing Day and St Patrick's Day concerts, and the annual Aonach concerts, which started in October 1921.

St Columb's Hall had its own amateur drama company, the St Columb's Guild's Dramatic Company, started in the early 1920s. As far as we know, it was the only amateur society in Derry to have its own 'Spiritual Director'. As with previous Catholic drama groups, it staged mainly Irish plays like *Arrah-na-Pogue* and J. Hartley

Manners' play *Peg O' My Heart*. It was this identification of Derry's Catholics with all things Gaelic and Irish that led to the foundation of the Feis Dhoire Colmcille in 1922.

Feis Dhoire Colmcille

For some time, it had been felt by many in the city that the Londonderry Feis, as it had become known, had lost touch with its roots in native Irish culture. It seemed to have more affinity with music festivals in Great Britain than with Dublin – a tendency that partition seemed destined to reinforce. The Feis Dhoire, by contrast, organised by a large, forty-three-strong committee and first held between Tuesday 27 and Friday 30 June 1922, was a self-conscious turning back to the original idea of a festival of Irish culture. Around 600 entrants competed in music, dancing and Irish, with five adjudicators: three in music, and one each in dancing and Irish. The city's Catholic choirs, singers and dancers came out in force, so much so that after four days' intensive competition the Feis Dhoire was declared a 'success far beyond the dreams of the promoters'.

Local composition was highlighted, with 'The Antrim Hills' from Conaghan's '98 *Cantata* as the test piece for the contralto solo. One of the music adjudicators, Dr Annie Patterson from Dublin, praised the song highly and claimed to be 'much charmed with it'. For this, and for saying that 'Derry possessed musical talent and ability second to no other city in Ireland', she was warmly applauded. Conaghan himself was not present. He had been ill for some time and died in December 1922, survived by his wife and seven children. The eldest child, his son William, succeeded him as organist of the Long Tower church.

By the early 1920s, the Guildhall was Derry's main concert venue, used for the two Feiseanna and the Philharmonic concerts, but, unlike the palmy days of H.B. Phillips, there were few concerts by distinguished visiting musicians. An exception was the Herman Van Dyk couple, 'Specialists as Piano Duettists', who in November 1922 performed concertos by Beethoven, Schumann and Grieg on a '200 Guinea grand piano'. The turnout, however, was disappointing. Later that month, the O'Brien Choir performed Haydn's *Creation* to a packed Guildhall audience, indicating that local performers could clearly count on personal support from family and friends. Yet this seems not to have translated into support for classical concerts in general.

The Musicians' Strike

Ownership of the Opera House was finally settled when the Dublin partnership of Izidore Bradlaw, his wife Juliet, and Robert Morrison bought the theatre in 1924. Bradlaw (1866-1933) had an unusual background: a Jew born in what is now Lithuania, his parents moved to Dublin when he was a boy. A dentist by profession, his main interests seem to have been in the theatre and horse racing, and by the early 1920s he and the Scots Presbyterian Morrison jointly owned Dublin's Olympia Theatre.[70] They appointed Percy Whittle as manager of their Derry theatre and broadened the programming to include circus acts and boxing tournaments, plays and opera festivals. They began the tradition of the Opera House Ball, the first being held in the Guildhall in October 1924. Since the city remained unsettled, patrons were promised 'curfew permits' to allow them to attend. However, a few weeks later the theatre gained unwelcome notoriety from a labour dispute that closed the theatre for three weeks and was covered extensively by the press.

The immediate cause of the dispute was the employment by Whittle of a new musician who was not a union member. The other musicians – all members of the 'Amusement Section' of the Transport and General Workers' Union – refused to work alongside him.[71] The management was accused of 'blacklegging' and being 'anti-union'. Within days, the entire Opera House staff (the manager excepted) had 'walked out', or, as some staff were to claim, were 'locked out'. This was only one of a series of charges and counter-charges levelled by each side at the other, and the arguments spilled over into the columns of the press. The situation was not helped by members of two separate unions, Bob Gray and another Opera House employee with the *nom de plume* of 'Striker', using the letters' columns of the *Journal* to trade insults, and to question each other's motives and good faith.

Whittle apologised to the public for the strike and reopened the theatre, replacing the scheduled live performances with films. But because of the bitter feelings aroused, he was only able to reopen with policemen on duty inside and outside the theatre. Whittle claimed that the strike was not of the Opera House's making, but was a dispute between two unions with the theatre caught in the middle. In a letter to the City Corporation, he cited threats made that the Opera House's electricity supply would be cut off by Corporation workers at the electricity supply station if the strike was not settled. The councillors, in turn, were alarmed that the city's electricity supply might be cut off if the Corporation failed to prevent the strike spreading to its own workforce. Whatever the rights and wrongs of the affair – and despite the extensive newspaper coverage, it is difficult to determine – the strike ended in late November 1924 with the (still unnamed) employee at the centre of the original dispute being reinstated.

Cinema Orchestras

By the early 1920s, the age of the lone cinema pianist had passed; small ensembles had taken over, and for the next decade in Derry the 'cinema orchestra' reigned supreme. Each theatre and cinema had its own group, usually named after the venue, made up of organists and music teachers glad of an extra source of income. Seddon's Picture

Palace was first, in 1914, with its exotically named Verni Continental Orchestra playing daily at the 'continuous' showings of films and weekly serials from 3 p.m. until 11 p.m. In 1918, Albert Cunningham led the first band at the new Rialto cinema, a small building in Market Street hastily constructed on ground formerly occupied by open-air stalls in Sir Edward Reid's market. It was run by the London Motion Picture Company and advertised (with an attempt at sophistication) 'Balcony, Parterre and Front' seats.

Willie Conaghan's Empire Orchestra provided the music at the (renamed) Opera House. His was the most varied ensemble, being eleven-strong with two violins, one cello, one double bass, two brass, three woodwind, a set of drums, and Conaghan himself on piano. The Empire was then showing silent movies several nights per week, guaranteeing his orchestra regular employment. Many other smaller groups emerged, such as the Rialto Trio and the Bohemian Bijou Band in 1924. The advent of silent films was as much a boon to amateur musical activity as the two Feiseanna – with payment into the bargain. Press advertisements and reviews raised the bands' status by listing the music played. Cunningham's Rialto Orchestra, for example, had a wide operatic repertoire, including Rossini's *William Tell Overture* and selections from Wagner's *The Flying Dutchman*, Gilbert and Sullivan's *Mikado* and Thomas's *Mignon*. In October 1922, these accompanied the films *Deep Waters* and *The Princess of New York*, representing a fairly typical evening's fare. Derry's cinema-goers were certainly not short-changed in the music provided, with selections from the classics, favourite Irish melodies and stirring marches carefully chosen to match and enhance the action on screen.

During the 1920s, there were many small 'orchestras' in Derry, although the great majority could more properly be described as dance bands. There was the Rialto Symphony Band, Robert Beattie's Orpheus Band and Alberto Macari's Band, all of whom at different times played at the Guildhall. Dances had long been held there but reserved to members of particular organisations. From the mid-1920s, however, the widely advertised Philharmonic Society Ball, the Opera House Ball, the Nazareth House Ball and Kathleen Watson's 'Dances' were open to the general public.[72] Most band members were engaged in 'double-jobbing', moving freely between cinema, hall and theatre, and it was not unusual to find the same musicians – Macari, Cunningham, O'Brien, Conaghan – in different venues, with differently named bands, on successive evenings.

Willie Conaghan was a multi-talented musician, like his father, but it was probably for his dance bands that he was best known. He was bandleader at the Opera House periodically during the 1920s, and even briefly in charge of the Rialto Orchestra. But Conaghan also had his own male voice choir, male voice quartet (The Bohemians) and his Chrysanthemum Orchestra, all regular performers at Guildhall dances and concerts and the Feis Dhoire. Conaghan's two orchestras (the Opera House and Chrysanthemum) probably had the same personnel but used different names to avoid contractual problems with Opera House management.

The Opera House held its second ball in the Guildhall in October 1925, with dancing starting at 11 p.m. and supper following at midnight. The late start suggests that patrons may have attended the theatre first, before moving to the Guildhall to dance to the Opera House Band. (The band presumably had to scurry down Shipquay Street to the Guildhall, clutching their instruments.) Around this time, photographs began to appear in local newspapers and this Opera House Ball was one of the first events where press reports were accompanied by photographs of those attending, in all their finery.

The Years of Festivals

The mid-1920s were notable in Derry's for 'festivals' put on by well-regarded visiting theatre and opera companies. Charles Doran's Theatre Company brought a week-long 'Shakespearean Festival' to the Opera House in January 1924, followed two months later by Joseph O'Mara's Dublin Opera Company. Doran's company returned for another festival of Shakespeare plays in spring 1926, followed some months later by the Royal Carl Rosa Opera Company. Like other Irish Shakespearean actors, Cork-born Doran had made his acting debut with Frank Benson's Company (in Belfast's Theatre Royal in 1899) and he had gathered many years' experience in theatres throughout Ireland before setting up his own company in 1920.[73]

In April 1926, Doran's festival programme was full to bursting. He presented nine different Shakespeare plays in six evening performances and three matinees, with Doran himself taking the lead roles in most of the plays. The plays were supplemented by what we would nowadays call 'educational outreach': Doran's lecture for teachers entitled 'Shakespeare in the Schools' in the Minor Hall of the Guildhall. The 'fairies' in *A Midsummer Night's Dream* were local children from Kathleen Watson's School of Dancing and were no doubt watched over with pride and trepidation by their parents. An anonymous critic observed – no doting parent, he – that 'not all of them [were] true to the shape and size demanded by the text'.

Charles Doran's Shakespearean Festival in the Opera House in January 1924. A feast for drama lovers – eight different plays in just six days. (Derry Journal, 25 January 1924)

OPERA HOUSE, DERRY
Resident Manager, L. M. Ewing.
THIS WEEK.
Once Nightly, at 7.30
SHAKESPEAREAN FESTIVAL.
VISIT OF
MR. CHARLES DORAN
And his Shakespearean Company in the following Repertoire :—
Mon.—**The Merchant of Venice.**
Tues.—**MacBeth.**
Wed.—**The Taming of the Shrew.**
Thurs.—**Othello.**
Fri.—**The Merry Wives of Windsor**
Sat.—**Hamlet.**
MATINEES :
Thursday, January 31st, at 2.30—
Julius Caesar.
Saturday. February 2nd, at 2.30—
A Midsummer Night's Dream.
Prices of Admission (including Tax)—No Extra Charge for Booking—Box Seats, 5/- ; Dress Circle, 5/- ; Upper Circle, 3/- ; Front Stalls, 3/- ; Back Stalls, 1/10 ; Gallery, 9d.
Tickets only available on Date of Issue.
Seats Booked at Theatre only 10 to 2. 'Phone 244

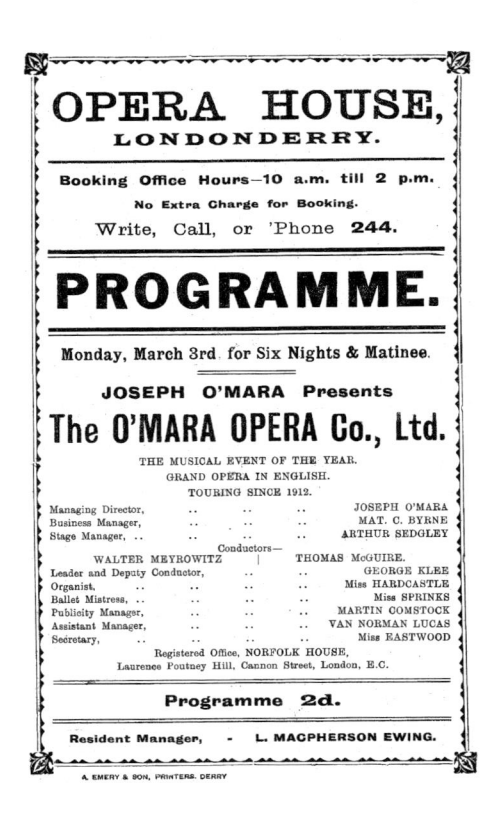

The programme cover for Joseph O'Mara's Dublin Opera Company's visit to the Opera House in March 1924. They presented seven different operas in just six days. (Author's collection)

Doran's broad repertoire was matched by that of the Royal Carl Rosa Opera Company, which staged eight different operas in just six days. Carl Rosa had visited Derry four years earlier, but the company's return in November 1926 was notable for the appearance of 'local' girl Ailne Phillips as principal ballerina with the company.[74] Advertisements promised 'Full Chorus, Orchestra and Ballet' and Derry's theatre-goers turned out in force for the entire week. 'By numerous demands' an extra matinee performance of ballet excerpts – in which Miss Phillips starred – was given on Saturday and it too packed the theatre. The newspapers provided comprehensive and glowing reviews of every performance, complimenting H.B. Phillips on his largesse in bringing so sizeable a company (over sixty performers) back to the city of his boyhood.

A sour note was introduced by a letter in the press, under the pen name of 'Granuaile', protesting about the reintroduction of the national anthem at the Opera House after 'a long and welcome absence'. The writer claimed to speak for the majority of Derry theatre-goers in requesting its discontinuance forthwith of this 'purely political anthem'.[75] The theatre ignored the request but the letter reflected a discontent about the anthem that would rumble on for another forty years.

By 1926, the Feis Dhoire was well established among Catholics as the musical – even cultural – highlight of the year. Like the Londonderry Feis with Alexandrina Stewart, the Feis Dhoire had its own tireless administrator in Rose O'Doherty, or 'Mrs Edward Henry' as she was known, a formidable music teacher and concert organizer. Her Feis Dhoire had four days of competition in which 14 cups, 123 medals and 45 junior medals were awarded, out of 700 entrants. Entrance fees formed the core of running costs, supplemented by a flag day later in the year, so the Feis Dhoire made a healthy profit, quite apart from its cultural benefits. The following year, for

OPERA HOUSE, LONDONDERRY.
FOR ONE WEEK,
Commencing Monday, 22nd November,

THE ROYAL
CARL ROSA OPERA COMPANY

Ethel Austen, Pauline Bindley, Olive Gilbert, Anna Catriona, Rosa Pinkerton, Helen Ogilvie, Doris Woodall, William Boland, Hubert Dunkerley, Leslie Jones, John Kelly, Kingsley Lark, Flintoff Moore, John Perry, Len Williams.

Monday—TANNHAUSER.
Tuesday—FAUST (with Ballet).
Wednesday—THE BARBER of SERVILLE.
Thursday (Matinee)—CARMEN.
Thursday Evening—CAVALLERIA RUSTICANA and I PAGLIACCI.
Friday—DON PASQUALE.
Saturday—IL TROVATORE.

Conductors—
CUTHBERT HAWLEY, THOMAS M'GUIRE.
Principal Dancer—AILNE PHILLIPS.

Full Chorus, Orchestra, and Ballet.

Reserved Seats — Dress Circle and Front Stalls, 5/9 (including Tax). Now Booking at Opera House. 'Phone No. 244.

Pirces (including Tax)—Upper Circle and Pit Stalls, 3/6 (Unreserved); Gallery, 1/6 (Early Door, 2/4).

Press advertisement for the 1926 visit of H.B. Phillips' Royal Carl Rosa Opera Company. (Derry Journal, 5 November 1926)

Derry-born Ailne Phillips, daughter of H.B. Phillips, a noted ballerina and dance teacher. She was Principal of Sadler's Wells Ballet School between 1946 and 1953, when her protégées included Margot Fonteyn and Moira Shearer.

the first time, a ninety-minute section of the prize-winners' concert was broadcast live on the BBC Northern Ireland Radio Service. (The whole concert lasted a marathon four hours.) The broadcast began with excerpts from Tchaikovsky's *Romeo and Juliet* on the Guildhall organ by O'Brien, followed by the prize-winning choirs, ensembles and soloists, well able, one would think, to take a radio microphone in their stride after the ordeal of the competitions.

While the Feis Dhoire was flourishing, the original Londonderry Feis, once an expression of the city's shared heritage, was beginning to struggle. The number of entrants had fallen away, largely because of pressure from within the Catholic community for their choirs and bands not to take part. Only two musicians, from different sides of the religious divide, Albert Cunningham and Orlando Cafolla, entered competitors at both Feiseanna. Cunningham's thirty-strong Bohemian Male Voice Choir was the most successful Derry choir of the inter-war years, winning the coveted Dublin An Tailteann award in 1924.

Orlando Cafolla: The Last of the Émigrés

Cafolla, known familiarly as 'OPF', was a gifted violinist and versatile music teacher, the latest in the long line of 'outsiders' – foreign musicians or those with foreign roots – to whom Derry's musical life owed so much. He was born of Italian parents in Ayr, Scotland, and first came to Derry around 1914, where his father, a linguist, was helping Italian immigrants settle in the city. As a young man, Cafolla cut a striking figure: he was tall, with well-defined features and a long mane of dark hair. Cafolla

Orlando Cafolla (1905-1997) pictured with one of his four orchestras, his 'Baby Orchestra' in the later 1950s. (By kind permission of Roma Cafolla)

later returned to the city, where he married his Derry-born wife, Sara O'Doherty, also a music teacher. Then, he taught all four traditional stringed instruments, plus piano, mandolin and guitar, music theory and harmony. From studios in Duke Street, and later in Strand Road, the couple set up four orchestras, three of them drawn entirely from their own pupils.

Up to this time, there had been only limited opportunities for learning classical string playing in Derry, but the Cafollas' tuition opened new horizons for Derry's youngest musicians. The most striking manifestation of this was his orchestra of 'baby' string players (all aged under five), wielding their quarter-size instruments, who became 'radio stars' on the BBC Northern Ireland Radio Service.

The Feiseanna and the Philharmonic

In 1927, the Londonderry Feis lost one of its main pillars when, following the death of her husband, Alexandrina Stewart moved back to Dublin. In recognition of her work for the Feis, the committee awarded her the honorary title of administrator and offered to pay her return journey to the annual Feis for as long as she was able to travel.[76]

Derry's Feiseanna attracted a number of distinguished adjudicators for their drama and music competitions. The Feis had composer Granville Bantock in 1923, with Irish composer Hamilton Harty the next year. In the 1920s, the Feis Dhoire had Colonel Fritz Braze (director of the new Military Band School in Dublin, and a former pupil of Joachim and Max Bruch), Irish tenor Joseph O'Mara and E. Godfrey Browne of the BBC. Adjudicators were generally appreciative of the efforts of competitors and spoke encouragingly of the musical talent of the city. The exception was Dr Charlton Palmer, organist of Canterbury Cathedral, who adjudicated the 1927 Feis. His comments on competitors and on the Guildhall organ were unusually biting. The boys' solo class was not very good; the work of most competitors in Musical Dictation was 'too terrible for words'. He accused Londonderry Corporation of having let the Guildhall organ deteriorate to the point where it was fit only for 'the scrap heap', and then, with scant regard for logic, waxed indignant that the city organists and their pupils were excluded from using it. He said it was 'a Perfect Scandal', etc., and he urged the press reporters to quote his remarks verbatim in their reviews.

A more celebrated, and emollient, adjudicator was Sir Frank Benson, the choice of the Feis Committee for 1928. Few, if any, of the entrants were old enough to remember this elder statesman of the theatre as a young actor in Derry's Opera House in the 1890s. Benson played to his Derry audience's sense of themselves as Irish by declaring that Ireland, with its much smaller population, had contributed 'far more writers of plays and actors than England and Scotland put together'. One of the minor awards he made in 1928 was to ten-year-old, Derry-born Noel Willman (third prize in elocution, nine-fourteen years), who went on to become a successful stage and screen actor and director.[77] Two of Northern Ireland's later professional musicians also found early success in the 1928 Feis: pianist Valerie Trimble and composer Dorothy Parke.

The once-thriving Philharmonic had its own problems; in particular, the poor health of its conductor Albert Cunningham necessitated a succession of temporary stand-ins, a situation partially relieved by the appointment of Henry Franklin in 1923. Franklin held the post of conductor for three years and under his baton, in spring 1924, the Philharmonic gave the first ever performance of Granville Bantock's *Grianan of Aileach*, inspired by the ancient ringfort of that name a few miles to the west of Derry.

In 1925, the Philharmonic's Silver Jubilee Year, it had a chorus of one hundred and twenty voices, a forty-strong orchestra and a non-performing membership of over three hundred. Committee members were drawn from the city's middle-class merchant and professional classes but all classes in society were in the chorus. As the city's premier music society, it enjoyed certain 'perks': the Synod Hall was lent for practices; the Northern Counties Hotel provided a room free of charge for committee meetings, and the Derry Boy Scouts served as stewards at concerts. H.B. Phillips, a good friend of the society, often provided Carl Rosa soloists from his opera company at greatly reduced rates.

In March 1928, the Philharmonic broke with tradition by giving a concert performance of Bizet's *Carmen*, a performance pronounced excellent by the reviewer for *The Irish Times*. By autumn 1930, Cunningham was sufficiently recovered to resume his position on the Philharmonic podium and conduct his fiftieth concert with the society, Handel's *Messiah*. In the society's annual report it was said that it had a thriving chorus, a 'brilliantly led' orchestra (the very words) and healthy finances. The future of the society seemed assured, in spite of 'competition from modern amusements', including 'those machines' – the gramophone and the wireless. The Honorary Secretary reassured members that 'the public [still] wanted the individual and human element'.

In the early 1930s, Derry's Philharmonic still had a strong, popular following and a local press that reported faithfully on its activities. It held an annual ball in the Guildhall, attended in 1933 by 300 people who were entertained in the interval by Kathleen Watson's ballet pupils. Cunningham's eyesight was failing, leaving him unable to conduct. So, after twenty-five years, he was replaced as conductor by J.A.G. (James) Mantz (b.1905), another military musician who was bandmaster of 2nd Battalion, the Leicestershire Regiment. Some of the original 'Phil' members were still singing with the society, but after thirty-four years numbers were declining. An appeal was launched for new members to fill the gaps in the chorus created by 'death, removal and other causes'.

Its 1933 winter *Messiah* in the Guildhall was notable for the first appearance in Derry of the young Belfast tenor James Johnston (1903-1991). Johnston, the son of a butcher, had no formal musical training but his tenor solos were judged 'excellent ... artistic [and] invested with a fine dramatic touch'. The *Sentinel* described the performance overall as 'a magnificent rendering [and] another triumph', and noted particularly that the 'fugal passages were cleanly taken'. There was praise, too, for the conductor, J.H. MacBratney, who had taken over from Mantz, who had received a military posting away from Derry. According to the press, the large audience 'composed of music lovers from the city and the North-west' had been privileged to listen to the oratorio 'in its full majesty'.

Apart from the Philharmonic concerts, there were others by church choirs and their organists. In April 1930, for example, Third Derry choir had their annual concert and organ recital in Great James Street Presbyterian church, which included 'Bach and Mendelssohn Choruses' and the 'Gloucester Cathedral Festival Cantata'. A week later, First Derry church hosted the Derry Presbytery Choral Union Festival, followed five days later by a performance of Stainer's *Crucifixion* in Carlisle Road Methodist church. The conductor was Richard Tolson, no longer working as a cinema pianist, with an augmented choir drawn from St Columb's Cathedral, Christ Church and All Saints', Clooney. Admittedly, these performances were concentrated around Easter time, but they indicate that choral singing continued to have an important place in the life of the city.

The Opera House in Decline

The mix of circus acts, music hall and boxing competitions by which the Bradlaw–Morrison partnership had tried to arrest the decline of the Opera House had only limited success. In late January 1927, a violent storm tore off part of the roof, forcing temporary closure of the building. Then a week later, Whittle, the manager, was prosecuted for permitting out-of-hours drinking on the premises. Although he claimed to have a special theatre-bar licence, he was found guilty, fined 20*s*, and told to (literally) set his house in order.

The cumulative effect of strikes, court cases and storm damage finally persuaded the Dublin owners to sell the theatre to 'Rialto Halls Ltd', a cinema chain, in October 1927. After some 'reconstruction, redecoration and refurbishment', the Opera House reopened as a cinema and was soon showing 'talkies' alongside the Rialto, the Palace, St Columb's Hall, the City and Midland Cinemas. It was a sign of the times. The Opera House undoubtedly had its own particular problems in the 1920s: the legal wrangling about ownership; the succession of short-term managers while it was under administration; the labour disputes under Whittle's management, and its absentee proprietors. But its fate as a theatre was effectively sealed by the change in popular taste away from live entertainments. The novelties offered by cinema came at a cost even the poorest could afford, with the cheapest tickets just 1*d*. With the advent of sound, cinema orchestras had also had their day, as musicians were superfluous at the 'talkies'. Fortunately, people continued to want, and to hire, musicians and bands to play live at dances and parties.

At Phillips' music shop, too, the main focus of the business was no longer musical instruments and sheet music, but gramophones, especially around Christmas time, when sales reached their height. New models of gramophones and 'His Master's Voice' records were the main items in Phillips' press advertisements, with long lists of the recordings available. There were promotional 'gramophone concerts', as in October 1930, when a representative of the Gramophone Co. Ltd demonstrated to a packed audience in the Guildhall the wonders of the new technology. Not to be outdone, Phillips' shop held a week of free gramophone 'demonstrations' in mid-November.

As live entertainments declined, the status of Derry's cinemas perceptibly rose, the appointment of their managers becoming a matter of public note in the local press. They now held 'Annual Dances' in the Guildhall – as the Opera House had once done – and photographs of cinema staff, neatly attired in uniforms, were published in the newspapers. By 1935, the theatre, its name now generally shortened to 'The Opera', advertised only films. For live theatre in Derry one had to look to a new generation of young and enthusiastic local amateur actors.

The Rise of Amateur Drama

The Londonderry Dramatic Society, founded in August 1930 by Hugh Weir, a solicitor's clerk from Belfast, was the second society in the city to bear that name. Its first actors and stage crew were recruited by Weir from members of the Presbyterian Working Men's Institute and early rehearsals were held in its rooms. Their first production was Charles Ayre's *Loaves and Fishes*, a three-act comedy well suited to their resources, having eight male parts and only three female ones. Shortly afterwards, the actors moved from their premises in the Diamond to the YMCA hall, which had more room for rehearsals and performances. From the start they kept up a fierce pace of three productions a year. In 1933 these were: Charles Hawtrey's farce *The Private Secretary* in March; T. King Moylan's three-act Irish comedy *Paid in His Own Coin* in October, and Lynn Doyle's Ulster comedy *Turncoats* in December.

These were truly local performances, staged for city charities and invariably drawing large and enthusiastic audiences from among the actors' friends and acquaintances. Local musical groups played interludes and incidental music at the plays, as when Albert Macari's band played in October 1933.[78] In the course of these productions, there were occasional incidents of unintended comedy, as in one performance of *The Merchant of Venice* when Shylock's nose, made from putty, began to melt under the heat of the lights and developed a marked droop at the tip. The audience, struggling to contain their laughter, couldn't take their eyes off it as it swung from side to side with every move Shylock (Hugh Weir) made.

Stage props and scenery were primitive in the early years, but Weir improvised with painted backdrops suspended from a wooden frame, including one with a dresser painted on it that was frequently used in 'Irish kitchen' dramas. Lighting was also of the most basic kind, consisting of two head battens and a foot batten fitted with bare electric bulbs.

The society specialised in Irish plays, especially works by George Shiels, Louis Walsh and Rutherford Mayne. Weir's production of Walsh's comedy *The Pope in Killybuck* in February 1937 drew large crowds to the Guildhall, including, on the second and last night, the playwright himself.[79] Among those who took their first steps in acting with the society were several who became leading actors in Derry in the post-war period: Fred Logan, Macrae Edmiston, Sidney Buchanan, Noel Atcheson, and Noel Willman, mentioned earlier, who left Derry in 1939 to make his professional debut at London's Lyceum Theatre. Fred Logan later recalled how he and his fellow actors were enthused by Anew McMaster's visits to Derry.

Anew McMaster's theatre company visited twice in 1936 and again in 1937, one of the last of such companies to play in the Opera House, and that only through the good offices of Hugh Weir's Dramatic Society, who negotiated on their behalf with the Opera House management. McMaster brought a range of Shakespeare plays (*Macbeth*, *The Merchant of Venice* and *Julius Caesar*), productions with enough gore and action-packed scenes to gratify Derry's young thespians. But there seemed a jinx on McMaster's visits to Derry. His first, in January 1936, coincided with the death of George V (and unusually arctic weather conditions), which caused performances to be cancelled, while the December visit was during the abdication crisis, when the local press ignored McMaster's visit to report on events in England.

The Guildhall Three

At this time, Derry enjoyed a trio of celebrity concerts the like of which it had not seen since before the First World War. They were preceded in October 1932 by John McCormack's first concert in the city for twenty-three years. It came just a few months after his performance at the 1932 Eucharistic Congress in Dublin, which had endeared him to many Irish Catholics. As on his 1909 visit, a large and appreciative audience flocked to the Guildhall to hear McCormack sing the Irish ballads for which he was famous and to call for a succession of encores.

McCormack's third Derry concert, in October 1935, organised by H.B. Phillips in association with London promoter Harold Holt, didn't match the success of his earlier visits. As Phillips had by this time largely severed his links with music in Ireland, it is unclear what prompted him to involve himself again in Irish concerts. Tickets were expensive, ranging from 5s up to 12s 6d, but it was probably assumed that McCormack's reputation would guarantee a full house. In the event, a number of empty seats in the Guildhall meant that the concert was unsuccessful from a financial point of view. Musically, however, McCormack continued to delight his audience with Moore's Melodies and other Irish ballads, and a sprinkling of classical songs from Handel to Rachmaninov. The event unexpectedly reignited the simmering national anthem controversy, as it was not sung at McCormack's recital, a rare omission at public concerts in the Guildhall. The *Sentinel* observed drily, or perhaps caustically, that its omission was 'customary at such [Irish?] concerts'. The *Journal*, by contrast, was only too happy to report the 'disappointment among a section of last night's audience'. Whatever the explanation, the anthem was played at Phillips' next two concerts, when, in the space of four months, he brought two more celebrated musical performers to Derry: Fritz Kreisler and Paul Robeson.

Kreisler's concert was on 16 January 1936. His career as a virtuoso violinist, initially dazzling, had faltered in the immediate post-war years, but by the mid-1930s he was once again ranked among the finest musicians in the world. His Derry concert attracted about 700 people, but, with a fifth of the seats untaken, it earned Phillips a paltry £6 commission (about £310 in today's money). In musical terms, however, it did not disappoint: Kreisler played Beethoven's *Violin Sonata No.3*, Chausson's *Poeme*, and a number of other showpieces in which the agility of his fingering and bow-work was displayed to brilliant effect. There were many calls for encores. One was

An autographed photograph of Fritz Kreisler, which was presented to the Phillips family during his visit in 1936. (By kind permission of Mrs Maureen Phillips)

his own arrangement of the 'Londonderry Air', which was predictably applauded with special warmth. The *Journal*, finding other words of praise failing it, fell back on the old chestnut of, 'The man with the fiddle was quick to produce his credentials. [Kreisler] was Kreisler.' The *Sentinel*, equally enthralled, concluded its review with a point of its own, 'The concert ended on a memorable note when the great violinist accompanied the singing of The National Anthem.' Four days later, George V died, plunging half the city into mourning.

Phillips' final concert, on 8 February 1936, featured Paul Robeson (1898-1976) and drew a huge crowd, estimated at 'at least one thousand'. The Guildhall was full to capacity with local people and those from farther afield avid to hear – and see – the legendary black singer, renowned for his singing of negro spirituals. Seats were added to the stage to allow more concert-goers to cram into the upstairs hall. Robeson was then at the height of his fame and popularity. A man of many parts, he had been an outstanding American League football player and athlete, had graduated from Law School, was a leading actor on stage and on the screen, and, above all, possessed a deep, rich bass voice. He had a commanding stage presence, and at over 6ft tall had to duck his head below the organ gallery to reach the Guildhall stage. The *Journal* – groping for an appropriate comparison – commented that 'one somehow got the impression that he was coming into a boxing ring', but then added sententiously, 'He had come for a battle of hearts, not fists.'

Robeson's performance met, and exceeded, all his Derry audience's expectations. The spirituals he sang, 'Poor Old Joe', 'Nobody Knows' and 'Swing Low, Sweet Chariot', were given added poignancy by the knowledge that his father, a clergyman, had been born a slave. His reading of William Blake's poem 'The Little Black

Paul Robeson photographed with members of the Phillips' family during his visit to Derry in 1936. (The Bigger McDonald Collection: by kind permission of Derry Central Library)

Boy' was the more moving for being spoken by a black man. He rounded off his programme with several encores, including 'My Old Kentucky Home' and 'Ol' Man River'. Alone of the three celebrity soloists, he made no attempt to ingratiate himself with the Derry audience by singing the 'Londonderry Air'. Nonetheless, it is doubtful if any singer, before or since, has filled – or thrilled – the Guildhall as did Robeson.

The St Columb's Hall Drama Festivals

McCormack, Kreisler and Robeson were like comets, spectacular but transient in the cultural life of the city. The bright lights in Derry's cultural scene in 1937 and 1938 were local and provided by two amateur drama festivals. Both were organised by the St Eugene's Building Fund and although their primary role was to raise money for the parish, they had a major influence on the development of amateur drama among Derry's Catholics. Seven societies competed in the first festival for a trophy presented by the President of St Columb's College, Dr Neil Farren. The *Journal* also presented a trophy, and a number of local businessmen donated gold medals. The following year there were fifteen drama companies competing for awards in three categories: one-act plays, three-act plays and 'plays of a religious nature'. Drama societies travelled from Omagh, Belfast and Donegal to participate, most associated with Catholic schools or charities. Religious divisions within Derry had hardened to such an extent that there was no question of any Protestant amateur drama society taking part. This had adverse consequences for drama on both sides of the religious divide, with the best actors, Catholic and Protestant, unable to work together and learn from one another.

The Discovery of James Johnston

James Johnston returned to Derry in March 1938 for a concert performance by the Philharmonic Society of Edward German's opera *Merrie England*. In the audience that night was Colonel Bill O'Kelly, on the lookout for soloists for his Dublin Grand Opera Society. O'Kelly was so impressed by Johnston's singing that he approached him straight after the concert to invite him to join his new company. After initially hesitating, Johnston agreed, and two years later, in November 1940, he made his professional debut in Verdi's *Rigoletto* at Dublin's Gaiety Theatre. This was the start of a glittering career for Northern Ireland's most celebrated tenor: he was to become principal tenor with Sadler's Wells in 1945, and take leading roles in opera there and at Covent Garden throughout the 1950s. He unexpectedly retired from the stage in 1958, wanting, he said, to leave 'while at the top', but thereafter he made occasional appearances as a soloist in oratorio.

The Opera House was rarely used for live shows in the later 1930s, a rare exception being the pantomime *Babes in the Wood*, staged by Ventom Smith's Company in January 1937. The last known live performance was in May 1938, when Kathleen Watson presented a 'Matinée Dansante' by her pupils. Shortly afterwards, the new owner, Wee ('Red') Willie O'Doherty, a popular local entertainer, closed the theatre for renovations, reputedly spending thousands of pounds covering up the ornately carved walls with smooth panelling, and replacing the older gallery and circle with a new 'commodious' balcony. St Columb's Hall was refurbished too, and reopened with 'all the modern facilities' for sound films, although these were often combined with live shows and concerts on Sunday evenings.

The Philharmonic, Derry's longest-lasting music society, finally called it a day in 1939. The tradition it had championed of large-scale oratorios at Christmas time had come to an end with its thirteenth and last *Messiah* in the Guildhall in 1935. Its veteran conductor Cunningham had died in 1935 and it had been unable to find a permanent replacement. The lack of settled artistic direction had an inevitable knock-on effect on its funds and the society had been struggling financially for years, incurring a loss of £55 in the 1936/7 season (over £3,000 in today's money). That year, a committee member complained, 'it is a disgrace that people should be sitting

Londonderry Philharmonic Society

(Thirty-Eighth Season.)

President :
HER GRACE THE DUCHESS OF ABERCORN.

SECOND GRAND
Subscription Concert,

"MERRIE ENGLAND"
(*Edward German*),
by permission of Messrs. Chappell & Co., Ltd.

AND MISCELLANEOUS SELECTIONS,

GUILDHALL, LONDONDERRY,

On Thursday, 31st March, 1938,

AT 7.45 P.M. PROMPT.

ARTISTES:

Miss OLIVE GROVES,	Soprano
Miss PATRICIA BLACK,	Contralto
Mr. JAMES JOHNSTON,	Tenor
Mr. HENRY GILL,	Bass-Baritone
Mr. LAWRENCE M'CANN, B.E.,	Leader of Orchestra
Mr. CECIL G. REID, L.T.C.L.,	Accompanist

CONDUCTOR:
Mr. J. CROSSLEY CLITHEROE.

Sentinel, Derry.   PRICE, SIXPENCE.

The Philharmonic Society concert in 1938, when tenor James Johnston (1903-1991) was 'discovered' by a talent scout. (Author's collection)

in cinemas listening to the crooning of songs while the Philharmonic had to appeal to the Carnegie Trust for help'. A disgrace it may have been, but complaining about it was not going to rescue the society's finances. It was, not to put too fine a point on it, broke. Nor was it the only city choir to go under. Cunningham's Bohemian Male Voice Choir fell apart with the death of its founder, and the Derry and Glee Madrigal Club, conducted by John Frankland, organist at St Columb's Cathedral, went the same way. Then the war came, and no one could foresee what its effect on the cultural landscape of Derry would be.

Wartime Concerts: 'It's a Long Way to Londonderry ...'

At first, the war seemed to make little difference. Rationing, censorship and identity cards were introduced, but there was neither conscription nor shortage of food.[80] In early September, the Feis was cancelled for the duration of the war, but, unlike England, where theatres and cinemas were closed in the autumn of 1939, Derry's halls and cinemas remained open. The people of Derry continued to go to films, church concerts and soirées, unaffected as yet by the war in Europe. Only one amateur group, the Doire Colmcille Dramatic Society, announced that it was cancelling its plans for the season 'owing to the present situation'. But it quickly reversed that decision, saying it didn't want to disrupt arrangements already made for future performances. One of the few definite signs of change was the coming together of a new generation of Derry's musicians, actors and variety performers for concerts in aid of war funds.

The first wartime concert in the Guildhall, on Saturday 28 October 1939, closely followed the format of such events during the First World War. It featured a medley of songs, comedy sketches, revue items and recitations, rounded off with community singing. Seven hundred people attended the first concert but audiences rose to almost one thousand at each of the two subsequent concerts before Christmas. They were repeated each lunar month throughout the war, always held on the Saturday night closest to the full moon to allow concert-goers enough light to find their way home. As elsewhere in Great Britain, the blackout was strictly enforced, and many accidents occurred in Derry when night-time walkers collided with pillar boxes and lampposts.

Over the war years, the concert format changed little, except that the city's amateurs were joined by church organists and music teachers, and increasingly by a wide range of military bands and individual airmen, soldiers and sailors. 'The Street Singers', a constantly fluctuating group of amateur performers, were the backbone of the concerts, delighting audiences with satirical skits, songs and jokes. In February 1940, they introduced their own 'Derry Soldier's Song', entitled 'It's a Long Way to Londonderry [*sic*]', made funnier by lots of local references. Hitler, Mussolini, and even Prime Minister Neville Chamberlain were the butt of musical sketches and comic songs. Derry's choirs, such as the Music Society Choir, appeared regularly. The role of compère at the concerts was taken in turns by Alex Rodgers and Joey (J.B.) Glover, then a young amateur actor and organist. All proceeds were donated to war charities, those from the first concert in 1939 going to the 'War Hospital Supply Depot'. Tickets were priced at 1s, with military personnel admitted free.

The Opera House Fire

But the war was not responsible for the great fire of 1940 that destroyed Derry's Opera House. Just before midnight on 9 March, the blackout was dramatically broken as flames from the Opera House lit up the Derry skyline. It could be seen for miles around. The *Derry Journal* described how, 'it dyed the waters of the Foyle with red, while the Waterside appeared as if in the rich glow of sunset'. People gathered in their hundreds on the Carlisle Road to watch the blaze develop as fire engines rushed to the scene. But the fire had already taken hold and within a few hours the whole building was gutted. According to the newspaper report:

> At midnight the whole place was blazing furiously. During the fire, explosions were heard at intervals, these being apparently caused by bottles bursting in the bar of the Opera House and the cracking of the slates on the roof. There were loud crashes as parts of the interior collapsed ... A gaunt roofless building burnt out to the walls was all that remained.

There was much speculation as to the cause of the fire. The Fire Chief put out a statement immediately that the fire was the result of faulty wiring and that the blaze had spread so quickly because of a draught between the older ornate wall panels and the recently installed wall panelling. The source of the fire, he said, was at the back of the building, to which no one had access but the Opera House's own staff. However, there were many in Derry who remained unconvinced. It was widely known that threats had been made by the IRA against the Opera House and six other Derry cinemas only three weeks before, warning them against screening British newsreels. All but the Opera House had stopped showing them. There had been incidents in the Opera House that had resulted in court cases and fines. A few weeks before the fire, one Albert Donahue and a fourteen-year-old boy were fined 21s for shouting, 'There will be no King and Queen after Easter', during a newsreel showing the royal couple. In a similar incident in March, there had been booing and whistling during another newsreel showing the Royals, when someone had called out, 'What about Hitler?'

These suspicions seemed to be confirmed two weeks later, when the Belfast branch of the IRA 'broadcast' a statement claiming responsibility for the fire.[81] This claim was given added credibility by the fact that a bomb had been discovered that same

BIG DERRY FIRE
OPERA HOUSE GUTTED
MIDNIGHT BLAZE LIGHTS UP CITY
DAMAGE ESTIMATED AT £30,000

Newspaper headline reporting the Opera House Fire. The site is now a car park. (Derry Journal, *11 March 1940*)

night on the roof of the Midland Cinema in the Waterside; it had failed to go off only because the fuse had been extinguished by rain.

Whatever the cause of the fire, the Opera House ended its seventy-three-year history as a charred skeleton, with jutting steel girders the only reminder of its once elegant, decoratively carved auditorium.

'Dancing Derry Mothers'

The reality of war was brought home to Derry just over a year later, on 15 April 1941, when two German parachute mines fell on the city, one killing fifteen people in Messines Park. Nine months later, with the United States now in the war, the first North American soldiers disembarked in Derry, evoking its history as a garrison town, as it became a transit point for American and Canadian servicemen gathering for the invasion of Europe.

Thousands more servicemen followed over the next two years. At its peak, there were 20,000 troops billeted in Derry and surrounding area, and 149 ships moored in the River Foyle. No other town or city in Ulster experienced so dramatically at first hand the impact of large numbers of Allied troops. Several city buildings were commandeered for war purposes, including the Apprentice Boys' Hall and the YMCA building. Full employment returned, with shirt factories once again making army

The booklet issued to North American servicemen arriving in Derry in 1942, outlining the city's amenities, entertainments and cultural venues. It was signed by the Mayor, Frederick Simmons, a bass singer in Derry's Philharmonic Society. (Author's collection)

uniforms and shipyard works geared towards armaments. Wartime brought newfound prosperity and more money to spend on cinema, dances and wartime amusements. From 1942 onwards, there was no shortage of musical entertainments, as every church hall, hotel, cinema and roadside shebeen vied to organise social events in aid of the war effort – and for the benefit of the North American servicemen. New local singers and musicians came to the fore, such as tenor Larry Hasson, pianist James MacCafferty, and the then relatively unknown local tenor Joseph McLaughlin (later 'Josef Locke').

In a short space of time, Derry became 'Americanized'. Jazz, swing, jitterbugging, square dancing and the 'big band sound' replaced the more sedate music society concerts and temperance soirées of the 1930s. Cinemas and dance halls were suddenly where 'things happened'. By 1942 there were seven cinemas in Derry, and in January that year the conservative and overwhelmingly Protestant Londonderry Corporation passed a resolution – no doubt through gritted teeth – allowing the Midland Cinema to open on Sundays 'for use by servicemen only'. Eight dance halls, including the Guildhall, provided virtually continuous employment for Derry's dance bands, the newest being the elegantly named Marlborough Salon Orchestra. But there was a downside. In November 1942, the *Sentinel* – with a shiver of embarrassment – remarked upon the new phenomenon of 'Dancing Derry Mothers' who left their children on their own to flock to the dance halls to meet the 'Yanks'.[82]

More respectable entertainments for the troops were provided by a local 'Hospitality Committee' in the form of concerts of 'recorded music' and musical evenings in the United Services Rest Room and Library above the Northern Bank in Shipquay Place. The war brought some well-known entertainers to Derry, such as George Formby (1904-1961), with his ukulele playing and naively risqué songs, but they came under the auspices of ENSA and were usually seen only by the troops.[83] Bob Hope and Al Jolson likewise came to Derry to entertain American servicemen.

This spread of American-style 'night life' was accompanied by a temporary decline in the performing arts. Large-scale concerts were abandoned and amateur drama was confined to small-scale productions. Many amateur actors, such as Joey Glover, Noel Acheson and Macrae Edmiston, were fully involved in the wartime concerts, leaving little time for drama. The Londonderry Dramatic Society did stage some plays, comedies and farces, such as *In the War Time* in the Guildhall in March 1940. Wartime scarcities meant that props were, once again, primitive and makeshift, with blackout cloths often doubling as backdrops. Interest in professional drama was kept alive only by twice-yearly visits from the Cork-based Carl Clopet Theatre Company, which brought plays to the Guildhall that were new to Derry audiences, such as Noel Coward's *Hay Fever*, Daphne du Maurier's *Rebecca*, G.B. Shaw's *Pygmalion* and Terence Rattigan's *French without Tears*.

Alongside dances and these occasional drama productions, the Guildhall was host to concerts and céilí dances organised by Derry's Catholics in aid of the Green Cross Fund, which supported the dependants of political internees. The *Journal* reported these entertainments in detail, describing the 'hour-long queues' that formed before concerts and the 'Irishness' of the programmes. The paper noted that the concerts ended with the singing of the national anthem, but whether it was 'God Save the King' or 'The Soldiers' Song', it did not say.

The Feis Dhoire, unlike the Feis, continued throughout the war years, seemingly unaffected by events elsewhere, and still attracting large numbers of competitors and equally large audiences. In 1942 their patron was Bishop Neil Farren, whose speech at the close of the event was infused with a kind of romantic nostalgia, appealing to the young competitors to uphold their Gaelic culture and not to 'despise our native dances for the sake of modern substitutes'. Had someone tipped him off about how Derry's young girls spent their wartime evenings?[84]

The thirteen-strong Jacques String Orchestra visited the city in October 1943. This was the first touring ensemble to be sponsored by the Belfast-based Council for the Encouragement of Music and the Arts (CEMA).[85] The concert provided a rare opportunity for Guildhall audiences to see and hear music performed by musicians other than a military, céilí or dance band. It was preceded by a short talk by Reginald Jacques on the music being performed. The same orchestra returned to Derry in early 1944, by special arrangement with the Home Office, which excepted it from the travel restrictions then imposed between Ireland and England in advance of D-Day.

'The Beginning of the End'

By early 1945, there were indications that wartime restrictions were gradually being relaxed. A prestigious Guildhall concert on 20 February, organised by the Newspaper Press Fund and featuring violinist Isidore Shlaen and Irish baritone Michael O'Higgins, had the novel feature of a 'Souvenir Programme', printed and published by Phillips' music shop. Throughout the war, paper had been so scarce that concert programmes were rarely printed and newspapers had fewer pages and barely any photographs. There was speculation in the press beforehand that the 39th Popular Saturday Night Concert in the Guildhall on 22 March might be the last of the war. And so it proved, with Derry's amateurs coming onstage for the last time to perform their songs, sketches, revues and recitations to well-earned – and probably relieved – applause.

THE THIRTY-EIGHTH POPULAR SATURDAY NIGHT CONCERT

IN AID OF UNITED AID TO CHINA FUND,

IN THE GUILDHALL,

TO-NIGHT, at 7.30.

Doors Open at 7 o'clock.

ADMISSION :   **ONE SHILLING.**

Early Door (Side Door), 6.30, Sixpence extra.

'By the Light of the Silvery Moon ...' The 38th Guildhall wartime concert, held on the night of the full moon in February 1945. (Londonderry Sentinel, 24 February 1945)

Seven

AGAINST THE ODDS, 1945-1979

The end of the war in June 1945 saw the first visit to Derry of the acting duo Micheál Mac Liammóir and Hilton Edwards and their Dublin Gate Theatre Company.[86] Their *Othello* in the Guildhall drew large audiences; a tribute to the reputation of the actors and a measure of the enthusiasm for live theatre in Derry. They staged two other plays, MacLiammoir's *Where Stars Walk* and the Brother Quintero's play *A Hundred Years Old*. Local reviews reckoned the visit 'a huge success … the sincerity of the players was most striking', and, in reference to Edward's direction of the plays, 'We have the secret of the superiority of the professionals.' However, the actors themselves considered that the Guildhall did 'not lend itself, to put it mildly, to the presentation of any worthwhile stage production'.

The *Sentinel* made the same point some months later, and criticised the City Corporation for its lack of interest in the arts. With the war over, local papers felt the time was ripe to press for a new theatre to replace the Opera House lost to fire six years earlier.

In March 1946, what was to become Derry's most active and longest-lasting amateur group, the City of Derry Drama Club (CDDC), arose out of the embers of the Londonderry Dramatic Society. (The latter was slowly disintegrating since the death of its founder, Hugh Weir, during the war.) Whereas the older society had been an informal affair, the new group had a properly constituted council and clearly defined aims. They agreed to produce two plays 'of proven worth' every year, with the profits to be used for 'scenery, lighting equipment, props and wardrobe essentials'. Control of the club was 'vested' in five council members: Jack Logan, Sidney Buchanan, Fred Logan, W. Macrae Edmiston and Noel Atcheson.

At first, the club had only basic props and equipment. As Logan later recalled, 'Productions were fraught because of shortages. Cloth was on coupons, timber could only be bought under licence, and electric equipment was in very short supply.' Logan

From Farquhar to Field Day

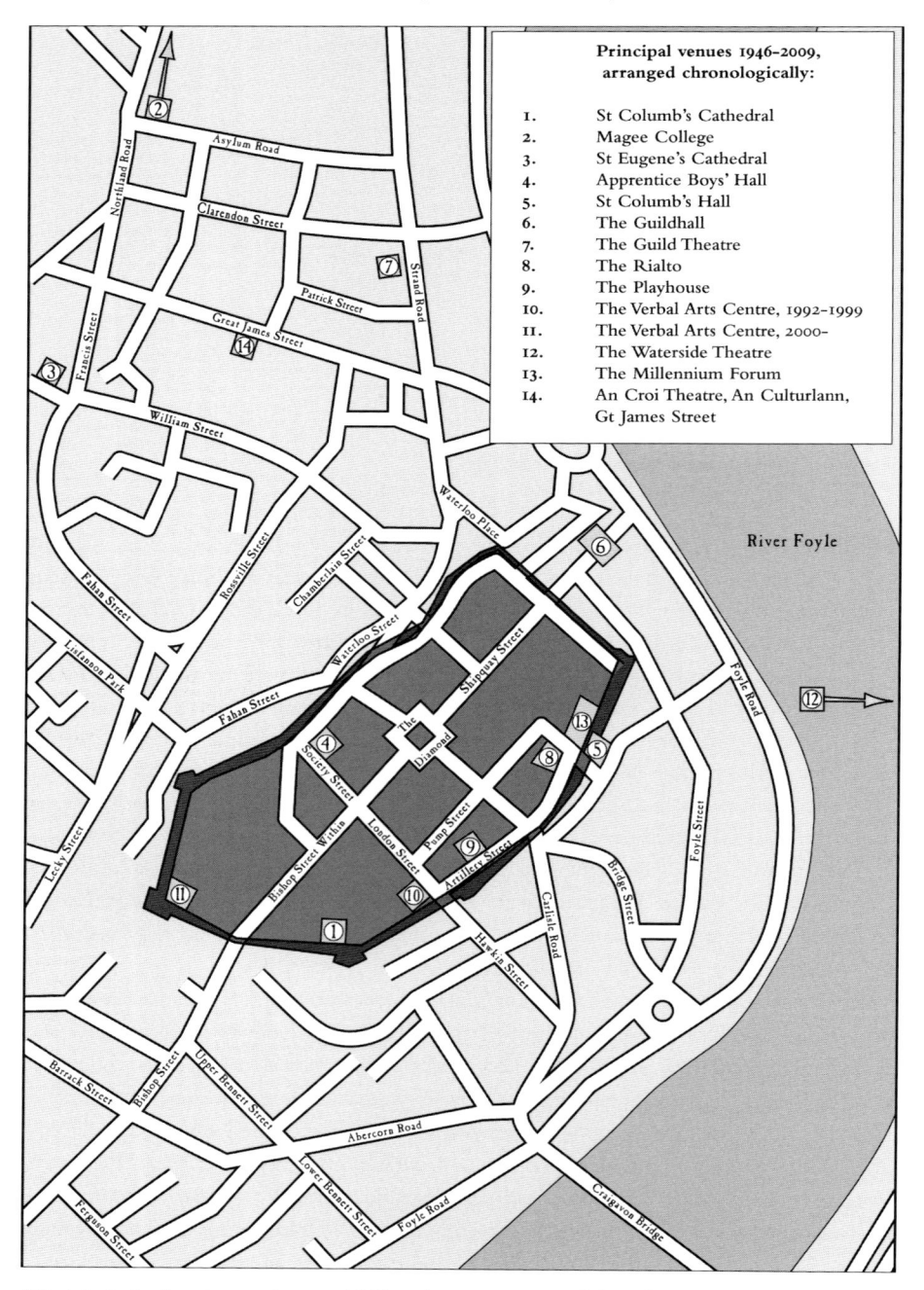

Principal venues 1946-2009, arranged chronologically:

1. St Columb's Cathedral
2. Magee College
3. St Eugene's Cathedral
4. Apprentice Boys' Hall
5. St Columb's Hall
6. The Guildhall
7. The Guild Theatre
8. The Rialto
9. The Playhouse
10. The Verbal Arts Centre, 1992-1999
11. The Verbal Arts Centre, 2000-
12. The Waterside Theatre
13. The Millennium Forum
14. An Croi Theatre, An Culturlann, Gt James Street

The principal cultural venues between 1946 and 2009, now spread throughout the city. The 'older' cultural quartier, centred on the East Wall, was given new life in the twenty-first century in the Playhouse, Millennium Forum and St Columb's Hall.

had been involved in drama since the early 1930s, when he was a young teacher in First Derry Primary School.[87] He took a leading role in the first production, a sell-out staging of St John Ervine's *Friends and Relations* in the Guildhall in October 1946. It was repeated six weeks later at the Guild Theatre.

The Guild Experiment

The Guild Theatre began life in a renovated building off Strand Road, and was unique ('the first of its kind in Ireland') in being run, financed and managed entirely by amateurs, under the auspices of the North-West Drama and Arts Guild. The actual theatre was in a disused factory in North Edward Street and held about 250 people. Under the name Clarendon Hall, it had been used for wartime céilís and dances. The Guild's first production, in September 1946, was Sean O'Casey's *Juno and the Paycock* by the Belfast Guild Players, when the hall was packed with patrons and subscribers and many more had to be turned away at the door.

The CDDC and the Guild Theatre were part of an upsurge in amateur drama in Northern Ireland after 1945. During the war there had been little live theatre in Derry, except for the occasional visiting drama company. Now amateur dramatics were all the rage and drama societies proliferated – at least ten by the end of 1946. They assisted one another and shared premises, equipment, props and even stage teams. In contrast, music in Derry was still divided along religious lines, with separate orchestras, choirs, music societies and venues.

The North-West Drama and Arts Guild concerned itself with drama, art and music, but drama initially was well to the fore. Its twelve trustees included Chairman Cecil King and Vice-Chairman Jimmy Mann of the YMCA Players. As an all-embracing arts organisation with responsibility for local cultural provision, it anticipated by several decades later concepts of community arts, cross-border funding and Arts Council subsidies. Its 1946 autumn programme was ambitious, with fifteen drama groups presenting twenty plays; six groups from across the border, six from Derry and three from elsewhere in Northern Ireland. Here, according to *The Irish Times*, was proof of Ireland's 'cultural unity' and that in the arts – as with Irish rugby – 'the border … is virtually non-existent'.

The city societies were St Enda's Dramatic Club, the City of Derry Drama Club, the YMCA Players, Kieran Dramatic Club, the Londonderry Dramatic Society and the Good Companions. Plays ranged from domestic dramas to thrillers and comedies, with a slight bias towards Irish plays. In addition, as part of its policy of joint learning and collaboration, the Guild organised lectures for producers, technicians and actors, for example in November on 'Stage Make-up' and 'Production'. It held its Annual Dance on Boxing Day and there was a three-day run of *Christmas Pie*, a variety show of 'Music, Song, Scenas, Comedy and Drama'.

> **NORTH-WEST DRAMA AND ARTS GUILD . . . .**
> have pleasure in announcing
> the OPENING of the *Guild Theatre* NORTH EDWARD STREET (off Strand Road), Derry,
> On **MONDAY, 30th SEPTEMBER**, with **THE GUILD PLAYERS**, Belfast, presenting
> "JUNO AND THE PAYCOCK," by Sean O'Casey. Production by Harry Coll, with Ann Gavin (B.B.C. and Olympia Theatre, Dublin), as "JUNO." Curtain 8 p.m.
> This will be Patrons' and Subscription Night. Subscription 5/- and 3/-. All Seats Bookable.
> Patrons' and Associate Members' Seats already Reserved.
> BOOKING at the Theatre Daily from WEDNESDAY, 25th September, between 12 Noon and 4 p.m. The Performance will be REPEATED on TUESDAY, 1st October, at the Usual Prices of Admission—2/6 and 1/6. All Seats may be Reserved. 'Phone 2091.
> Late-comers will not be admitted until after the First Act.

The opening advertisement for the Guild Theatre in North Edward Street. (Londonderry Sentinel, 24 September 1946)

There was usually some orchestral music before each play, conducted in rotation by Orlando Cafolla, Mrs Caldwell and Mrs F.E. McCarroll. Of the three, Cafolla was the best known. He then had three ensembles: his 'Baby' and 'Junior' strings, and the Polychordia String Orchestra. (He also combined with his wife Sara in a 'Palm Court' duo in seaside towns during summer months.)

There were even Guild-organised concerts: in December a 'Gramophone Recital' of music by Beethoven, Mozart and Elgar compered by Redmond Friel, and a second, 'Farewell', concert for local mezzo-soprano Angela McGovern before she left for music studies in London. This was the debut of a 'new and promising young singer', Derry-born William Loughlin, and the beginning of his long association with music in Derry. He became a frequent Feis prize winner in the later 1940s, when at least one adjudicator suggested that his rich bass voice would not be out of place at Sadler's Wells Opera. However, Loughlin decided not to pursue a professional career in music, preferring to give his services as an amateur at concerts in North-West Ulster for the next fifty years.[88]

Caoilte the Critic

Popular interest in drama was reflected in two columns in the *Journal*, 'Round the Shows' and 'Drama with the Amateurs', the latter written under the pen name of 'Caoilte' – reputedly Kevin Doherty, a Buncrana pharmacist. Caoilte made weekly contributions, discussing theatre companies, individual actors and their plays.[89] At first he was full of praise for the Guild, 'Once inside I was deeply impressed. It's a beautiful little theatre ... I was full of admiration for the little band of enthusiasts who are responsible for giving us this – the first amateur theatre in Ireland.'

But soon his penchant for plain speaking was raising hackles. He got embroiled in arguments with named individuals from the theatre and was sharply critical of some productions, saying that they were ill-produced and under-rehearsed. He antagonised producers, actors and even some in the audiences, who thought his criticisms unfair, ill-judged or too severe for what were, after all, amateur productions. He began once piece by saying, 'I expect that what I am going to write in this article will make me very unpopular in different quarters', and went on, 'Generally speaking, the standard is not good enough. In some cases, it is not good enough for a small town or village, not to mention Derry, with its magnetic counter-attraction – the cinema.' He counselled the theatre committee to 'wake up from their sleep' and apply stricter standards by excluding weaker drama companies. His review provoked a furious response in the *Journal* from two correspondents signing themselves 'Improved Drama' and 'Justice'. They were caustic about Caoilte in their turn, questioning his fitness to pass judgment on amateur drama. The upshot was that Caoilte declared himself reluctant to attend performances at the Guild Theatre, fearful of his reception.

According to the newspapers, audiences for some plays were 'surprisingly small' and full houses were reported only for the better-known societies, such CDDC and the YMCA Players. Caoilte's criticisms cannot have helped. In addition, there was competition from St Columb's Hall, which provided a varied programme of plays, dances and films during the winter months. And of course, the 'counter-attraction' mentioned by Caoilte – Derry's cinemas.

The Guild Theatre closed finally on 16 January 1947, with the Omagh Players in Edward Percy's three-act thriller *The Shop at Sly Corner*. At the end, 'wave after wave of applause rolled through the crowded auditorium', but the applause could not hide a sizeable debt of £50. The theatre had been totally self-funded, relying on box-office takings, membership fees and voluntary subscriptions. CEMA provided neither subsidy nor guarantee against loss. Guild members may in any case have been reluctant to seek a subsidy from CEMA, given its insistence that the national anthem be played at all its events. There was disappointment at the failure of the theatre, but no attempt to lay blame. The *Sentinel*, in keeping with the general mood, concluded that the closure was 'definitely not to the discredit of the Committee or those connected with the Guild Theatre'.

The Guild Theatre was the first example in Derry of actors, producers, artists and musicians working collaboratively. After its demise, amateur actors and musicians continued to perform, but dispersed across different venues – the YMCA Hall, St Columb's Minor Hall, Magee and the Guildhall – although Caoilte's weekly column in the *Journal* continued for another decade. But there was one lasting legacy of the Guild: the Londonderry Music Circle, which grew out of its music section, was to become the first Derry music society to organise and promote concerts, rather than have the members performing themselves.

Magee University College Londonderry

MONDAY, MARCH 5th, 1956
at 8 p.m.

Mozart Bicentenary Concert

LAWRENCE McCANN	- Violin
JOHN NOURSE	- Piano
BARBARA MORRIS	- Soprano
ANTHONY KNOWLAND	- Piano
HUBERT EVANS	- Piano

and

The Senior Choir of the Londonderry High School

Conductor - HEATHER PARR

The Common Hall   Magee University College

PROGRAMME - - PRICE 6d.

A Londonderry Music Circle concert in March 1956. Held in Magee's Common Hall, it featured a local school choir singing Britten's 'A Ceremony of Carols'. (Author's collection)

The Londonderry Music Circle

Redmond Friel was the key figure in the founding of the Circle in 1947, alongside wartime concert stalwarts Joey Glover and Walter Aickin. It ran two sorts of concerts: live recitals by visiting musicians provided by CEMA and gramophone concerts. The latter were held in the City Café, where recordings of classical music were preceded by a short talk on the composers featured. As gramophones were still luxury items, the concerts attracted a regular clientele, keen to hear music on 'good quality equipment'. Often the evenings ended with music quizzes which Friel invariably won.

Redmond Friel (1907-1979) was a stalwart of Derry's musical life for almost fifty years, through his long association with the Feis Dhoire, his GPO Choir, his many years teaching music at St Columb's College, and, finally, his numerous compositions. His compositions were varied: orchestral music, music for orchestra and voices, chamber music, church and choral music, film and incidental music. As an arranger of Irish traditional melodies, Friel was also one of the most prolific Northern Irish musicians of the post-partition period and he will be remembered principally for his arrangements for orchestra and choirs. Between 1937 and 1939, he was one of the musicians engaged by the BBC to orchestrate the traditional folk music of Ulster, with his arrangements broadcast in the popular radio programme, *Irish Rhythms*.

The Circle's live concerts were held in a number of venues: Magee, the Memorial Hall (the 'Mem') in Society Street, and the Guildhall. A typical example of the Circle's small-scale chamber concerts was the piano and vocal recital that Havelock Nelson and Mary Johnston gave in the 'Mem' in January 1949. But at the society's AGM that year, committee members registered complaints about the lack of interest in the live concerts, with on average only thirty-four people attending each – a desperately poor turn-out for a city of Derry's size. Nonetheless, the Circle continued to operate well into the 1960s, when it operated in tandem with the North-West Music Society, founded in 1957.

The City of Derry Drama Club

The City of Derry Drama Club's high level of organisation and planning enabled it to survive and prosper where the Guild Theatre had failed. It persuaded Londonderry Corporation to buy a proscenium, complete with curtains, and to extend the existing stage of the Guildhall. The proscenium, a portable steel structure, cost £200 and was hired out to drama clubs at 10*s* a night. The club also established its own fund for drama coaching and payment of outside producers, which within ten years grew to £5,000. As the leading amateur drama society in Derry, it worked in association with CEMA, handling the local arrangements for visiting drama companies, such as the Colchester Repertory Company's October 1949 production of d'Usseau and

Derry's amateur actors at a rehearsal in the 1950s. (By kind permission of Derry City Council Museum Service)

Gow's play *Deep Are the Roots*. This play, which deals with the tensions in an inter-race relationship and had a racially mixed cast, may have evoked memories of the African-American servicemen who had passed through Derry during the war. The costs of the visit were underwritten by CEMA, but the club introduced its own pricing structure to attract last-minute play-goers. Tickets booked in advance were 2*s* and 3*s*, but there were 130 tickets at the door for 1*s*.

Thanks to the club's collaboration with CEMA, Derry had no shortage of visits by other professional companies in the 1950s: the Belfast Arts Theatre, the Ulster Group Theatre and Anew McMaster's Company. His fifteen-strong 'Full London Company' returned for their fourth visit in 1957, bringing six plays to the Guildhall, including two by Oscar Wilde, *Lady Windermere's Fan* and *An Ideal Husband*, and two Shakespeare, *King Lear* and *Julius Caesar*. But the jinx on McMaster's Derry visits continued. On the afternoon of Saturday 16 November, the last day of their one-week visit, their rehearsals were 'dramatically' halted by three explosions which rocked the Guildhall. Smoke and fumes then billowed through the building, filling the upstairs hall, where McMaster's company was – ironically enough – rehearsing Janet Green's play *Murder Mistaken*. The cause of the fire was a malfunction in the boiler room, the doors of which had been locked for several months, 'as a precaution against activities by an illegal organisation' – a reference to IRA activities in the later 1950s.[90] The play went ahead regardless that evening, albeit in a chilly, unheated

Guildhall. The Town Clerk was confident that 'there was no reason to believe that the explosions were other than an accident'. At this stage in McMaster's career (he was sixty-three years old), he was prone to forget what play he was acting in and launch into a Shakespearean soliloquy. Other cast members had to then somehow get him back on track.

The *Sentinel*, whose editor, Sidney Buchanan, was one of CDDC's leading members, reported extensively on the club's activities and printed sympathetic reviews of its productions. The substantial financial and material reserves which it built up in its early years enabled it to survive well into the 1970s. It was generous about lending props and lighting, and even providing stagehands to other drama groups for their productions. The Magee University College Drama Society, which in December 1956 thanked Fred Logan and Sidney Buchanan for help with lighting, curtains, make-up and stage management, was one of many groups that benefitted from CDDC's largesse. This kind of co-operation was typical of drama groups in the city at this period.

However, there were still striking differences in their activities and repertoire. Some, like the Mercy Convent Past Pupils' Union Dramatic Club and the St Columb's Club, performed in Derry and also competed in drama festivals throughout Ireland, travelling with busloads of boisterous supporters. Trips to drama festivals in Donegal were particularly welcome, for the chance to smuggle eggs, cheese and butter, still rationed in Northern Ireland, in the bus going back to Derry. CDDC, on the other hand, staged plays only on home turf. The older YMCA Players staged mainly 'kitchen' dramas, while the CDDC, again, experimented with more modern plays.

Derry Feels the Draught

While amateur drama at least was in a healthy condition, Derry's music was in the doldrums. Apart from occasional visits by the Boyd Neel and Jacques Orchestras, few outside musicians of note visited. CEMA was widely perceived as neglecting Derry. An editorial in the *Sentinel* in May 1947 tackled this neglect head on, comparing 'what Belfast gets' with 'what Derry gets' and arguing that there was a huge discrepancy between them. Two years later, the newspaper took up the cudgels again in a series of editorials which deplored the lack of a choral or operatic society in the city. It looked back nostalgically to the 'glory days' of the Philharmonic, noting that even Bangor now had an operatic society, whereas Derry did not.

On the other hand, the *Sentinel* was quick to spring to Derry's defence when it was an outsider who was the critic. When the adjudicator at the 1949 Feis, the celebrated theatre director Tyrone Guthrie, was somewhat disparaging of Derry's young actors, the newspaper went to town in repeating criticisms of Guthrie himself, dismissing his comments as 'unjustified' and claiming he 'was rather out of touch with the standard of verse-speaking in the province'.

There were a certain number of local concerts in the early post-war years, and several small choirs regularly performed operettas, cantatas and excerpts from oratorios. Mrs I.M. McClean's Maiden Singers staged operettas in the Guildhall in aid of charities, and James Moore's various choirs (he had three) sang selections from oratorios at Christmas time and Easter. Moore, born in Ramelton, County Donegal, was organist at Fourth Derry Presbyterian church in the later 1940s. He founded and conducted a forty-strong ladies' choir, The Londonderriaires, whose name must have raised an eyebrow or two at their Guildhall concerts.

The Guildhall also hosted an annual Diocesan Choral Festival, which brought together Anglican choirs in a celebratory, rather than competitive, spirit. And when a large choral society finally did emerge in 1952, it was under the new St Columb's Cathedral organist, Sligo-born Michael Franklin (1903-1990). He was not new to Derry; he lived there while his father was the Philharmonic's conductor in the mid-1920s. Franklin had a varied career, having spent some years as cinema pianist in Manchester and Dublin, until the 'talkies' ended that employment. He studied music at Trinity College Dublin and from there went to a post in Limerick Cathedral. His return to Derry in 1948 enlivened both Cathedral and city music. Within a year, he gave Derry's first public organ recital for twenty-five years, and followed this up by founding Templemore Male Voice Choir. His main achievement, however, was to set up Derry's first choral society since the Philharmonic and to revive their tradition of performing major choral works.

St Columb's Cathedral Oratorio Society

The St Columb's Cathedral Oratorio Society held their first concert in the Guildhall in December 1952, singing Bach's *Christmas Oratorio* (Parts 1 and 2) and some excerpts from Handel. The guest organist was Evan John, music lecturer at Queen's University, Belfast. The next year they sang Haydn's *Creation*, and then Mendelssohn's *Elijah* in April 1954. By this time, the chorus had grown to ninety-three, with ladies – as usual – outnumbering men by almost two to one. In addition, *Elijah* featured fourteen choirboys; an opportunity for the young trebles of the Cathedral to get their first taste of oratorio.

Other oratorios followed, including several *Messiah*s, Handel's *Samson* and *Acis and Galatea*, Mendelssohn's *St Paul* and Parry's *Blest Pair of Sirens*. Soloists were brought in from outside; usually Northern Irish singers such as Heather Harper, Marjorie Wright and Jean Allister, frequently joined by local bass Willie Laughlin. James Johnston made several return visits to the city where he had been 'discovered'.[91] The spring concert was usually a lighter piece; for example, the society's eleventh subscription concert in April 1958 featured Edward German's *Merrie England*, its first Derry performance for twenty years.

A number of those in the new society had been members of the Philharmonic before the war, notably Muriel Anderson, the violinist and leader of the orchestra, and her brother Willie, also a violinist. Another long-serving musician was Nellie McGhee. Like the Philharmonic, the society's patrons were the Duke and Duchess of Abercorn, and it had a large subscribing, but non-performing membership. Thanks to an annual grant of around £250 from CEMA, it avoided incurring the large debts of its predecessor. Yet although the Cathedral society was in many ways a reincarnation of the Philharmonic, and had a similar repertoire of oratorios and light operettas, its membership and office-bearers were almost exclusively Protestant. It did not have the cross-community mix of the earlier society – an indication of how, by the 1950s, musical life had become polarised into separate Protestant and Catholic music societies and choirs. And it was from the latter, St Eugene's Cathedral Choir, that there came one of Derry's most beloved singers, Josef Locke.

Josef Locke

Locke was born Joseph McLaughlin in Creggan Street in 1918, one of eight children. In 1944, his stage name was shortened to 'Josef Locke' to fit on a theatre playbill and he retained the name, thinking it more exotic than his birth name. After some years as a policeman – and earning the nickname 'The Singing Bobby' – Locke accepted an offer to sing opera in Dublin. There, he was advised by John McCormack to concentrate on a 'lighter repertoire', as McCormack himself had done.

Success came quickly. Within a few years, Locke was singing at the Victoria Palace in London and working in Blackpool with George Formby. By the later 1940s he was at the height of his popularity: he had a charismatic rapport with his audiences, sold over one million records and was reputedly the highest paid entertainer in England, earning £100,000 per year. Yet with characteristic generosity he still returned frequently to his hometown to give concerts for local groups, such as the concert he gave in the Guildhall in January 1953 in aid of Derry Football Club, which sold out within three hours and attracted a capacity 850 audience. His career took a downward turn in 1958, when he was unable to pay a large bill for tax arrears from the Inland Revenue. He fled England for the Republic of Ireland, where he dabbled with farming and kept race horses, but he never regained his former position as a singer.[92]

Barbirolli, Cafolla and the Hallé Orchestra

In May 1951, there was a concert in the Guildhall by the Hallé Orchestra conducted by Sir John Barbirolli. The visit, part of the Empire Year celebrations, was jointly organised by the Feis committee and the Londonderry Music Circle. Orlando

Programme of the 1951 Hallé Orchestra concert, autographed by John Barbirolli. (Author's collection)

Cafolla, who had known Barbirolli from his days in Manchester before the war, was invited to 'guest' in the violins for the Guildhall concert and Lady Barbirolli made him a gift of Barbirolli's own violin bow as a memento of the occasion.[93] The programme included Tchaikovsky's *Romeo and Juliet Overture* and Beethoven's *Seventh Symphony*. As an encore, Barbirolli led the orchestra in Hamilton Harty's arrangement of the 'Londonderry Air', a particular favourite with the local audience and one which, according to the *Sentinel*, left 'hardly a dry eye in the Assembly Hall ... Very seldom had music ever created the same wave of emotion in a Londonderry audience.' A five-minute ovation followed and Barbirolli was recalled to the platform several times. He gave an impromptu speech, praising the acoustics of the Guildhall, which he thought 'admirably suited for musical performance' and 'even better than the Festival Hall in London'. This, as one might imagine, was well received.

Although there were other classical music concerts in the Guildhall during the 1950s, there were sometimes complaints in the *Sentinel* that the music was 'too highbrow for ordinary people'. Tickets were usually priced at 7s 6d, 5s and 2s 6d, with 6d for programmes, making them expensive for most working people. That was, of course, if work could be found. Unemployment in the city stood at well over 35 per cent of the adult male population for most of the decade.

Among these concerts were several by the Raidió Éireann Symphony Orchestra. Their programming was adventurous, in regularly including original music by contemporary Irish composers such as Brian Boydell and John Larchet. The City of Belfast Orchestra visited Derry too, and significantly, on their second visit, in November 1956, the soloist was Lawrence Glover in Prokofiev's *Third Piano Concerto*.

Lawrence Glover

Glover came from a Derry family.[94] He was an outstanding pianist. It was said that Gordon Green, his teacher at the Manchester College of Music, rated his talent above that of his fellow student John Ogdon. In its review of the concert, the *Sentinel* praised him cautiously for 'his interesting interpretation of a rather difficult work', and of course played up his Derry origins. Overall, the concert was 'splendid', the paper commending the orchestra for 'a very noticeable improvement in technique' from the strings, but adding, lest that should go to their heads, that they had 'on one occasion sounded a little off tone'. Glover was later appointed to the Royal Scottish Academy of Music and Drama in Glasgow, and became Head of Piano there. He occasionally toured as a concert pianist, but increasingly found greater fulfilment in teaching.[95]

Willie Loughlin's first opportunity to sing solo with a full professional orchestra was in October 1958, when the City of Belfast Orchestra was again at the Guildhall. He sang two arias from Mozart's *The Magic Flute*, while Joseph Cooper (many years later the host of the BBC2 programme *Face the Music*) was the soloist in Beethoven's *Emperor Piano Concerto*. This time, the *Sentinel* was severe about both orchestra and pianist. The playing of the Belfast Orchestra 'could have been better', while Cooper's performance 'lacked the colour and sparkle of the performance in Belfast'.

A few months earlier, in May 1958, there had been the first Guildhall concert by the BBC Symphony Orchestra, conducted by Rudolf Schwarz. The concert programme was one of the first in Derry to ask patrons to 'refrain from smoking' during the performance. Until then, smoking at concerts and the theatre was quite common. Indeed, during the 1930s the practice was *de rigueur* at Derry's 'smoking concerts'. By the later 1960s, however, the smoking of cigars and cigarettes was forbidden at most concerts (although it took another two decades before tobacco advertising was banned altogether from concert programmes).[96]

Apart from the larger orchestral concerts at the Guildhall, Magee hosted smaller chamber concerts during the winter months. The North-West Music Society, founded in 1957 by Redmond Friel, James MacCafferty and Dr McCallum-Walker, engaged many well-known musicians for the latter, including guitarist Julian Bream in January 1958. However, the fact that orchestral concerts and some smaller concerts were run in association with CEMA, which required that the national anthem be played at the concerts, alienated Nationalists in Derry and led to the events being shunned by many Catholics.

Pianist Lawrence Glover (1931-1988) photographed with Leon Spierer, leader of the Berlin Philharmonic Orchestra during their 1974 tour of Northern Ireland. Their itinerary included a chamber music recital in Derry, birthplace of Glover's father. (By kind permission of the Arts Council of Northern Ireland)

It was quite otherwise at St Columb's Hall, which provided 'live' entertainments, sandwiched between its film shows. Its Boxing Day concerts, January pantomimes, St Patrick's Day concerts and annual musicals showcased local Catholic talent. These actors and musicians did not belong to a specific society but were drawn together by Edward O'Doherty and his wife Rose, a leading music teacher. In February 1958, for example, they staged a two-week run of the musical *The King and I*. Special buses ran from Buncrana and Moville, attracting as many people from Donegal as from the city itself.

James MacCafferty

Derry's Catholics have long had their own musical leaders, and none was more influential than James MacCafferty, who directed and dominated the community's musical life for five decades. MacCafferty was a musical polymath: a singing and piano teacher, choir trainer, accompanist, conductor and musical director. His career began in the mid-1930s and he was still teaching music a few weeks before his death. MacCafferty formed, trained and conducted almost twenty choirs, and he was the linchpin of both the Feis Dhoire (as accompanist) and St Columb's Hall (as its musical director).

Unlike other key musicians in Derry's history who came to the city from elsewhere – Malmene, H.B. Phillips, Daniel Jones, Joseph O'Brien, and MacCafferty's contemporary Michael Franklin – MacCafferty had deep roots in Derry. His parents were local people and had first met during rehearsals for O'Brien's operas in the 1920s. His father Patrick had sung in the 1898 and 1900 performances of Conaghan's *'98 Cantata*, while his mother, Cissie Meehan, was a well-known amateur soprano. Theirs was a 'musical' marriage, and James inherited both their love of music and a gift for teaching and choir training. And it was as choirmaster that MacCafferty made his most lasting contribution to music in the city. Indeed, it was mainly due to him that Derry developed its twentieth-century reputation for choir singing. He founded the Little Gaelic Singers in 1956, in partnership with Brendan De Glin, an Irish-dance teacher, and together they toured America four times, playing for presidents and movie stars. The MacCafferty Singers followed next, an amalgamation of the male voice choir of St Eugene's Cathedral and the (by then teenage) members of The Little Gaelic Singers. All his choirs sang from memory in public, as MacCafferty felt that the use of scores hindered communication between singer and audience.

MacCafferty was a skilled performer in his own right but always preferred a supporting role. Although a versatile pianist with a gift for sight-reading and transposing at sight, he preferred to be out of the limelight. In the 1950s, his friendship with Josef Locke led to his being in demand as the latter's accompanist for several summers in Blackpool.

Self-Help in the 1960s

In the 1960s, Derry experienced a series of economic body blows. Decline in the shirt industry and the closure of the shipping link between Glasgow and Derry brought huge loss of employment in both factories and the port of Derry. Most painful of all was the recommendation of the 1965 Lockwood Report that the main campus of the New University of Ulster, with its associated job opportunities, be located in Coleraine rather than Derry. Indeed it was a double blow, as the university opened a purpose-built theatre on the new campus. Here was confirmation that the Northern Irish establishment, including its arts arm, the Arts Council of Northern Ireland (ACNI), as CEMA was now called, had given up on 'west of the Bann'.

Thrown back on their own resources, the people of Derry pursued a policy of self-help, creating their own entertainments, in concerts, variety shows, pantomimes, drama productions and musicals. 'All-Star Variety Concerts' were already running in St Columb's Hall in the early 1960s, organised by Fr Aidan Mulvey. He put together a varied line-up for his Sunday shows: well-known Irish singers such as Eileen Donaghey and Nita Norry; Belfast comedian Frank Carson, billed as the 'Variety King'; local man Don O'Doherty as compère, and James MacCafferty as musical director.

In 1962, the concerts were renamed the 'Sunday Night Variety Shows' by Fr Edward Daly, then curate at St Eugene's Cathedral, and given a new lease of life.

For six years the shows started in autumn and reached a 'Grand Finale Concert' with a talent show on the last Sunday before Lent. For each show there was a 'big star': from Ireland, actor Milo O'Shea, singer Ruby Murray, crooner Val Doonican and the folk group the Clancy Brothers; and from further afield, Roy Orbison, Jim Reeves, the Bachelors, Scottish singer Moira Anderson and The Seekers. Such was the reputation of the 'Sunday Night Shows' and the size of their audiences, that Daly was able to book artists from television's *Sunday Night at the Palladium* and have them appear on his show the following Sunday. All acts were supported by MacCafferty and his MacCafferty Singers, Little Gaelic Singers, the Ten Columbians, and the Sunday Revue Orchestra, with Frank Carson as resident 'variety entertainer'.

The Derry Pantomime Players, who produced annual pantomimes in St Columb's Hall, were an offshoot of the 'Sunday Night' concerts. Their greatest coup was persuading Frank Carson to appear in *Ali Babi and the Forty Thieves* in January 1964. Although Carson broke his wrist towards the end of the run, he refused to stand down. Eighteen thousand people attended the pantomime, one of the most successful shows in Derry's theatrical history.

The Feis Dhoire continued to enjoy phenomenal success. Waldemar Rosen, conductor of the RTÉ Singers, was music adjudicator in 1962 and praised the 'extraordinarily good singing' of the Colmcille Mixed Choir. He lamented that the city had no choral society, and argued that the formation of a 'well-organised' society with 'practices and performances all year round' would lead to a musical revival in the city. Obviously no one had told Rosen of the St Columb's Cathedral Oratorio Society (renamed St Columb's Cathedral Musical Society in 1956), which was still going strong and celebrating its tenth anniversary that year. Another music society did start up in Derry later in 1962, but it had nothing to do with the Feis Dhoire.

The Londonderry Light Opera Society

The Londonderry Light Opera Society was founded by New Zealander Belinda Story, who had come to Derry as a teacher in 1959. Known as Linda, she had a passion for Gilbert and Sullivan operettas. So, with teaching colleague Mary McCann, she gathered together eleven enthusiasts, including Fred Logan, Scott Marshall, Donald Hill and Edgar Bigger, and started auditions and casting for their first production. Rehearsals were held in each other's houses and in the vestry in Christ Church. From this small nucleus of friends developed fifty years of Derry musicals, which continue to the present day in the Londonderry Musical Society.

Their first production, in May 1963, was a two-night run of the short Gilbert and Sullivan operetta *Trial by Jury*, supplemented with some other Gilbert and Sullivan songs, in Londonderry High School. At first there was an acute shortage of men for the chorus but gradually their numbers increased. The society grew quickly and soon

Against the Odds, 1945-1979

The Londonderry Orchestra, led by Muriel Anderson (pictured right), taking a bow at the Strand Road (Second Derry) Choir's performance of Handel's Messiah in the Guildhall in 1954. The conductor was Winifred Thompson. (By kind permission of David Burke)

had over 100 members. They rented a one-room 'studio' in Great James Street, on the top floor of an electrical shop beside Third Derry, and there they rehearsed to a piano for their second production, *HMS Pinafore*. It ran in the Guildhall for three nights in May 1964, with eleven principals and a mixed chorus of thirty. Amongst the leads were Scott Marshall, Donald Hill and Billy Carruthers, pillars of the society for the next thirty years. A twenty-four-piece ensemble called 'The Londonderry Orchestra' was put together for the performance: eleven strings, five woodwind, six brass and two percussion, with Mrs Hazel Gordon on piano. It included several members of the Britannia Band. The leader, as with so many other Derry orchestras, was Muriel Anderson.

By 1966, the society was searching for premises with better rehearsal space. With the help of the Londonderry Port Commission, the society rented the vacant 'Derrycraft' premises, above a grain store on the Strand Road. That same year, four of its actors were judged 'outstanding' in *The Mikado* at the Waterford Light Opera Festival and Scott Marshall won the 'Best Director's Award'. Those early years were the heyday of the Londonderry Amateur Operatic Society (its name since 1965). As soon as booking for its musicals opened, queues formed outside Beethoven House in a rush to buy the best seats in the Guildhall. Leading members of city drama clubs helped out behind the scenes. Fred Logan of CDDC was their skilled set builder and served for several seasons as stage manager, while fellow actor Joey Glover helped out as répétiteur.

The North-West Arts Festivals

The first publicly funded arts festival in Derry, encompassing drama, music and visual art, in April 1964, was organised by a local Arts Festival Council chaired by Professor F.J. Healey of Magee. It was funded by the City Corporation and The Honourable The Irish Society, with an ACNI guarantee against losses. Highlights included a 'Television Concert' in the Guildhall by the BBC Northern Ireland Light Orchestra, which included the first showing of *A City Solitary*, a film with screenplay by John Hume and music by Redmond Friel. The soprano Joan Hammond gave a concert a week later; there was a scramble for tickets and the concert sold out within hours.

There were plays by CDDC, the St Columb's College Union Drama Group and the Young Irish Theatre. The local press reviewed all the performances and, although Caoilte had long since departed for Dublin, the *Journal*'s drama critic continued in his acerbic tradition. The Magee Drama Society's production of John Osborne's *Look Back in Anger* was described as 'over-ambitious', and the young actors as 'obviously out of their depth'. The St Columb's Group was the only Catholic drama group to participate in the festival. The old standoff over the national anthem persisted. Aware of people's sensitivities, the festival committee compromised by agreeing to leave the decision whether to play it or not up to individual event-givers. But when the festival ended with a 'Masked Ball' in the Guildhall, some middle-class Catholics were in a quandary whether or not to attend an event where they knew the anthem would be played. Referring to the Masked Ball, an *Irish Times* journalist commented, with tongue in cheek, 'I foresee all sorts of delightful opportunities for involuntary ecumenism.' He could not have foreseen how masks would be used in Derry in the decades that followed.

The second festival, in April 1967, opened with the presentation of a painting and original music to the Festival Council. The painting, entitled 'Phoenix Derry '67', was by Derry artist Brian Ferran; the music was 'Air and Eight Variants in Dance Form' by Redmond Friel.[97] Riding a wave of optimism, three of Derry's drama societies joined forces to form the West Ulster Festival Theatre Company. The combined talents of the YMCA Players, St Columb's past pupils and CDDC performed G.B. Shaw's *John Bull's Other Island* under director Jack Gallagher. The festival concluded with Bach's *St John's Passion* by the St Columb's Cathedral Music Society, conducted by Havelock Nelson. There were twelve other events, the festival having greatly expanded under its new chairman, veteran actor Sidney Buchanan. Overall it was deemed a huge success, with the organisers looking ahead three years to the next festival.

The festival had included a Viennese concert by the newly formed Ulster Orchestra, their third visit to the city. Their first concert, in September 1966, was an all-Beethoven programme in the Guildhall, and they returned three months later to accompany the St Columb's Cathedral Music Society in Handel's *Messiah*. This forty-strong ensemble – Northern Ireland's first full-time professional orchestra – replaced the City of Belfast Orchestra. It became a frequent visitor to Derry, often in demand to accompany the city's music societies.

By the later 1960s, Derry had an established calendar of musical entertainments. St Columb's Hall had its Christmas pantomime, followed by the Sunday Night Variety concerts and the St Patrick's Day concert. The Feiseanna then took over the Guildhall in Easter week and in early summer. An easing in Catholic attitudes towards the Londonderry Feis meant that both communities now competed together. The Londonderry Amateur Operatic Society staged their operettas in May, followed in autumn by the North-West Music Society's chamber concerts. Finally, the St Columb's Cathedral Music Society presented its Christmas oratorio.

But these were mainly local events, staged by city people. In the absence of arts leadership from the city fathers, Derry people had had to construct their own cultural life. The new order differed from that of former years. Gone were the large music societies with their twice-yearly concerts, wealthy patrons, prestigious operatic artistes and organist-conductors. In their place were variety shows, talent contests, pantomimes and musicals, and oratorios by a smaller choral society. The cultural leaders were no longer the church organists, as in the 1920s and '30s. Instead it was drama and music teachers who started and led amateur activity: James MacCafferty, Redmond Friel and Belinda Story in music, and Fred Logan, Sidney Buchanan, Michael Gillen and Eithne McCloskey in drama. It was their teaching, enthusiasm and passion for music and drama which kept Derry culturally alive during the depressed 1960s.

What Derry lacked above all was a purpose-built theatre, and a small, informal group of campaigners, including Brian Friel and Risteard Mac Gabhann, had begun meeting regularly at Magee to discuss possible ways of bringing this about. Other leading voices openly criticised Londonderry Corporation's perceived inaction in this matter. In 1968, Scott McCarter, chairman of LAOS, complained that 'little had been done by the City Fathers to improve the facilities [of the Guildhall]'. He added, 'Of course what we really want is our own theatre. Then we would have some chance of giving the public the shows which they would like to see. Any kind donor willing to head a subscription list with, say, £5,000?' His invitation went unheeded.

Post-war Derry was characterised by economic decline and social deprivation, with political stagnation and blatant gerrymandering over four decades inducing despair and frustration. Out of this frustration arose the Civil Rights Movement. And it was a banned Civil Rights march on Saturday, 5 October 1968, that marked the beginning of the Troubles in Derry and in Northern Ireland as a whole. Over the weekend, violence erupted on the city streets and was relayed on television screens worldwide.

From Farquhar to Field Day

The Collapse of the Old Order

On Sunday night, 6 October 1968, The Dubliners folk group played to a packed house at St Columb's Hall while disorder raged nearby. The performance was quite unlike their usual uninhibited and joyous renderings of Irish songs, and they were no doubt glad to escape back to Dublin later that night. With political turmoil continuing, the city's governing body, the Londonderry Corporation, was abolished on 22 November, to be replaced two months later by the Londonderry Development Commission.

Despite the deteriorating political situation, the third North-West Arts Festival, run jointly by ACNI and the new Londonderry Development Commission, went ahead in April 1970. It had an ambitious programme, with an Ulster Orchestra concert, an all-Beethoven recital by German pianist Michael Braunfels, and Bach's *St Matthew's Passion*. Not surprisingly, the festival incurred a substantial loss: costing £1,981 but taking in only £582. Although originally envisaged as a triennial event, this festival was the last in Derry for several years.

The 1970s brought ever-rising levels of conflict and violence, which shook Derry to its foundations. In particular, Bloody Sunday on 31 January 1972 set off a decade of bombings and killings that resulted in the city losing more than a tenth of its buildings to bombs – more than any other town or city in Northern Ireland – and cost the lives of 353 people from Derry (out of the 3,633 in Northern Ireland who died in the conflict between 1969 and 1999). In a major movement of population, the majority of Protestants on the west bank of the Foyle – around 15,000 – left their homes for the Waterside, leaving the city side almost totally Catholic.

The commercial effects of this were felt very quickly. In 1971, Ken Phillips, nephew of H.B. Phillips and owner of the Beethoven House music shop, said that it

A billhead from Phillips' Beethoven House. The shop finally closed in 1980, after almost ninety years. Latterly it sold smaller electrical goods as well as pianos and sheet music. (By kind permission of the Foyle Civic Trust)

had experienced a 25 per cent drop in turnover in the previous year. His shop windows had been broken twice, the premises hit by an incendiary bomb and then raided by gangs six or seven times. Understandably he had boarded up the shop windows and was running down his stock. The final straw came in January 1975, when a bomb in a nearby alleyway caused major damage to the building. The shop limped along for a few more years before it finally closed in 1980.

Amid the gathering gloom, there were occasional shafts of light. The singer 'Dana', otherwise local girl Rosemary Brown, won the Eurovision Song Contest in 1970 with 'All Kinds of Everything'. As a teenager she had won many prizes at the Feiseanna and appeared regularly at St Columb's Hall concerts and pantomimes. When she returned to Derry from her Amsterdam victory, it was a moment of rejoicing for thousands in the beleaguered city. Success in the Eurovision Song Contest was nothing new for Derry. Three years earlier the composer of the winning Eurovision entry 'Puppet on a String' was Phil Coulter, also from Derry. Coulter, a student of St Columb's College in the 1950s, also composed one of the iconic songs of the Troubles about his native city, 'The Town I Loved So Well'.

The '71 Players and The Theatre Club

In the early 1970s, Edward Daly was among the first to recognise and harness the power of community involvement in culture as a means of social regeneration. In September 1970, he held a meeting in St Columb's Hall, hoping to start some musical activity for the women of his parish. It resulted in the formation of a choir and a drama society, the Colmcille Ladies' Choir and the '71 Players.

The '71 Players took their name from the year of their first production, Lennox Robinson's *Drama at Inish*, staged in the Little Theatre. This was the renamed minor hall of St Columb's Hall, hastily refurbished as a 100-seat auditorium. Here the '71 Players rehearsed several nights a week and presented three, sometimes four, productions a year. At first they concentrated on plays by Irish authors like Brian Friel, Hugh Leonard and John B. Keane. Friel was a particular favourite, and the '71 Players often gave Derry audiences their first taste of a new Friel play. But their repertoire soon expanded to include other twentieth-century playwrights, such as Arthur Miller and J.B. Priestley. Among their members were the cream of the city's amateur actors: local teacher Scott Marshall, Anne Craig, Carmel McCafferty and Pauline Ross, then working at the Derry Credit Union, the community 'bank' set up by John Hume. By the time of their fifteenth production, Hugh Leonard's *Da*, in spring 1975, the group had over seventy members and several plays in rehearsal simultaneously.

The Theatre Club, which also began in 1971, was equally busy, staging four plays in its first year and every subsequent year for the next decade, by playwrights ranging from Muriel Spark to Ugo Betti. They began with Brian Friel's *Lovers* in February

A poster for the Theatre Club's production of Patrick Kavanagh's Tarry Flynn, *staged in the Little Theatre, part of St Columb's Hall, in October 1975. (By kind permission of Pauline Ross)*

1971, directed by Sean McMahon. He was to direct their productions on a number of occasions. Other directors rose from their own ranks, including well-known local actors Scott Marshall, Art Byrne and Eddie Mailey.

Few actors or musicians of note visited Derry during the Troubles. An exception was Belfast-born actress Siobhan McKenna, who gave two appearances at the Shantallow Festival in July 1972. The first was her own one-woman show; in the second she acted in several scenes from Brian Friel's *The Loves of Cass Maguire*, assisted by members of the Theatre Club. In those dark days, Derry's drama societies provided entertainment for local audiences and a social outlet for their amateur actors, but, more importantly, they kept drama and theatre-going alive at a time when few professional drama companies came to the city.

Likewise, music was kept alive by Derry's organists, singers and music teachers – Billy West, Willie Laughlin, Michael Mason and James MacCafferty – whose organisation of concerts and organ recitals helped maintain some semblance of 'normality' in the midst of mayhem. The North-West Music Society continued to promote concerts but had to contend with bomb scares, tightened security measures and falling audiences. There was little financial encouragement to keep going. In 1972/3, ACNI awarded them a meagre £50, only £5 more than it gave to the 39th Old Boys' Flute Band in Belfast. (The Belfast Philharmonic Society received £7,250.) There was a marginal improvement in 1973/4: the Music Society received £463, the band £95.

'To see how a town could be brought to its knees'

As the Troubles worsened after Bloody Sunday, the activities of Derry's larger drama and music societies largely ground to a halt, each having suffered in its own peculiar way. CDDC lost all its scenery, stage equipment and costumes in 'a malicious fire', forcing its closure. The Amateur Opera Society suspended productions between 1972 and 1974, and the Feis followed suit. Its losses were both material and personal. Its office in Waterloo Place was bombed, destroying many years' irreplaceable archives. Then its treasurer, Joey Glover (b.1916), the accomplished singer, organist, actor and compère of the Guildhall wartime concerts, was shot dead by the IRA. On the evening of his death, he was due to act in Jean Anouilh's *Antigone* at Magee, directed by Scott Marshall. The performance was cancelled as a mark of respect. When it was performed a month later, in Glover's memory his part was left unfilled. The Feis Dhoire also suspended activity in 1972. The Guildhall, its home for fifty years, was bombed twice that year and rendered unusable. The Britannia Brass and Reed Band stopped concerts too, as members were unable to attend practices in their city-centre rooms. The St Columb's Cathedral Music Society disbanded, never to regroup.

By the mid-1970s, few outside music or drama groups were willing to come to Derry. Media coverage of the city's relentless decline and the threat of disruption by bomb scares or actual explosions put off most performers. Nonetheless, ACNI continued to maintain its touring schedule of orchestral concerts, opera, plays, ballet, exhibitions, films and literature readings. Around 100 groups a year played in provincial theatres, town halls and makeshift venues across Northern Ireland. But they tended to be smaller ensembles, rather than the larger visiting orchestras of the 1950s. They were mostly Northern Ireland artists too, such as Havelock Nelson's Studio Opera Group, which brought Mozart's *Don Giovanni* to Magee in February 1973. The following year, their two-night run of Rossini's *Barber of Seville* attracted a large turnout of 440 people. This company and Theatre North were Derry's most faithful visitors, their performances in Magee providing some relief in what was otherwise a cultural wilderness. But often Derry was omitted from ACNI tours, as was the case with some of Lawrence Glover's chamber concert tours in the mid-1970s – a surprising omission given his links with the city. Most ACNI events were held at Magee, as the Guildhall was undergoing repair after its double bombing. It was also considered a safer venue, its location away from the city centre making it less likely to be bombed.

Audiences, understandably, were low. A piano recital by Peter Katin on 12 June 1973 attracted 130, whereas the following night 213 people attended the same concert in the small town of Glenarm. A touring ACNI literature production, *At Home to The Honourable*, on 7 March 1975, was attended by just six people. Its next performance in Holywood attracted an audience of eighty.

The Beginnings of Recovery

The first hint of recovery was an announcement in 1975 that a new umbrella arts body, the Londonderry Arts Association, was to be set up. Then Derry's three key arts organisations started up again: LAOS and Feis Dhoire in 1975, and the Londonderry Feis in 1976. LAOS was first, staging a one-week run of *The Merry Widow* in Glendermott Intermediate School in February, which reunited many actors and singers from its 1960s operettas. (In 1969, the society had diversified away from Gilbert and Sullivan to stage other musicals, starting with *Oklahoma* and *The Gypsy Baron*.) Their new musical director was Jim Goodman, a veteran member of the Britannia Brass and Reed Band.[98] In March, the Feis Dhoire was relaunched, with competitions spread across five venues. Three years after its actual fiftieth anniversary year (1972, when it was suspended) it celebrated its Golden Jubilee. Redmond Friel composed a *Choral Scena* for the celebrations, which were officially opened by Bishop Edward Daly and the Mayor of Derry. The Feis Dhoire seemed to have taken on a new lease of life, with 6,000 entrants from America, England and Ireland; a return to the heady days of the early 1960s.

A Theatre Club production of Brian Friel's Philadelphia, Here I Come! *in the Little Theatre in December 1975. (By kind permission of Pauline Ross)*

In 1976, there were other signs of progress. In January, the St Mary's Choral Society pantomime attracted 19,000 people to nineteen performances and there was a LAOS production of *Hello Dolly*. These were followed by the '71 Players in Friel's *Freedom of the City* (its amateur premiere), J.B. Keane's *The Field*, and J.B. Priestley's *An Inspector Calls*. The Theatre Club also performed three plays, one each by Shakespeare, Arthur Miller and Brendan Behan, a continuation of their tradition of ambitious and eclectic programmes which had seen twenty-two different plays staged since their founding in 1971. CDDC signalled its return to 'business as usual' with an anniversary staging of *Friends and Relations*, their inaugural production in 1946. And Dublin's Abbey Theatre gave its only Northern Ireland performance in Derry, in Eamon Kelly's one-man show *Bless Me Father*, in a three-night run at Magee.

The Foyle Singers kept up Derry's tradition of choir-singing by winning the 1976 Oireachtas competition in Dublin. So many choirs (thirty-one) from Derry were entered for the competitions in the Feis Dhoire that there had to be preliminary rounds 'to ease the burden' during Feis week. An early indication of the 'American money' that would later flow into the city was the award of $1,500 to the Derry School of Irish Harping on Strand Road. When the Londonderry Feis resumed, all three of Derry's main music organisations were up and running. It restarted in a shortened two-day format but with the familiar name of Claude Herdman as Honorary Secretary. Soon, most of its competitions were restored, with the older favourites of ballet and elocution drawing a new generation of young dancers and actors. However premature, therefore, there was some justification for the City Council's decision to designate 'The City of Song and Dance' as the theme of the 1976 'Civic Week'.

There were also signs of a new commitment by ACNI to the arts in Derry. The Derry Players received £550 from ACNI in 1978/9. The next year, the North-West Music Society was awarded £2,549 in its twenty-first season, a huge increase on previous years. The new emphasis on 'regional arts', outlined two years earlier by ACNI Director Kenneth Jamison, aimed to provide 'equity of opportunity for people throughout the province'. Coupled with this was first mention of 'community development in the arts'. Community arts were nothing new in Derry, which had been adept in creating its own entertainments. There were any number of 'community' cultural groups already present in its choirs, music societies, Feiseanna committees, drama societies and writers' groups. What the city lacked was a theatre.

In the twenty years since the *Sentinel* had first called for a theatre in Derry, it had received the backing of the local press and of numerous private individuals, all of whom were ignored by the Stormont Government and the City Corporation. In the 1970s, however, pressure for a new theatre began to build. In December 1973, the Theatre Action Group (TAG) was founded at Magee by a small circle of drama enthusiasts, including Scott Marshall, Michael Gillen and Risteard Mac Gabhann. Four months later, the City Council gave its 'official support' to the campaign with a £300 grant towards the launch of a worldwide appeal for funds. It was then estimated that

Ticket for the City of Derry Drama Club's May 1976 production of Friends and Relations, *a repeat of their inaugural play thirty years earlier. (By kind permission of Derry City Museum Service)*

the theatre would cost just £200,000. Within Derry itself, fundraising for the theatre was vigorous, with 'bricks' of the new theatre offered for sale. *The Irish Times* boosted morale by reporting that a theatre was 'in the offing' and with rumours that a model of the 'proposed theatre' was stored somewhere at ACNI headquarters in Riddell Hall.

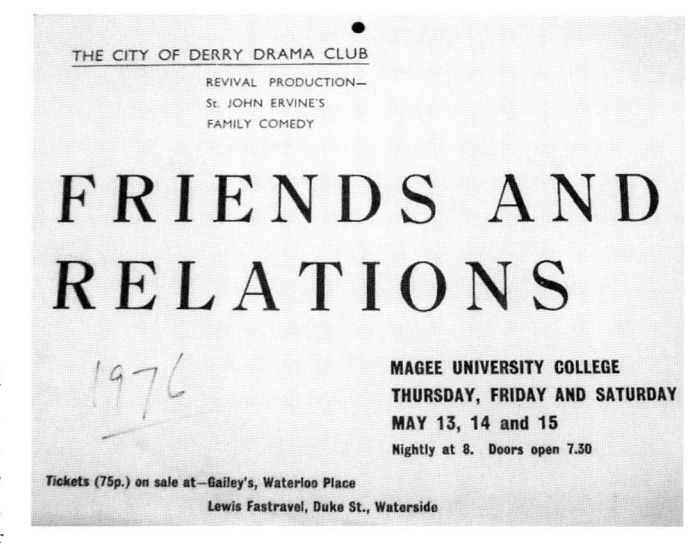

TAG kept the pressure up by organising a week-long arts festival, including a 'Theatre in the Community' symposium, at Magee in 1975. Eminent speakers were invited, including playwright Denis Johnston, Abbey Theatre director Thomas MacAnna, and the Derry poet and critic Seamus Deane. The *Journal* hailed the event as 'particularly appropriate', given that the City Council was 'currently considering plans for a new civic theatre in the city', a reference to the Council's inclusion of a theatre in its five-year strategic plan. The Council, it is true, also considered short-term fixes, such as the leasing and refurbishment of the vacant YMCA Hall on Derry's East Wall. This, however, came to nothing.

As the 1970s drew to a close, hopes were buoyant. The last ACNI report of the decade spoke of '[the] major scheme for a new theatre at Londonderry' being at 'sketch-plan stage', intimating that it would be built by the mid-1980s. But with no political solution to the Troubles in sight – and the 1981 Hunger Strike was to signal an intensification of violence across Northern Ireland – whether these plans would ever be acted upon was one of many uncertainties in Derry's future.

Eight

THE FOYLE RENAISSANCE, 1980-1995

The announcement on 6 June 1980 that the city's Guildhall had been chosen by Field Day productions for the world premiere of Brian Friel's new play, *Translations*, was a turning point for the arts in Derry. The novelty of having Friel's play opening in the city caught the imagination of both Derry newspapers, which reported on the preparations for the production in obsessive detail. There were photographs of the Guildhall stage under renovation and lengthy interviews with the actors, publicity assistants, costume and set designers – a distant echo of the cultivated hullabaloo that had preceded Madame Albani's visit to the city in 1892. Although there have been arguments, since, over Field Day's long-term legacy, it is undeniable that the staging of *Translations* in Derry ushered in a period of cultural renewal in the city, a veritable Foyle Renaissance after the doldrums of the 1930s and the post-war years. Nor was the choice of the Guildhall, for so many years the seat of Unionist government and the perceived home of 'Derry-mandering', without its significance: it seemed to herald a new era in which Nationalists and Unionists, instead of keeping apart, would work together and acknowledge and develop their joint cultural heritage.

The opening night of *Translations*, 23 September 1980, was a festive occasion which brought together Ireland's theatrical and literary elites, and the leaders of Derry's cultural and political life. Apart from Friel himself, there was Seamus Heaney and Nell McCafferty, with others from south of the border (Cyril Cusack, Thomas Kilroy from Galway and the Abbey Theatre's Joe Dowling), alongside John Hume and Marlene Jefferson, the Ulster Unionist Mayor of Derry, and city councillors. For Cusack, it may have had a special poignancy, returning to the city where he had been a child actor on the Opera House stage, more than sixty years before. According to *The Irish Times*, it was 'a night of high excitement and deep emotion … Derry on show and the show was for Derry.' It was a welcome change for the city to be

The Foyle Renaissance, 1980-1995

FIELD DAY THEATRE Co.

BOOK NOW FOR
TRANSLATIONS
by BRIAN FRIEL

**WORLD PREMIERE
IN DERRY CITY GUILDHALL
TUESDAY, 23rd SEPTEMBER, 1980**
at 8 p.m.
**CONTINUES UNTIL AND INCLUDING
SATURDAY, SEPTEMBER 27**
(Late comers not admitted until interval)

Booking at the Orchard Gallery (Telephone: Derry 69675)
Booked tickets must be collected before 7.30 p.m. on evening of performance

TICKETS: £2.50 (Students and O.A.P.s £1.50)

Directed by *ART O BRIAIN*
Designed by *CONSOLATA BOYLE*
Lighting by *RUPERT MURRAY*

THE CAST:

★ LIAM NEESON   ★ RAY McANALLY
★ STEPHEN REA   ★ ROY HANLON
★ BRENDA SCALLON   ★ ANN HASSON
★ SHAUN SCOTT   ★ NUALA HAYES
★ MICK LALLY   ★ DAVID HEAP

*Press advertisement for Brian Friel's Translations. Its premiere, in September 1980, began Derry's cultural rebirth. (*Derry Journal, *19 September 1980)*

receiving attention for theatre, rather than exclusively for the riots and shootings that had provided the real-life dramas and tragedies on its streets. *Translations* had an outstanding cast in Stephen Rea, Liam Neeson, Ray McAnally and Mick Lally; a group of actors whose like had not been seen in Derry since the visits of Anew McMaster, Hilton Edwards and Micheál Mac Liammóir in the 1940s. But there were local actors too: Ann Hasson, daughter of local tenor Larry Hasson, as the mute Sarah, and Fermanagh-born Brenda Scallon as Bridget.[99]

If Field Day was one of the cornerstones around which the Foyle Renaissance was built, scarcely less important were the many arts festivals and new arts centres. And, unlike previous eras, much of this cultural rebuilding was started and maintained by local people. Pauline Ross founded The Playhouse Arts Centre, which was followed by similar community-based ventures, the Nerve Centre, Verbal Arts Centre and An Gaelaras. In the two decades leading up to the millennium, hardly a year seemed to go by without some new landmark production, the opening of a new arts venue or some further step towards the 'normalisation' of Derry's musical and theatre life. In addition to long-established institutions like the Feis Dhoire Colmcille, the Londonderry Feis and the Londonderry Amateur Operatic Society, a newcomer, the Classical Music Society, began a series of ambitious concert seasons. So for all the continuing violence of the 1980s, the Derry theatre- or concert-goer enjoyed a range of drama and music such as there hadn't been in the city since the mid-1920s.

Yet there was still no venue capable of hosting major productions, the long-awaited theatre still on the 'drawing board' awaiting funding. In the interim, Derry City Council bought the Rialto, latterly known as the ABC Cinema, and renamed it 'The Rialto Entertainment Centre', a continuation of the 'make do and mend' policy that had characterised Derry's cultural life for so many decades.

Brian Friel and Field Day

Brian Friel was born in Omagh, County Tyrone, and attended St Columb's College in Derry, an *alma mater* he shares with writers Seamus Heaney and Seamus Deane, and architects Liam McCormick and Tom Mullarkey. He began writing short stories and plays in the 1950s, but *Philadelphia, Here I Come!* (1964) was his first international success. Since then, Friel has written twenty-four original plays, several of them set in the fictional town of Ballybeg, and adaptations of works by Chekhov and Ibsen. Recognition of his status as Ireland's greatest living playwright has come with his membership of Aosdána and election as one of its 'Saoi', the highest honour that can be bestowed by fellow Aosdána.[100] Since his schooldays, Friel has lived in or around Derry. He was a school teacher in the city through the 1950s, and since 1960 has lived in Derry, and latterly across the border in Donegal, on his earnings from his writing.

Brian Friel (b. 1929) at the Charles Macklin Festival in October 2011. (By kind permission of Sean Beattie, Macklin Festival)

Translations was the first Field Day production. The company name was loosely derived from the names 'Friel' and 'Rea', evoking both the earthiness of the word 'field' and the casting off of inhibitions, as in the expression 'having a field day'. The primary object of its founders – Friel, a Tyrone-born Catholic, and Rea, a Belfast Protestant – was to establish a 'fifth province' of the arts, beyond the familiar four provinces of Ireland, with their existing political and religious associations. However, the need to secure Arts Council funding for productions required the formal structure of a theatre company and the setting up of an executive board (the latter consisting of themselves, Seamus Heaney, Tom Paulin, Seamus Deane and the musician David Hammond). Thus Field Day became, almost by default, Derry's first professional theatre company since Edward Heffernon's company at the Queen's Theatre in the 1860s.

Field Day's production of *Translations* coincided with a revival in amateur drama in Derry that recalled the immediate post-war years. Among the groups staging productions in the Guildhall, St Columb's Hall, Magee and Union Hall were The Derry Players, The Colmcille Players, The Theatre Club and the '71 Players. (The '71 Players were celebrating their tenth anniversary year with a season of Irish plays, including another revival of Friel's *Philadelphia, Here I Come!*) But whereas the earlier resurgence reflected a climate of post-war optimism, the activity of the 1980s took place against a background of rising violence, as the Troubles entered a new and bitter phase.

The City of Derry Drama Festival

Politically, circumstances could hardly have been less propitious when the City of Derry Drama Festival took place between 22 and 29 March 1981 at Magee. The key figure behind the festival was school principal Michael Gillen, who drew together a cross-community team from local drama societies, including veterans Fred Logan, Sidney Buchanan and Thelma Arthur, alongside Kevin McLaughin and Ian Doherty. Maureen Gallagher and Michael Sheerin, whose association with the festival continues to the present day, were members of that first organising committee and remember the early days when meetings were held in Gillen's house. Together they ran the first nine-day festival, relying on the generosity of local businesses for sponsorship and the City Council for a financial guarantee against losses.

Gillen (1927-1992), the driving force behind the festival during the 1980s, is now remembered for his long and illustrious contribution to amateur drama in Derry and elsewhere. Over many years he acted with the St Columb's College Union Drama group, The Theatre Club and the Derry City Players. He was also a founder member of the Theatre Action Group (TAG) and as its chairman was a persistent lobbyist for Derry's long-awaited civic theatre.

The first festival attracted entries from both sides of the border, from Ballymena, Cushendall, Dublin, Ballybofey, Eslin and Sligo. The adjudicator was Moville-born actor Ray McAnally, fresh from his highly praised performance as Hugh O'Donnell in *Translations* six months earlier. The winning plays reflected the breadth and variety of the festival, from the Slemish Players, with *The Playboy of the Western World*, to St Michael's (Enniskillen) with *The Killing of Sister George* and the Butt Drama Circle's *The Days of Wine and Roses*.

Their venue, Magee's Great Hall, held about 100 people; sufficient for the small audiences in these early days. But as the festival grew, more space was needed for both theatre companies and audiences, and in 1986 it moved to the Rialto Entertainment Centre, its home until 2000. In its first twenty years, the festival attracted amateur groups from all over Ireland, with several making return visits. Many outstanding productions were staged, including the Butt Drama Circle's own *Translations*, the Slemish Players' *The Last Burning*, and the Silken Thomas Players' *The Normal Heart*, which then won both the Ulster and All-Ireland titles. The festival organisers aimed to include a mixture of tragedy, comedy, classical and contemporary works, with at least one new company every year.

There was an unintended drama in the 1987 Festival, in Ballymoney Literary and Debating Society's production of Alan Bennett's *Habeas Corpus*, which features a hanging in the first act. At the crucial point the safety harness failed, leaving the actor, Mac Pollock, literally hanging at the rope's end. To the rapt audience it must have seemed that Pollock's portrayal of a man being slowly throttled was a *tour de force*. Luckily, the other cast members realised what had happened and immediately brought the curtain down (to sustained applause) before they had a real body on their hands. Their prompt action saved the City of Derry Drama Festival from its first on-stage fatality.

Field Day's second production, on 8 September 1981, was Friel's adaptation of Chekhov's *Three Sisters*, directed by Stephen Rea. The cast included James Ellis and Sorcha Cusack, whose father Cyril had acted in the 1968 premiere of Friel's *Crystal and Fox*. The first night again attracted a distinguished audience, but at one point in the performance there were disturbing reminders of life outside, when the actors' voices were almost drowned out by army helicopters circling overhead. This, and the imperfect acoustics in the Guildhall, prompted *The Irish Times* to join in the call – made by local papers for many years – for a theatre for Derry, 'May it soon arise and give Field Day the home it deserves and Derry the theatre it needs.'

'The Theatre Story' Part 1, 1981-1989

In fact, the council had already commissioned plans for such a theatre from Clarendon Street architects McCormick, Tracey & Mullarkey, and a model of Tom Mullarkey's design for the new building was on display in the Guildhall that night. It was to have a 500-seat auditorium, with facilities to house a repertory company, at an estimated cost of £2.6 million. It was planned for the East Wall, home of the former YMCA building, on a site recently bought by the Council.[101] TAG Chairman Michael Gillen hailed the plans as 'another major landmark on the long road'. The *Journal*, ever optimistic, ran a headline, 'Civic Theatre Plan Gets Green Light', announcing that work would begin in the latter half of 1985.

But nothing happened. TAG stepped up its lobbying, frequently meeting with city councillors and ACNI, pressing for work on the theatre to be started. At one meeting in April 1983, TAG met with both the Director and Chairman of the Arts Council, Kenneth Jamison and Arthur Brooke, and city councillors to discuss three aspirations: for a resident repertory theatre company; for the appointment (within eighteen months) of an artistic director to liaise with arts societies, and, of course, for a theatre. Again, nothing came of it. The reality on the ground belied ACNI's annual reports, which, as in 1983/4, mentioned 'theatre centre projects for Londonderry' as being either 'confirmed' or at the drawing-board stage. As a result, local shows and touring productions continued to struggle with the cramped and out-of-date facilities of the Rialto, while the City Council considered yet another renovation scheme, this time to convert the Rialto into a theatre. This idea was rejected in 1983 and the old cinema remained as it was, stretched to the limit by new productions.

Festival City

Notwithstanding the lack of a theatre, arts festivals proliferated in the 1980s, with drama, dance, poetry readings, jazz, Ulster Orchestra and chamber concerts telescoped into a few weeks each year. The North-West Arts Festival resumed in November 1980, providing two weeks of drama, concerts, string quartets, films and organ recitals, ending with an Ulster Orchestra concert in the Guildhall conducted by Adrian Thomas. Tickets were priced just £2. The festival then became an annual two-week fixture in later November, run by the Londonderry Arts Association with direct funding from ACNI.

In 1985, the festival received a huge uplift in support from ACNI (£10,000 – more than six times its previous level) under a new 'block grant scheme' for regional festivals. This made possible a wide-ranging programme, with three different plays, the Dublin City Ballet in *Giselle*, organ recitals, jazz concerts and weekend seminars on theatre and music. 'Light Entertainment' was promoted alongside 'Community Arts', art and photographic exhibitions, and featured Acker Bilk, Mick Lally and Nuala Hayes, amongst others. Financially the Derry festival still lagged behind the Queen's Festival, which that year received over £75,000, but it was a feast of culture for a city that had been starved of outside performers for many decades. Over the next five years, Derry once again shared in Belfast's cultural life, as the Charabanc Theatre Company's staged Marie Jones's plays in Magee, and George Melly and the John Chiltern Feetwarmers brought jazz to the Guildhall.

Other festivals followed: the North West Story-Telling Festival, the Foyle Film Festival, the Colmcille Festival and the Maiden City Festival. In all, there were over twenty-five different arts festivals in Derry in the two decades after 1980. A number of major figures in the arts came to Derry, eager to help in the city's regeneration. They included newer artists such as Shaun Davey's sixty-strong orchestra with uilleann piper Liam O'Flynn in the Rialto in 1987. The culmination of all these initiatives was Derry's first year-long festival of the arts, the controversial but ground-breaking Impact '92.

In 1982, the LAOS briefly returned to its roots by staging Gilbert and Sullivan's *Mikado*. Its orchestra was similar to that of the pre-war Philharmonic; thirty strong, with many wind and brass players borrowed from the Britannia Band. The orchestra was now led by Pat Bergin, veteran leader Muriel Anderson having finally laid aside her violin and bow after many years' service. But the soloists and stage team still included many stalwarts of the 1960s – Fred Logan, Donald Hill, Thelma Arthur and Scott Marshall – alongside a younger generation of actors and singers. By the later 1980s, the LAOS was the city's major music society, its productions attracting a large and faithful following. The year 1990 saw the beginning of their collaboration with the Britannia Brass and Reed Band for annual concerts for charity, a partnership which continues to the present day in 'Showstoppers'.

Field Day in the 1980s

Field Day's third play, *The Communication Cord*, was premiered in the Guildhall on Tuesday, 21 September 1982, and, as before, was as much a roll-call of Ireland's social and cultural elite as a theatrical occasion. Stephen Rea returned with local actor Ann Hasson in a smaller, but no less distinguished cast for this, the latest of Friel's Ballybeg plays. *The Irish Times* gave the production an excellent review, describing it as both 'dramatically intriguing and ... hilariously funny', and saluting Friel's courage in mocking travesties of the very themes of culture and identity so movingly expressed in *Translations*.

In its first phase, Field Day produced and toured eleven plays, including world premieres of Derek Mahon's *High Time*, Tom Paulin's *The Riot Act* (both in 1984), Thomas Kilroy's *Double Cross* (1986), Stewart Parker's *Pentecost* (1987), Friel's *Making History* (1988), Terry Eagleton's *Saint Oscar* (1989), and Seamus Heaney's adaptation of Sophocles's *Philoctetes*, *The Cure at Troy* (1990). The succession of premieres was interrupted in 1983 by *Boesman and Lena*, an anti-apartheid play by South African author Athol Fugard. For the most part the productions addressed themes of identity, history and language, which were central to Field Day's conception of its mission. All were staged in the Guildhall, which every autumn welcomed back familiar faces from Ireland's theatrical world, journalists and critics from the national press, and Derry theatre-goers lucky enough to secure tickets.

Press reviews were generally enthusiastic, particularly for the earlier plays, but became more mixed and critical as the decade progressed. Friel's plays invariably had enthusiastic reviews, but Eagleton's 1989 play was criticised as 'dramatically inert and linguistically glib', although the 'Daliesque' sets by Bob Crowley were highly praised. Field Day's reputation and connections were such that it was able to draw upon well-established Irish artists and musicians, as in Basil Blackshaw's frequent designs for poster and programme covers (for *Translations*, *Three Sisters* and *The Communication Cord*) and Mícheál Ó Súilleabháin's incidental music (for *Three Sisters*).

Throughout the 1980s, Derry's drama scene was lively and inventive. The combination of Field Day, the City of Derry Drama Festival, visiting companies, and amateur drama created an atmosphere of expectancy which drew in enthusiastic audiences. Productions were now almost all year round, as outside companies, such as Belfast's Themus Theatre Company, brought contemporary Northern Irish drama to Derry audiences. Martin Lynch's play *Dockers* was well received in the Guildhall in October 1982, a few months after its Belfast premiere. Local amateur societies thrived too. The Theatre Club continued its productions, as did the Derry Players, the Colmcille Players and the City of Derry Drama Club. There was huge variety in their productions, from plays by Hugh Leonard, Neil Simon, Arthur Miller and Noel Coward to the standard works of the Irish repertoire, O'Casey, St John Ervine and Oscar Wilde. Understandably, Brian Friel's plays were particular favourites, with *The Freedom of the City*, *The Aristocrats* and *Philadelphia, Here I Come!* often staged by Derry's amateurs. A wide range of venues were brought into service: the Guildhall, Magee, the Union Hall, the Little Theatre and the Rialto (run since 1983 by DCC as an 'entertainment centre'). Yet these productions had difficulties to overcome; actors often struggled to attend rehearsals, with bombs exploding in the city centre and constant security alerts.

Music in the 1980s

While drama took centre stage in Derry during the 1980s, there was also a recovery in music. There were thrice-yearly concerts by the Ulster Orchestra and concert seasons by the Londonderry Arts Association at Magee. Even at the height of the Troubles, ACNI continued to tour concert parties and drama companies throughout Northern Ireland, although lamenting in its annual reports that, while there was initial enthusiasm for events, actual turnouts were often disappointingly small – not surprising, perhaps, given the recurring levels of violence at this time.[102] Havelock Nelson's Studio Opera Group continued to visit Derry about twice a year until the early 1990s, always attracting a devoted following to the Great Hall at Magee, a venue well suited to their small-scale chamber operas.

However, in Derry a younger generation of musicians and music lovers was beginning to emerge, eager and well qualified to rejuvenate the city's musical legacy. The Londonderry Arts Association began a series of 'Music in Magee' monthly chamber music concerts during the winter months. These developed into the Classical Music Series of the mid-1980s, which by winter 1987 included regular seasons of four concerts. Donal Doherty, organist at St Eugene's Cathedral from 1982, reached out to new audiences with his Cathedral choirs and orchestra, rising above the then current fashion for 'folk masses' encouraged by the Second Vatican Council.[103] Their concert of Mozart's *Requiem* coupled with Britten's *Missa Brevis* in the Cathedral in April 1988 was a foretaste of Doherty's later forays into choral music in the 1990s.

Muriel's 'Molitor'

Muriel Anderson, who had first played violin with the Philharmonic orchestra as a ten year old, died in 1992 after a lifetime of music-making. She had been a member of the Philharmonic for twenty-five years, latterly as its leader, had led her own string orchestra in regular Sunday-night concerts in the YMCA Hall in the 1930s, and worked with other orchestras in the city in the post-war years. As she recalled in 1976, aged seventy-one, the two musical high points of her life were playing before Queen Elizabeth II in the Guildhall in 1953 and being called upon at short notice to replace the Martin Quartet's second violinist (who had gone down with flu) in their concert tour of Northern Ireland.

In 1989, following the death of her brother William, a fellow violinist and organist in Culmore Parish church, with whom she lived in the family home in Aberfoyle Terrace, she gave their Stradivarius violin to the Derry branch of the Red Cross. (She and her brother had benefited from its Meals on Wheels service in their later years, but her family's involvement with the Red Cross went back to the First World War, when her father, James Anderson, had been a tireless worker with the organisation.)

CHORAL CONCERT

in

St. Eugene's Cathedral

on

Sunday, April 10th, 1988 at 8.00pm.

Presented by

St. Eugene's Cathedral Choirs and Orchestra

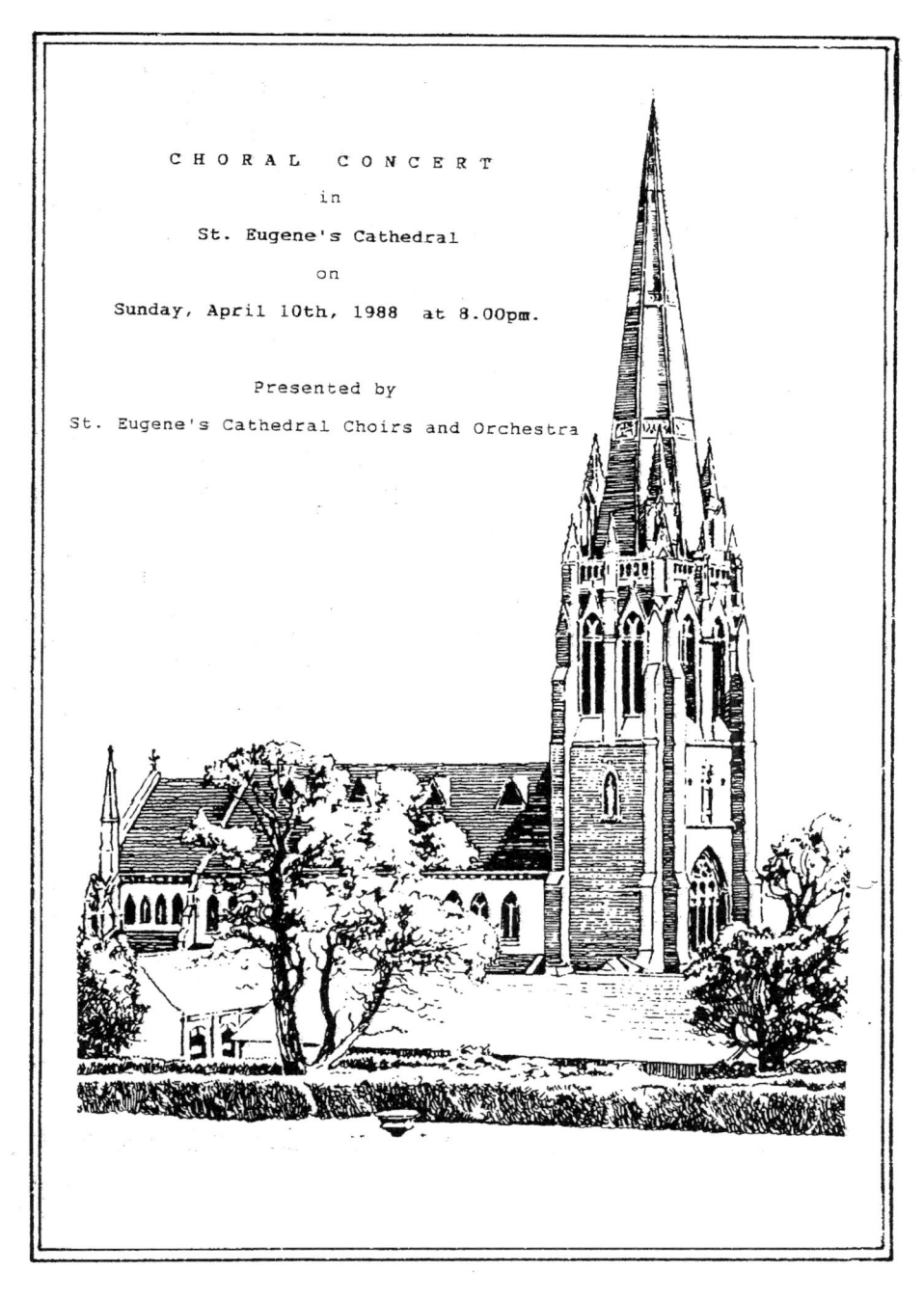

Programme of one of Donal Doherty's first choral concerts in St Eugene's Cathedral in April 1988. (By kind permission of St Eugene's Cathedral)

Muriel Anderson's 'Molitor' Stradivarius violin, reputedly once owned by Napoleon Bonaparte. (By kind permission of the Tarisio Auction House, New York)

When the violin was sold through Christie's of London it realised £195,000, which, together with a further legacy upon her death, funds the Muriel Anderson Trust to the present day. Subsequently, in October 2010, Muriel's 'Molitor' Stradivarius violin was sold at auction in New York for $3.6 million, the then highest price ever recorded for any musical instrument – an astonishing sum for a violin that for thirty years had been owned and played by two unassuming Derry musicians. Its present owner, the Californian violinist Anne Akiko Meyers, has said of it, 'It was love at first sound. Its power, feel and range of colour are extraordinary.'

Muriel Anderson's legacy to the city was thus two-fold: in the lifetime of musical performances in which she took part and in her final gift of her violin to a charitable foundation that continues to benefit her local community.

The Foyle Renaissance, 1980-1995

The Tercentenary Commissions

The tercentenary of the Siege of Derry was celebrated by the city's citizens in 1989-90, although the celebrations took different forms from those in previous centuries. There were two compositions commissioned by Derry City Council for the anniversary. The first commemorated the 'Shutting of the Gates' by the Apprentice Boys (in December), the second, the relief of the city by Williamite forces (in August). In light of Derry's contested history – both distant and recent – these were sensitive commissions. Perhaps for this reason, the works were commissioned respectively from a Derry-born Catholic and a Belfast-born Protestant.

The first commission was *From the Besieged City*, a cantata for mezzo-soprano and orchestra from Kevin O'Connell, a classical composer in the modern idiom.[104] It was first performed by the Ulster Orchestra in the Guildhall on 26 October 1989, appropriately under Derry-born conductor David Jones. The work was based on a poem by the contemporary Polish poet Zbigniew Herbert about an unnamed city under siege at an unstated – but probably ancient – time. (It was dedicated to Kevin McCaul in recognition of his encouragement of young creative artists.) The result was more sombre than celebratory: O'Connell's work, a modern, post-serial composition, had few moments of optimism. Only the last few lines of the poem/music gave any hint of hope or relief:

> We look in the face of hunger the face of fire face of death
> Worst of all – the face of betrayal
> And only our dreams have not been humiliated.

The second commission was from Belfast-born Shaun Davey, who had a reputation for accessible music framed in classical mode. His *Relief of Derry Symphony* likewise was premiered by the Ulster Orchestra in the Guildhall, on 5 May 1990. It was an altogether different work, with traditional musicians and two local pipe bands playing alongside the orchestra. The composition itself was in conventional symphonic form, with four movements, but ended with a triumphant coda representing 'the city's thanks for deliverance'. The premiere of the piece was part of a 'Siege Pageant', a huge celebratory event organised by the City Council with funding from several sources: The Ireland Funds, ACNI and The Honourable The Irish Society. The pageant included an open-air play by Andy Hinds acted out in Guildhall Square amid giant puppets and music by additional pipe bands.

The Council commissioned a further work from O'Connell, a violin concerto which was premiered by the newly formed Northern Sinfonietta during the 1990 North-West Arts Festival. At this time, spending on the arts by the city had reached an all-time high – much higher than for any local council elsewhere in Northern Ireland. However, not everyone was happy about this, with one Official Unionist

Programme cover of the 1989 Siege of Derry Pageant celebrating the tercentenary of the siege. (By kind permission of Derry City Council)

councillor, John Adams, on record as complaining that spending on the arts (and on Derry's local airport) was too high. But a boost came in later 1991, when the 'Deane Report on the Performing Arts', commissioned by the Arts Council and Department of Education from Professor Basil Deane, favoured Derry as the location of a new performing arts academy, a recommendation which provided hope to those who saw the city as the cultural capital of the north-west.

Impact '92

'Impact '92', a rather contrived acronym for 'International Meeting Place for the Appreciation of Cultural Traditions', was a year-long arts festival directed by Sean Doran, and funded by Derry City Council and ACNI.[105] For Derry, this festival was unprecedented in length and breadth, encompassing film, dance, poetry readings and jazz. It also marked Derry's first significant engagement with *avant-garde* and 'cutting edge' arts, with new and innovative productions alongside the more traditional offerings in drama and music.

Doran proved to be an inspired choice as artistic director.[106] He chose to focus upon the 'International' aspect of the title, and this, combined with his success in persuading so many well-established names to come to Derry, provided a memorable year. This was all the more remarkable given the city's embattled image in the media. The festival was launched in the Guildhall with readings by the Field Day triumvirate of Seamus Heaney, Seamus Deane and Tom Paulin. This was followed by performances from the Royal Shakespeare Company, the Maly Theatre from St Petersburg, the Philippe Genty Company and The Opera Factory – a range of drama companies and music ensembles of a quality not seen in Derry since before the First World War. The highlight here was perhaps the RSC's performance of *Electra*, starring Fiona Shaw, which was staged in the Templemore Sports Complex for four nights in February 1992. Four months later, the sports complex was again refitted as a theatre for the National Theatre's production of Lope De Vega's *Fuente Ovejuna*. Local pride was assuaged by Dublin theatre company Rough Magic's production of Farquhar's *Love and a Bottle*, its first staging in Derry for more than 150 years. Other highpoints were Frank McGuinness's play *Observe the Sons of Ulster Marching towards the Somme*, a (second) performance of Shaun Davey's *Relief of Derry Symphony* at the Rialto, and a recital by Arturo Pizarro on the new Steinway grand piano in the Guildhall.

Among the many notable drama productions was the Derry premiere of McGuinness's play *Carthaginians*, by the Galway-based Druid Theatre Company in March 1992.[107] The play is set in Derry and shows a group of relatives of the Bloody Sunday dead, waiting in a graveyard in hope of the resurrection of their loved ones. Perspective on their situation and black humour is supplied by an outsider, the central character Dido, a drag queen. However, the play almost did not reach Derry's

> **DRUID THEATRE COMPANY**
> presents:—
> **IMPACT '92**
>
> # CARTHAGINIANS
>
> (By Frank McGuinness)
>
> The plot tells of seven people in a Derry graveyard, waiting for a miracle. They believe the dead will rise. And so they remember the day a city died, January 30th, 1972, the day of Bloody Sunday. For some members of the audience the programming and performance of this production may be an unnerving and challenging experience.
>
> ## RIALTO — OPENING TUESDAY, 10th to FRIDAY, 13th MARCH 8 p.m. Nightly
>
> ADM. £5.00 Full Price/£3.00 Concessionary
>
> *For Bookings and tickets, contact*
> **RIALTO BOX OFFICE 260516**

Press advertisement for Frank McGuinness's Carthaginians *in March 1992 in the Rialto. (Derry* Journal, *6 March 1992)*

Rialto, as some city councillors, having attending a preview in Galway, were adamant that it should not be brought to Impact '92. The festival organisers pressed for its inclusion, and – predictably – it was the presence of a homosexual character in the play that attracted protests in the streets outside the Rialto, rather than any political content. Inside the theatre, the Derry audience received it warmly; McGuinness himself confessed that it was only when he heard them laughing at the comments of Dido that he felt able to relax and enjoy the occasion.

Midway through the year of Impact '92, there were press reports of 'inter-personal tensions', and financial and administrative problems.[108] In particular, Derry City Council withdrew £65,000 funding from Field Day for their staging of Friel's *The Freedom of the City*, unhappy, it was said, at providing so large a subsidy for a nineteen-year-old play. In its place, Field Day held a play reading in the Guildhall of David Rudkin's 1973 radio play *Cries from Casement as his Bones are Brought to Dublin*. Later in the year, Friel's *Dancing at Lughnasa* was staged in the Rialto – described sniffily, if correctly, by *The Irish Times* as a 'converted cinema'. The five-night run in October

The Foyle Renaissance, 1980-1995

Sean Doran (b. 1960), Artistic Director of Impact '92 and the 1993 Octoberfest. (By kind permission of the West Australian)

attracted packed audiences and left 500 people on a waiting list for returned tickets, a testament to the enduring popularity of Friel's older plays.

The year ended strongly with a Field Day sponsored reading by the Poet Laureate Ted Hughes in the Guildhall on 13 October. A few days later there was Derry's first three-day Guinness Jazz Festival, which brought back favourites from the 1980s in Acker Bilk and George Melly. Later that month, the experimental Gardzienice

Group from Poland performed a double bill of *Carmina Burana* and *Avvakum*, the latter described as 'physically reckless and thrillingly well-sung'. The two pieces were performed in two different venues, with the members of the group taking a 'staged walk' between The Playhouse and the Guildhall accompanied by their audience.

The First Two Cathedrals' Festival

As a spin-off from Impact '92 there was also, in October, the first Two Cathedrals' Festival, started by Derry's two Cathedral organists, Donal Doherty and English-born Tim Allen, a newcomer to the city. A Cambridge graduate in music, Allen was organist in Chelmsford Cathedral, Essex, before being appointed to St Columb's in 1991. Supported by funding from Impact '92 and the local business sector, the week-long festival broke new ground in secular and church music. It opened with an orchestral concert with organ concerto; it had a varied programme of solo recitals (organ, tenor, classical accordion and guitar), and was brought to a stirring conclusion by Verdi's *Requiem* performed by the Festival Chorus (made up of the two Cathedral choirs) and the Ulster Orchestra. The range of music performed was wide, from Dowland to Britten, and with modern works by Takemitsu and a newly commissioned 'Festival Anthem' from Kevin O'Connell.

For all the mid-term misgivings about its financing, Impact '92 was phenomenally successful in attracting audiences, and in the range and number of performances. Between April 1992 and April 1993, there were 120 amateur and professional drama performances in Derry, almost four times, per head of population, the number in Belfast during the same period. Yet the festival faced criticism both then and after the event for its supposed lack of community involvement and what was seen as the 'cultural elitism' of its programme.

This was not a charge that could be levelled at The Playhouse Arts Centre, whose opening in April 1992 was another significant date in Derry's cultural renaissance.

The Playhouse

The Playhouse was situated in two convent schools in Artillery Street (previously Artillery Lane). The choice of location was chance rather than design, being the only city-centre properties which Pauline Ross could afford to rent.[109] It was close to the former Artillery Lane and Fountain Street theatres, then the cultural hub of the city. By the early 1990s it was again the cultural quarter, containing the Rialto, St Columb's Hall and the Orchard Gallery. But the Troubles had taken their toll of many inner-city premises, and, although 'listed' as being of historic interest, the school buildings were derelict and had lain empty for eight years.

Ross (b.1952) was an amateur actor and director with a wide-ranging interest in the arts. Having 'cut her teeth' with the '71 Players, she then worked at Derry's Orchard Gallery, where she began to form ideas for a community arts centre. She initially persuaded local businessman Joe Mulheron to rent her the convent buildings, and undeterred by the scale of repairs needed, she pressed ahead seeking sponsors and benefactors. Armed with a rudimentary business plan, Ross first obtained a £300 grant from the British Enkalon Foundation; she then persuaded her compliant landlord to allow her to 'buy' the premises from him, on the understanding that she would pay him back when she had raised the money.

In its early years, The Playhouse had a small, ninety-seat theatre – inadequate for a city whose population approached 100,000 – but offering an intimate space for local and experimental drama. Its first production, on 14 April 1992, was Charabanc Theatre Company's premiere of Andy Hind's *October Song*, a play set in Derry and focusing on a family's attempts to deal with the past. The Playhouse specialised in international plays dealing with the effects and aftermath of conflict, but it also featured new and contemporary Irish works, such as the premieres of Eddie Kerr's *Guildhall Clock* (1993) and *Packie's Wake* (1994). A succession of performing troupes took up residence: the Derry Youth Theatre, the Lilliput and Ridiculusmus theatre companies, and the Echo Echo Dance group, followed in 1995 by the O'Casey Theatre Company, under Sean O'Casey's daughter Siobhan. The Playhouse offered short-term residencies for arts groups, and ran outreach arts workshops in prisons and credit-bearing courses in the arts. It was, in the truest sense, a community arts centre with particular emphasis on education, outreach and collaboration.

In its first two years, The Playhouse hosted over 100 productions, many of them sold out before their opening nights. By autumn 1995, 61,000 people had visited the arts centre, of which more than half had attended drama productions – an indication of both the appetite for drama in Derry and the need for a theatre. By this time, Ross had persuaded twenty-five funders to donate £226,540 to The Playhouse and had garnered valuable supporters in the President of Ireland Mary Robinson, author Jennifer Johnston, and the two Bishops of Derry, Mehaffey and Daly.

The Playhouse was not alone, however. The Foyle Arts Centre, funded by DCC and the Arts Council, was housed in the former Foyle College building, and it too had a theatre space. In the years after 1992, the centre housed a myriad of arts organisations, including Field Day, the Classical Music Society, a jazz group, a speech and drama group and a contemporary dance group. In the absence of a purpose-built theatre in Derry, it also played a vital role in presenting play readings, drama performances, dance workshops and exhibitions.

Meanwhile, other arts centres had sprung up in the city. In 1992 the Verbal Arts Centre (VAC) was set up by local poet and writer Sam Burnside, with its core objective 'the promotion and support of spoken and written literature'. Like The Playhouse, VAC was an expression of community arts, described as access to 'imaginative experiences ... and creative expression' for everyone. It opened in the former Cathedral School in London Street, another disused and rundown city-centre building. By 1996, expansion in the centre's activities forced Burnside to look for larger premises, which he found in the former First Derry Primary School, set into the walls at Bishop's Gate. It too was in a badly decayed state, closed since 1995 and deteriorating with each passing year. Burnside launched an energetic fundraising campaign and raised £1.7 million for the purchase and refurbishment of the building. The foundation stone was laid on 5 December 1998 by Irish poet John Montague, yet another 'brick' in Derry's cultural regeneration.

A fourth arts centre, the Nerve Centre in Magazine Street, had opened in 1990 as a 'focus for youth culture'. It grew out of the North-West Music Collective, a group of musicians who met together informally to play and compose. Not to be left out, in July 1993, Derry city's heritage body, the Foyle Civic Trust, organised a joint play reading by local architects and Theatre Club members. The play was *Development* by Czech President Vaclav Havel, which appropriately, given the Trust's remit, addressed 'planning and city development issues'.

If it is hard to think of original music inspired by the Troubles, the opposite is true of the theatre, where a host of plays addressed themes of conflict, identity and sectarianism. One in particular provoked a reaction in its Derry audience reminiscent of that in the Opera House 100 years before.

Plus Ça Change: At the Black Pig's Dyke

The incident was prompted by the Galway-based Druid Theatre Company's staging of *At the Black Pig's Dyke* in the Guildhall in July 1993. The play centred on the consequences of a 'mixed', that is to say Catholic–Protestant, marriage in a divided community, a theme sure to resonate in Derry's own divided community. The play ran for four nights without disruption, but near the end, on the fifth and final night, members of the local Frontline Community Theatre group brought the performance to a halt by invading the stage. Wearing masks and wrapped in Union Jacks, the protestors chanted, 'Here comes Mr Major and His Men', a self-conscious parody of a line in the play. According to those involved, their protest was aimed at what they later described as 'the play's sophisticated naivety'. The cast took flight, understandably enough given Derry's reputation for sectarian violence, but were persuaded to come on stage once again to finish the play. It is said that they and the protestors met later that night in the Dungloe Bar, and that the evening ended amicably, with the theatre company promising to return to the city. Is it fanciful to think – in a city with such a long memory for grievances – that the 1993 protestors were getting their own back for the Opera House riot of 1885 organised (it was said at the time) by the 'denizens of the Bogside'?

At the Black Pig's Dyke, the play which provoked a stage invasion in 1993. (Derry Journal, 18 June 1993)

Octoberfest 1993

Impact '92 was followed in 1993 by the shorter, month-long 'Octoberfest', with Doran again as artistic director and Steve Blunden as financial director. Despite its more restricted time scale, it was another ambitious and wide-ranging festival with over 100 events in fourteen venues by artists from nine countries, and ranging in content from 'liturgical music to cartoon comedy'. By this time, levels of violence in Derry were decreasing compared with Belfast, and it was hinted that Derry, once the 'cockpit' of the Troubles, had opted out of the armed struggle in anticipation of a political settlement. Octoberfest was able to proceed without any major terrorist disruption. It styled itself 'a festival of festivals', inasmuch as it incorporated The Languages of Ireland Festival, with Roddy Doyle and Edna O'Brien, a World Theatre and Dance Festival, and the second, now eagerly awaited, Two Cathedrals' Festival.

Elgar's *The Dream of Gerontius* was the opening concert of the Two Cathedrals' Festival, in St Columb's Hall on Saturday 16 October 1993, again with the combined Cathedral choirs and the Ulster Orchestra. This 1993 Cathedrals' Festival was the second of eight such annual events, which, in musical terms, were definitive of the 1990s in Derry, as they brought individual musicians and ensembles of the highest rank to the city: Harry Christophers and the Sixteen, tenor Ian Partridge and his accompanist David Owen Norris, the Jacques Loussier Trio and Musica Antiqua Köln. The Sixteen, in particular, returned to Derry several times, building up a close rapport with the Cathedral choirs in rehearsals and workshops.

The main draw in the 1993 festival was soprano Victoria de los Angeles (1923-2005), who gave a song recital in St Columb's Cathedral on 18 October. Just two weeks off her seventieth birthday, she gave a lengthy and largely romantic programme, consisting of songs by Brahms, Fauré and Granados, and ending with songs from her native Catalonia and others by the poet and playwright Federico Garcia Lorca. While it was generally agreed that age had robbed her voice of some of its power, the press described her delivery as imbued with a 'beguiling girlishness that would be the envy of many a singer half as young again'.

Major to the Rescue

The 1993 Two Cathedrals' Festival had the unusual distinction of being mentioned in a House of Commons debate, when Sir Patrick Mayhew, the Northern Ireland Secretary, cited it as an indication of how much had changed in Northern Ireland, and in Derry in particular, 'If one goes to Derry, pride in what the city has achieved and faith in what the future holds are at once apparent.' He went on to quote, approvingly, Donal Doherty's words, 'Don't talk about the Two Cathedrals' Festival being cross-community. This is the community.'

Even in 1993, all was not entirely peaceful: the Choir of Notre Dame cancels their concerts in Derry, and throughout Northern Ireland. (Derry Journal, *10 July 1993*)

MALE VOICE CHOIR OF NOTRE DAME

Due to the recent bombings, the Notre Dame Choir have CANCELLED their Northern Ireland Tour

What Mayhew didn't say was that, behind the scenes, the Prime Minister John Major had had a crucial role in securing the survival of the festival. The events, as recalled by Tim Allen years later, were as follows. In the immediate aftermath of the Warrington bomb, Allen had written to Major telling him of the positive 'musical' moves in Derry towards reconciliation. To his surprise, he received a reply from Major's Private Secretary conveying the PM's personal support for the festival and inquiring if they had funding in place for the event that year. When Allen indicated that it might have to be cancelled due to a shortfall of £25,000, he was told, 'Leave it with me.' A couple of hours later, Allen was summoned to the Londonderry Development Office to be told that instructions had come 'from the top' that the festival should receive the money required. In effect, Major had personally authorised that the money be paid. His intervention – and his interest – in the festival remains to this day gratefully remembered.

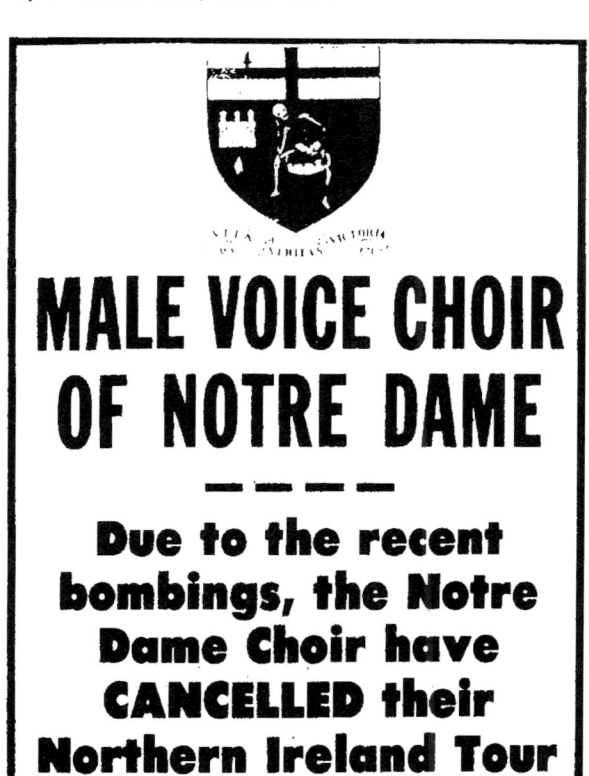

With Octoberfest completed, Doran warned the city fathers that the festival, which he had run 'on a shoe-string', and without any personal remuneration, needed to be adequately funded to survive. Mayor Annie Courtney's response was to claim in her 1993 Christmas message that Derry was already 'a city of culture'. Although Derry City Council was then spending more per person on culture than any other council in Northern Ireland, the councillors couldn't agree among themselves about whether another festival of the scope of Octoberfest was affordable – or even desirable. The familiar arguments resurfaced over finance, alleged elitism and failure to get city people involved. In July 1994, *The Irish Times* reported on 'Dissension in the

Derry Air' and 'a dream gone sour'. That autumn, the Council ran a more modest and populist Banks of the Foyle Festival, which lacked the flair and artistic high points of the previous two years. Doran, by this time, had taken his talents elsewhere: initially to the Belfast Festival at Queen's, then as Director of the Perth International Arts Festival in Australia. In 2003 he was appointed Director of English National Opera.

One major legacy of Impact '92 was the Two Cathedrals' Festival. Not since the headiest days of the Philharmonic had choral performances in Derry attracted so large and faithful a following or been recognised both within the city and beyond as major events in the musical calendar. Nor since the Londonderry Musical Union of the 1890s had the singers and musicians of the city's main religious denominations co-operated to such good effect.

The festivals often premiered music by young Irish composers as well as that of their internationally recognised contemporaries, such as Arvo Pärt. Central to all of them was the local Festival Chorus, drawn from the choirs of both Cathedrals, which performed large choral works at either the opening or closing concerts; sometimes modern works such as Tippett's *A Child of Our Time* (1994), at other times old favourites such as Mendelssohn's *Elijah* (1998). Concerts were held in venues across the city: the Guildhall, the two Cathedrals, First Derry church, St Columb's Hall, and the Methodist church. Not all of these lent themselves readily to the wide range of liturgical or secular music that characterised the festival. One *Irish Times* reviewer, in October 1995, complained about the unsuitability – the 'totally flat [and] dead acoustic' – of St Columb's Hall for a performance of Bruckner's *Te Deum* and criticised in particular the Ulster Orchestra's 'unduly prominent trumpets'. However, he was at pains to stress the positive, acknowledging 'performances that tried very hard' and praising 'this worthy cross-community venture'.

The Classical Music Series/Society

In the balmier atmosphere of the 1990s, long-established societies such as the Londonderry Arts Association took on new life. Already, in 1988, it had renamed its concerts the Classical Music Series, its organising committee was revamped, and it began to be more professional in its fundraising and marketing of events, building up an impressive list of funders and sponsors. Initially its concerts were small scale: piano recitals, string quartets, violin and piano duos, and song recitals with piano accompaniment. But by 1990 it was hosting ten concerts per season, with orchestral music and opera appearing for the first time. There were regular visits from Opera Northern Ireland, pianist Nikolai Demidenko and the Brodsky Quartet, all of whom returned to play at least three or four times during the 1990s. The London-based Brodsky Quartet was a particular favourite with Derry audiences, not least perhaps because violist Paul Cassidy was from the city.

The mid-1990s saw a sea change in the role of the Arts Council of Northern Ireland (ACNI) when it became a development and funding agency for the arts, ending fifty years of direct arts provision. This meant the end of its touring events, the last in Derry being a concert by the Vanburgh Quartet in March 1993. The changed system of funding put the onus on local councils, arts bodies and individual artists to promote, organise and market their own cultural events. This was in some ways a return to the situation in the early twentieth century, when responsibility for music and theatre was devolved locally. Here Derry, more than any other council area, had the advantage of a strong tradition of local activity, rooted in the 'self-help' approach of the 1960s.[110] ACNI was generous towards Derry in the later 1990s, with The Playhouse, Verbal Arts Centre and the Two Cathedrals' Festival all benefitting, their awards further augmented after 1995 by National Lottery funding. The Playhouse in particular did well, allowing it to expand its innovative programme of community drama, music and visual art. Derry City Council, for its part, was generous in its arts expenditure, exceeding by far the average per capita spend in Northern Ireland. In 1997-8 Derry City Council expended £876,400 in arts provision, averaging at £8.37 per head of population, second only to Belfast, with £10.31.

'The Theatre Story' Part 2, 1990-1995

To the frustration of many in Derry, lack of funding meant that the plans of the early 1980s for a new theatre were continually put back. So much so that in 1989, Gerry Downey, a founding member of the Theatre Action Group (TAG), suggested changing their acronym to TIG, Theatre *Inaction* Group. In 1990, Derry City Council went so far as to consider conversion of the then-vacant Third Derry church into a theatre, but, as with previous schemes, it was rejected as unworkable. Meanwhile, the Rialto remained stretched to the limit by new productions, as in October 1992 when IOU's production of its multimedia show *Boundary* required the almost complete overhaul of the theatre, and it took almost three days to set up the stage equipment, props and lighting. Quite apart from its limitations as a theatre, it was estimated that the former cinema cost six times more to run than it earned.

Hopes were raised by the ACNI annual report for 1992, in which the recently appointed Director, Brian Ferran, cited the success of Impact '92 as grounds for raising the priority of a new Derry theatre. He was echoing the 1992 Priestley Report on the arts, which had recommended 'a 350-500-seat theatre, drama school and resource centre' for Derry as part of the decentralisation of the arts in Northern Ireland. Again, lack of funding in the short term prevented any of the three being pursued. Additional salt was rubbed in the wound in August 1993, when Donal Deeney, Chairman of ACNI, was quoted in the press as saying that the Derry campaign for a theatre was 'inadequately coordinated'.

In 1993, Derry City Council commissioned a report from Eddie Friel, the Derry-born tourism and marketing guru credited with transforming Glasgow's image for its year as European City of Culture. He recommended a riverfront location for the theatre, combined with a museum. However, when the Council finally issued a prospectus for the theatre and invited tenders in a 'Design and Build' competition, the winning bid, from Fermac Properties of Ferryquay Street, was for a site on the East Wall, chosen for its accessibility and centrality. The architect was Martin O'Kane of HMD Chartered Architects. Opponents of the East Wall site were quick to raise objections. The General Secretary of the Apprentice Boys described the location as 'idiotic', with the theatre 'squeezed' on the site and disfiguring the walls. A phone-in poll around the same time showed 84 per cent of those taking part held a similar view. In a related but separate argument, papers were passed to and fro between DCC and ACNI regarding the size of the theatre, with the latter favouring a smaller auditorium and the Council holding out for a large, 1,000-seat, theatre. Putting the funding together took even longer, as £14 million had to be raised for the project. Meanwhile, city dwellers held their breath as months passed with still no sign of building.

By the mid-1990s, Derry had turned itself around culturally, socially and physically, in a transformation achieved by no other town or city in Ulster during the Troubles. The city had three art centres, two museums and a host of small venues. With all their limitations, the Rialto, Guildhall and St Columb's Hall were putting on concerts and plays direct from Belfast's Opera House and Waterfront Hall. Pride in (if in some quarters only a hazy knowledge of) the city's musical and theatrical past had returned after the doldrum years between 1930 and 1979. But just as music and theatre had been kept alive at an earlier period in the city's history by the efforts of a few musicians and drama lovers, so the renaissance of the 1980s and '90s owed everything to the vision and determination over many years of a handful of local figures, including Sean Doran, Tim Allen, Donal Doherty, Pauline Ross and Kevin McCaul.

The End of Field Day in Derry

Field Day likewise had been a major influence in Derry's cultural rebirth, but Frank McGuinness's version of Chekhov's *Uncle Vanya* in February 1995 was to be their swan song. Directed by Peter Gill, with Stephen Rea in the lead role and Denys Hawthorne as Serebryakov, it was their fourteenth play since *Translations* but their first production in Derry since 1992. Reviewers did not hide their disappointment. *The Irish Times* headlined its review, 'No Field Day for Field Day', and described Rea as too young for the role. It was not said outright but the implication was that, theatrically, Field Day was a spent force, and there was little in the production to remind the reviewer of the company's earlier glory days. Brian Friel left the board at the end of 1994, having for some time previously premiered his plays elsewhere; that for

> **FIELD DAY THEATRE COMPANY** presents
>
> **UNCLE VANYA**
>
> a version by **FRANK McGUINNESS**
>
> **THE GUILDHALL, DERRY**
>
> **MONDAY 20-SATURDAY 25 FEBRUARY** at 8.00 p.m.
>
> with Stephen Rea (Uncle Vanya), Helena Carroll, Pauline Delany, Denys Hawthorne, Gerard Lee, Enda Oates, P.G. Stephens, Kim Thomson, Zara Turner Directed by Peter Gill; Set Design Hayden Griffin; Costume Design Pamela Howard; Music Terry Davies, Lighting Design Andy Philips.
>
> Tickets are £7, concession £5 from
>
> **RIALTO BOX OFFICE, MARKET ST. (0504) 260151**

The last Field Day play in Derry, Frank McGuinness's version of Chekhov's Uncle Vanya, in February 1995. (Derry Journal, 14 February 1995)

Dancing at Lughnasa, arguably his most successful play in commercial terms, was in the Abbey Theatre in 1990.

Publishing became an increasingly important part of Field Day's activities after 1983. The initial three pamphlets a year were followed by the *Field Day Anthology of Irish Writing* in 1990, controversial for its omission of many female writers and alleged political leanings. By then, Field Day's main performing days were over and it had changed to being more a discussion forum for literary topics, viewed by some of its critics as promoting 'green nationalism and divided culture'. The theatre company had never had a physical base in Derry, so its departure from the city passed almost unnoticed. By the mid-1990s, the association with Field Day that had shed lustre on the city was at an end.[111]

In November 1981, when Field Day was in its first flush, Brian Friel wrote an epigraph for the programme of the St Columb's College Union Dramatic Society's production of one of his plays, which seemed to acknowledge the inevitability of just such a parting of the ways:

> Writers are spiritual locusts. They descend and squat on a chosen terrain for as long as it sustains their imagination and then move on.

Nine

EPILOGUE: AN EMBARRASSMENT OF RICHES? 1996-2009

> Given time, perhaps, and the right direction the theatre in Derry can become the third Foyle Bridge.
>
> Tom Mullarkey, 1985

Those citizens of Derry who had campaigned for forty years and more for a proper theatre for the city found themselves, in the early years of the twenty-first century, in the position of a traveller waiting for ages at a bus stop, who, when his bus finally comes along, sees three others come along simultaneously. When the long-awaited Millennium Forum opened its doors to the public for the first time in 2001, it was joined over the next eight years by three other theatres: the Waterside Theatre, An Croi and the refurbished Playhouse Theatre. If there is anything to Tom Mullarkey's vision of a theatre being a third Foyle Bridge, then the banks of the Foyle were on their way to becoming dangerously – or perhaps one should say gloriously – crowded.

Developments were not confined to new theatres. By 2000, the Verbal Arts Centre had moved to its new home in Stable Lane; the city's two music societies, the Londonderry Amateur Opera Society and the Classical Music Society, were in rude health, and there was Derry's successful amateur drama festival. On the political side, Derry City Council had commissioned its first arts strategy, confirming the arts as a priority in the city's post-Troubles regeneration.

Nonetheless, there were still underlying problems. Street violence had decreased dramatically from its height in the mid-1970s, but low-level civil disorder persisted, often surfacing at sensitive times, such as during the 'marching season'. The events of Bloody Sunday still cast a long shadow, although people's grievances were now being given an airing by the Saville Inquiry, which, from March 2000, took over the Guildhall for four years, displacing the concerts, dramas and the Feis Dhoire which had previously used its facilities.

Epilogue

The Theatre Trust and Millennium Forum

In March 1996, the Derry Theatre Trust was set up as a charitable, limited company to oversee and manage the new theatre project. Its board included city councillors, Risteard Mac Gabhann, a former chairman of TAG, and figures from the arts in Derry such as Brian Friel and the novelist Jennifer Johnston. Thirteen months later, details of the project were unveiled and it was announced that Derry's new theatre would open on the East Wall in just over 1,000 days.

Excavation work on the site finally started early in 1999 and almost immediately there was a crisis when a ten-metre section of the city wall adjoining the site collapsed, leading the *Journal* to quip that the builders had finally succeeded where 'the bombardment of three siege armies in the seventeenth century had failed'. In fact, this was the *third* time Derry's walls had been breached. It had happened in 1826 and again in 1940. There was similar amnesia about the historical significance of the site, few realising that the once-elegant terrace on the East Wall had been Derry's cultural quarter during the nineteenth century. Here, the musicians Logier, Perois and Bartowski had lived and worked, and later the YMCA Hall had hosted drama productions, concerts and soirees. Directly opposite, St Columb's Hall had been the scene of concerts by John McCormack, Edward Sousa and the Hallé Orchestra.

The Two Cathedrals' Festival

The Two Cathedrals' Festival continued to thrive, becoming Derry's equivalent of the English Three Choirs' Festival. It acquired a 'fringe' in 1996, in the shape of music-making by local schools in local venues and even in shopping centres. Choral music was particularly strong that year, with Harry Christophers' Sixteen joining the 100-strong Festival Chorus in Mozart's *Requiem*, and a semi-staged performance of Purcell's *Dido and Aeneas* by the Amersham Festival Chamber Orchestra and Singers. The next four festivals brought other celebrated musicians: harpist Marisa Robles, the Jacques Loussier Trio, Cleo Laine and Johnny Dankworth, and the tenor Philip Langridge. In a lighter vein, there were concerts by The Demon Barbers (with their 'razor-sharp' barbershop and rugby songs) and the BBC Big Band. The Percy French Concert Party brought French's humorous songs to the Guildhall in 1999, exactly 100 years since the composer himself had sung there. The highlight of the 1999 festival was a thrilling performance of *Messiah* by Harry Christophers' Sixteen in St Eugene's Cathedral on 22 October.

When the Two Cathedrals' Festival came to an end the following year it was not because the event had run out of steam, but because the two organists responsible had moved on from their Cathedral positions: Doherty to a new post in music education and Allen in 2000 to a post as organist in St Louis, USA. As might have

The Ulster Youth Orchestra concert which opened the Millennium Forum, Derry's long-awaited theatre, on 17 August 2001. (By kind permission of the Ulster Youth Orchestra and McCabrey Design)

been said about Malmene in 1868, Derry's loss was Missouri's gain. Not that Donal Doherty gave up working with choirs: he has continued to lead the City of Derry Civic Choirs (formed in 1997) and, since 2001, their adult chamber choir Codetta which, under his direction, has acquired an international reputation.

Derry's long tradition of choral singing goes back to the Scottish Presbyterian choirs of the nineteenth century and continues into the present day. Apart from Doherty's choirs, there is currently the Altnagelvin Hospital Choir (formed in 1994), the Calgach Singers (1996), and the Brow o' the Hill Choir, composed of past pupils of the Christian Brothers' School, who in 1998 gave a memorable centenary performance of Edward Conaghan's '98 *Cantata* in the Rialto – due recognition of Derry's first local musician of note. Although some claimed to detect a falling away in choral singing in Northern Ireland as the twentieth century drew to a close, the evidence from Derry suggests otherwise.[112]

Amid the success stories there was one notable casualty: the Londonderry Feis. Falling entries and attendances made its demise in 1998 inevitable, depriving Derry of its oldest surviving musical institution. In contrast, the Feis Dhoire continued to go from strength to strength, notching up 6,000 entries in 1999, as it celebrated its 75th Anniversary Year.

About another area of growth it is hard not to feel a certain ambivalence, namely in the increasing layers of bureaucracy involved in every cultural event. Each theatre or arts centre now had its manager, marketing assistant and educational outreach officer to play up the role of the arts in bringing the community together or regenerating the local economy – a far cry from the days when it was individual enthusiasts, many of them musicians or actors themselves, who were the driving force behind the city's cultural activities.

The Waterside Theatre

2001 was an exceptional year for Derry, with two new theatres opening within the space of six months, on opposite banks of the river: the Waterside Theatre in March and the Millennium Forum in August. The Waterside Theatre on Glendermott Road was housed in the former Young & Rochester Factory, built in 1892, when shirt manufacturing was at its height in Derry. One hundred years later the building was derelict and was only rescued from demolition by the Maydown Community Group led by Glen Barr, a former loyalist politician and leading figure in the Ulster Defence Association. The new, rather makeshift theatre opened with a seating capacity of 372, initially without any public funding. It quickly built up an exciting and diverse repertoire of plays, concerts, opera and dance events that persuaded ACNI and other funders to support the work it was doing with the young and the community in general on the East Bank. The physicality of some of the Waterside Theatre's events was designed to appeal particularly to younger people, such as visits by the North-West Circus School, the Lakota Native American Dancers and Project X, a one-day project of 'stage combat and hip hop dancing'.

The Millennium Forum

The completion of the Millennium Forum marked the final chapter of the longest-running saga in Derry's cultural life. It opened to a capacity audience on 17 August 2001 with a concert by the Ulster Youth Orchestra. Past disagreements about its location were for the moment forgotten, as eighty-six young musicians, including a large percussion section, filled the stage and provided a first stern test of the building's acoustics. The programme was demanding for such a young ensemble: Berlioz's *Carnival Overture*, Rachmaninov's *Second Piano Concerto* and Walton's *First Symphony*, the last of these chosen for its Irish connection (it was dedicated to and premiered by Irish composer and conductor Hamilton Harty). The soloist in the Rachmaninov concerto was twenty-five-year-old Dublin pianist David Quigley, who received a three-minute standing ovation; some of it, no doubt, for the new theatre as well as for the young pianist and orchestra. Belfast pianist Barry Douglas was spotted backstage, fulfilling a promise made three years before to attend the Forum's inaugural concert.

A scene from Dave Duggan's play, Still the Blackbird Sings *staged by the Playhouse. Based on an episode from the First World War, the popularity of the play confirmed Derry's enduring fondness for plays on a military theme. (By kind permission of The Playhouse)*

Among the first-night audience and the public at large there was widespread agreement that the design and layout out of the building was an imaginative response to a difficult site. The new Forum was a 'fine building' and built on a 'grand scale', and, if its 1,100-seat capacity was not quite the compact repertory theatre envisaged by TAG's campaigners of the 1960s, the ceiling of the auditorium could be lowered to convert it into a medium-sized theatre space of 700 seats, or, for smaller events, a stalls area of around 360 seats – in effect, providing three theatres in one.

The 'official' theatre opening was on 7 September. Following the nineteenth-century practice, Michael Poynor gave the traditional manager's speech, describing – and demonstrating – the theatre's 'state-of-the-art' facilities, computerised sound system and generous stage (reputedly the largest in Ireland). Poynor, an experienced actor, producer and director with strong links to amateur drama, was a popular choice as the theatre's first Chief Executive.

One of the opening shows, the musical *Rent*, was described as the 'First West End Show' to be brought to Derry. This is perhaps literally true, but it showed scant awareness of the many celebrated London actors who over the years had performed on Derry's stages, from the Artillery Lane Theatre of the 1820s to the glory days of the Opera House.

Several amateur groups quickly adopted the Millennium Forum as their new home, including the Classical Music Society, the City of Derry Drama Festival, and the Londonderry Musical Society (the renamed Londonderry Amateur Opera Society, now with a healthy membership of over 100 singers and actors, and nineteen patrons). The Classical Music Society, too, seemed to be growing in strength, building up new audiences and developing a network of 'friends'. Kevin Murphy from Derry, a professional clarinettist, was now their Audience Development Officer and organisational mainstay. The Forum was their preferred venue for concerts; with the upper balconies partitioned off, an intimate atmosphere could be created for their chamber music concerts, song recitals and opera. Many noted musicians and ensembles appeared, including Barry Douglas, cellist Julian Lloyd Webber, the RTÉ Concert Orchestra and the Joachim Piano Trio. The Brodsky Quartet, with its Derry-born violist Paul Cassidy, were frequent and popular visitors. The City of Derry Orchestra, set up by local professional musicians in 2000, added a further dimension to the society's Christmas concerts. The future seemed bright and unthreatening.

'Teething' Problems

The first sign of trouble came towards the end of the Forum's first year, when it was revealed that it had incurred debts of £750,000, vastly in excess of the projected figures. There was a confrontation between the Derry Theatre Trust and the manager, with Poynor initiating legal action, claiming he was being made a scapegoat for the theatre's under funding. Newspapers reported him as having been 'sacked' by the Trust in an attempt to avert the theatre's closure. At a series of hastily convened crisis meetings with the principal funders, an emergency rescue package was put together, with Atlantic Philanthropies and ACNI the main contributors. Finally, in September 2002, Deputy Manager David McLaughlin was appointed in Poynor's place. According to the *Belfast Telegraph*, the Theatre Trust offered Poynor financial compensation in exchange for him dropping his legal challenge, in order to 'prevent a lengthy and expensive court battle'.

The controversy rumbled on into 2003. In March, arts commentator and journalist Ian Hill argued that the Trust had 'let go [*sic*] the experienced Michael Poynor for not doing the impossible' — the 'no bricks without straw' defence — and a director of ACNI put the blame for the debt squarely on what he called 'inappropriate programming'. Whichever was right, the Forum management took the hint, and over the next few years settled into an unashamedly populist and financially 'safe' diet of musicals, tribute shows and pantomimes, with only occasional visits by touring ballet companies and repertory companies to pull in the *cognoscenti*. Attendance figures climbed, attracted by popular entertainers like Billy Connolly, Kris Kristofferson, Brian Kennedy and Jason Donovan, but while this made good sense in box-office terms, it seemed something of a come-down from the high hopes that many in Derry had had for the theatre.[113]

Meanwhile a new Centre for the Creative and Performing Arts opened at Magee College in October 2003. Housed in the former Foyle Arts Centre on Lawrence Hill, it centralised undergraduate and postgraduate teaching in the performing arts (music, dance and drama) on one campus of the university. The building chosen had been Foyle College in the later nineteenth century, where organist Patrick Mulholland, bandmaster Henry Stoll and polymath Jerzy Renczynski had all taught. But its transformation to its new use was made possible only through the continuing generosity of Chuck Feeney, whose Atlantic Philanthropies gave US$2 million to buy and renovate the building. The move of music to Derry, in particular, was soon felt within the city, with Shaun Ryan's university choir losing no time in establishing a reputation for thrilling performances of new and difficult works by contemporary composers.

Ilex-urc, the city's urban regeneration company, might have seemed an unlikely source of cultural renewal. Established by the government in 2003, with Derry-born Eddie Friel as its first Chairman, its original remit was to develop two disused city locations: Fort George and Ebrington Barracks. But within a few years, Ilex was interpreting its brief more widely, identifying culture as its preferred means of regenerating the city. Thus it was Ilex, in partnership with Derry City Council, which submitted the Derry~Londonderry bid to be the first UK City of Culture in early 2010, finally using the city's divided history and cultural heritage to its advantage. It was the submission's emphasis on culture as a unifying factor and as a means of reconciliation that was said to have swayed the judges to choose Derry.

The Playhouse Restoration Campaign

While the Millennium Forum went down the route of popular, 'crowd-pulling' shows, The Playhouse persevered with its grassroots theatre, dance and community outreach programmes, all the time struggling with an ageing building in constant need of repair. A possible solution to its problems presented itself in the BBC2 *Restoration* programme in 2004. If The Playhouse could win the competition, the prize money would be sufficient to totally refurbish the building. It passed the first hurdle, winning the regional round. For the London final, a campaign of support began in Derry – and throughout Northern Ireland – with the City Council providing free phone calls from the Guildhall for voters. Backed by a city united in goodwill, a deputation of Playhouse directors, staff and supporters, accompanied by Radio 3 presenter Sean Rafferty, set off for London on 5 August. The Playhouse failed to win, but the publicity generated by its participation in the competition proved almost as good, as subsequent applications to the Heritage Lottery Fund and the Arts Council, among others, raised sufficient funds to completely restore the building and redesign the interior.

Epilogue

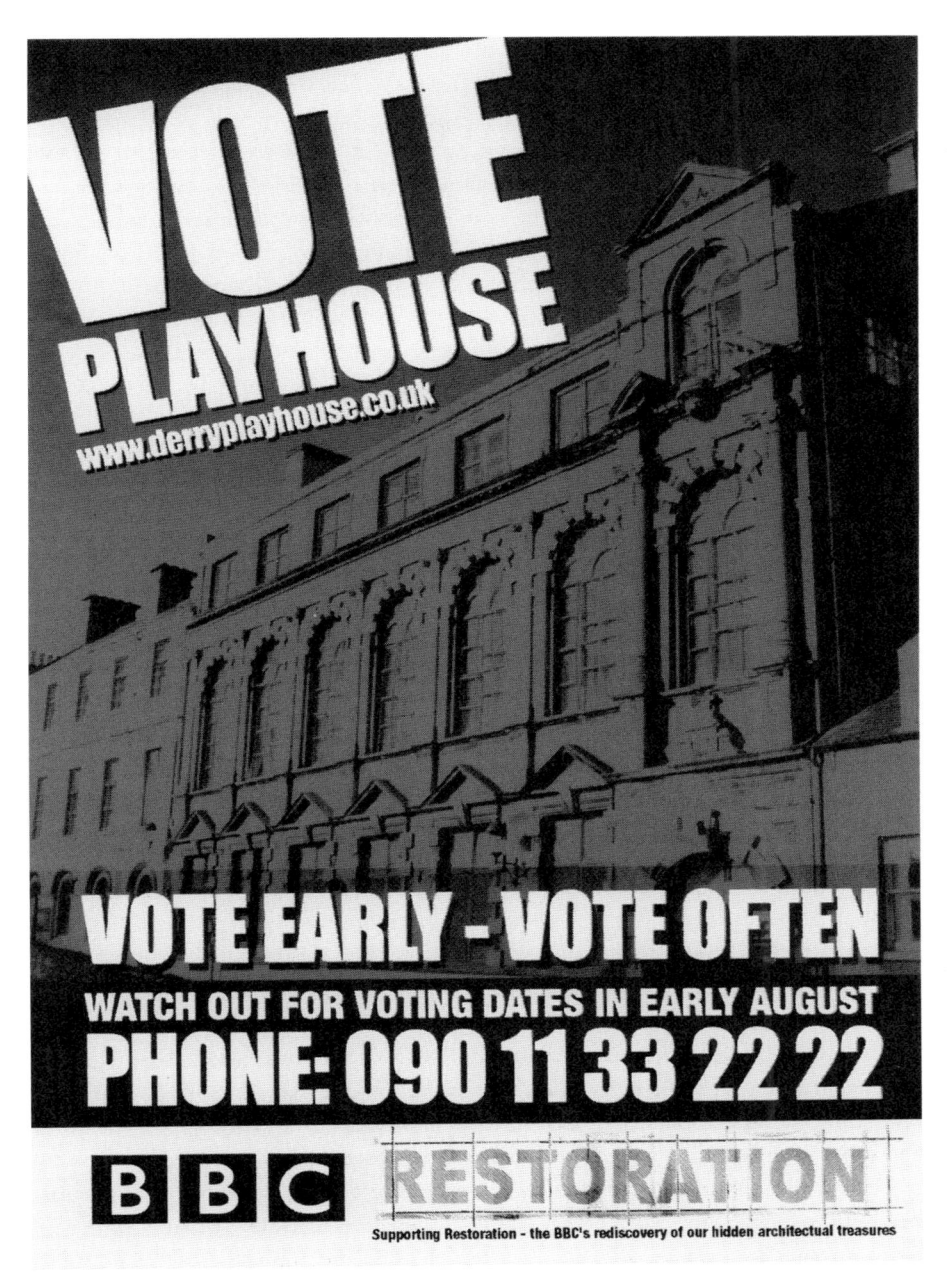

'Vote Early-Vote Often!' The Playhouse campaign flier for the 2004 BBC2 Restoration *competition. (By kind permission of The Playhouse)*

Music 55-7 or What's in a Name?

In 2006, with healthy concert seasons and annual weekend festivals well established, the Classical Music Society's name was changed yet again, to the jazzier 'Music 55-7', a reference to the city's latitude. Its status, too, was altered from a charitable organisation to a limited company. The new company then established a base in Magee, with ambitious plans for school-based projects involving collaborative work with professional musicians. However, the educational focus of Music 55-7 broadened at the expense of its other activities. Instead of seasons of concerts taking place at regular intervals during the year, there were concentrated one-off festivals of music: The City of Derry Guitar Festival, the City of Song, Walled City Festival and Fiddle Fest – arguably more festivals than a city of Derry's size could support. By 2008, the society's regular concert seasons had ceased.

In retrospect, those responsible for running Music 55-7 were perhaps rash in making so many radical changes of direction all at once, without ensuring that they had their existing audience base, used to regular concerts in the winter months, behind them. The outcome was all too predictable. By the beginning of 2010, the company was in financial difficulties, faced with mounting debts and with its ACNI funding suspended. This, combined with the departure of artistic director Kevin Murphy to another arts post and the resignation of chairman Brendan Devlin, left Music 55-7 still existing in name, but for all practical purposes defunct. By then, another concert-giving group had emerged in pianist Cathal Breslin's 'Walled City Festival'.

Three Openings and a Festival

By autumn 2009, theatre-goers in Derry were, in terms of venues, enjoying an embarrassment of riches. There was, of course, the city's main civic theatre, the Millennium Forum, but, remarkably, three other new or refurbished theatres opened or reopened their doors in the space of a few weeks. First was An Croi, the new 200-seat theatre in the Irish language arts centre, An Cultúrlann, which opened on Friday 4 September. This £4 million state-of-the-art building in Great James Street also housed a multi-purpose arts centre, classrooms and a bookshop. Although its focus in the main was on the Irish language and culture, the theatre provided a wide range of plays, lectures and concerts designed to appeal to all of the city's culture lovers.

Next was the Waterside Theatre, which reopened on 17 September, its £1.2 million refurbishment bringing a new entrance and foyer, rehearsal rooms and exhibition space. Its parent body, the Maydown Group, had by this time changed its name to the International School for Peace Studies, to reflect its dedication to reconciliation. The theatre's new auditorium was officially inaugurated by local young people performing excerpts from Felicity McCall's drama *We Were Brothers*. There was potent

James Lecky (left) and Gerry Dorrity (right) in the Waterside Theatre's production of We Were Brothers. *(By kind permission of the Waterside Theatre)*

symbolism in the choice of this work, given its poignant dramatisation of the bonds between two young soldiers from North-West Ulster, drawn from each side of the religious divide, who had fought together at the Battle of Messines during the First World War. Since then, the play has been revived several times in the theatre, and the International School for Peace Studies continues to use the piece in their international outreach work in conflict zones in Bosnia and the Middle East.[114]

The Waterside Theatre has now established its own place in Derry's cultural life, specialising in local drama, ballet, opera and music. Since 2006, it has hosted the City of Derry Drama Festival, its smaller, unfussy auditorium providing a more intimate space for plays, audiences, and the crucial, and often lively, post-show discussions. Its annual Hidden Treasures Children's Theatre Festival has featured many Northern Irish drama groups such as Cahoots, Sticky Fingers and Replay Productions. With its programming and warmer atmosphere, the theatre in many ways comes closer to the kind of theatre originally envisaged for Derry by TAG, a fact acknowledged by both Brian Friel and Frank McGuinness individually agreeing to become its patrons.

Finally, the restored Playhouse reopened on Friday 27 November 2009 to reveal its £4.6 million makeover, which included a new compact 175-seat auditorium. The historic buildings, redesigned by London's Blonski Architects, have been 'restored sympathetically, and yet fused with very modern interior design'. Since then, the centre has housed the Playhouse Players, an innovative repertory company which

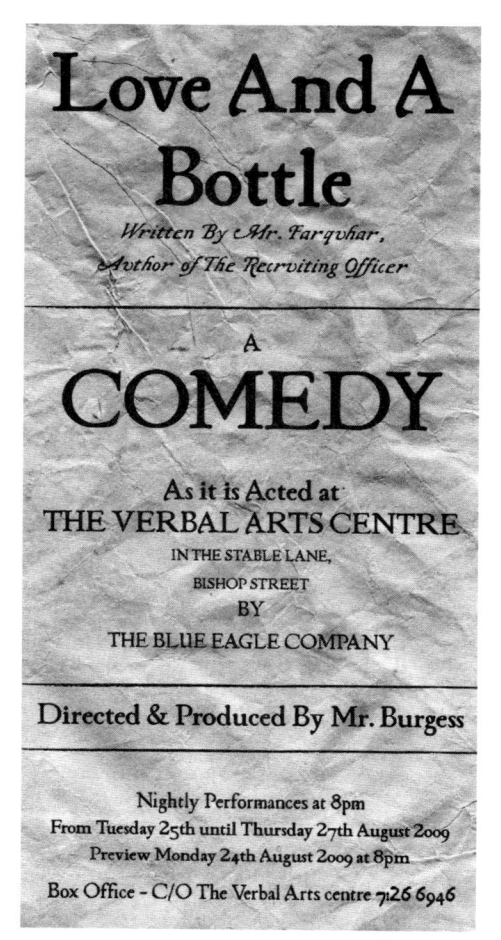

Blue Eagle Productions' staging of Farquhar's Love and a Bottle *in August 2009 to mark the unveiling of a Blue Plaque to Farquhar at the Verbal Arts Centre. (By kind permission of Jonathan Burgess)*

commissions, produces and tours plays throughout Ireland. With this, and through its repertoire of local and experimental drama, art workshops, lectures and concerts, The Playhouse has made itself into the kind of theatre hoped for by so many theatre-lovers of the post-war period. Patrons of The Playhouse include novelist Jennifer Johnston, playwright Frank McGuinness, and the three Cusack sisters (Sorcha, Niamh and Sinéad), mindful perhaps of their Derry-born mother, actress Maureen Kiely.

The story of Derry's theatrical life began with George Farquhar and it might appropriately, for the time being, close with him. In the spring of 2008, an event took place in the city of his birth that was probably without precedent in the long history of the stage. The brainchild of Jonathan Burgess, it was the George Farquhar Theatre Festival, a celebration of the playwright's works and the first to present all seven Farquhar plays in succession to the public over the course of a few days. Three were given full-dress performances by Blue Eagle Productions and the others were given as play readings. Spread across six venues, the festival was a reminder to his fellow citizens of the abiding wit and humour of one of the city's finest writers. Farquhar is commemorated, finally, in a blue plaque that was unveiled at the Verbal Arts Centre in Stable Lane on 25 August 2009. It says simply, 'George Farquhar, *c.*1677-1707, Playwright, attended the Free School near this site.'

APPENDIX 1

DERRY~LONDONDERRY CULTURAL CALENDAR, 1677-2009

1677	Birth of George Farquhar, playwright, in Bank Lane.
1703	Birth of Charles Macklin, actor and playwright, in Culdaff, County Donegal.
1741	First record of a theatre company in Derry, Dublin's Smock Alley Theatre Company.
1769	First visit by Thomas Ryder's Theatre Company.
1774	Derry's first theatre opens on the Shipquay.
1778	St Columb's Cathedral organ is damaged by vandals.
1779	First Derry performance of *The Beggar's Opera*.
1780	Derry's first music society, the Londonderry Musical Society, is founded.
1788	Siege centenary commemorations.
1789	Derry's second theatre opens in Artillery Lane.
1791	Thomas King, actor, appears in the Artillery Lane Theatre.
1796	First visit of Count Joseph Boruwlaski, dwarf guitarist.
1802	First recorded use of a piano in a Derry theatre.
1810	Montague Talbot becomes manager of the Artillery Lane Theatre.
1813	Michael Lacy, virtuoso violinist, performs in the theatre.
1817	First performance in Derry of excerpts from Handel's *Messiah*.
	Derry's second music society, also called Londonderry Musical Society, is founded.
1820	Mozart's *Don Juan* (*Don Giovanni*) is performed in the Artillery Lane Theatre.
1823	Edmund Kean plays Othello in the Artillery Lane Theatre.
1825	Corporation Hall opens in the Diamond.
1829	Angelica Catalani, soprano, gives a concert in Corporation Hall.
	Ira Aldridge, the 'African Roscius', makes the first of four visits.
1832	Weber's *Der Freischütz* first performed in the Artillery Lane Theatre.
1833	Artillery Lane Theatre finally closes.
1835	Guilio Regondi gives concerts in Corporation Hall.
1843	Derry's third theatre, the Theatre Royal, opens in Fountain Street.
	James Hunter opens Derry's first music shop.
1847	Derry's first orchestral promenade concert.
1849	Derry's third music society, the Londonderry Musical Association, is founded.
	Band concerts first held in the grounds of Gwyn's Institution.
1851	Derry's first choral concert, in Glendermott Presbyterian church.
1854	Derry's first choral society, the Londonderry Harmonic Society, is founded.
1855	Patriotic Fund Concerts held in aid of the Crimean War.

1857	First visit of Catherine Hayes, the 'Hibernian Nightingale'.
1858	Final closure of the Theatre Royal in Fountain Street.
1859	Concert by Louis Jullien and Henryk Wieniawski in January.
	Concert by Jenny Lind and Joseph Joachim in October.
	First piano recital in Derry by Frederick Eavestaff.
1860	The Maiden City Band of the Apprentice Boys is founded.
1862	Derry's fourth theatre, the Queen's Theatre in Chamberlain Place, opens.
1863	Concert by pianist Sigismond Thalberg in Corporation Hall.
1866	The Britannia Brass and Reed Band founded.
	First series of 'Popular Concerts' by Waldemar Malmene.
1873	Grand concert to celebrate the first organ in St Eugene's Cathedral.
	Fisk Jubilee Singers give a 'service of song' in First Derry church.
1874	Final press advertisement for the Queen's Theatre, Chamberlain Place.
1875	Root's *Belshazzar's Feast* becomes the first full-length oratorio to be performed in Derry.
1876	Derry's first public organ recital, All Saint's church, Clooney.
1877	Premiere of Patrick Mulholland's cantata *Brian Boru* in Corporation Hall.
	New Royal Opera House opens.
	Apprentice Boys' Hall opens in Society Street.
1878	Derry's first complete choral and orchestral performance of Handel's *Messiah*.
	Carlisle Road Choir is founded.
1879	Arthur Lloyd, music hall entertainer, first appears at the Opera House.
1880	Barton McGuckin and William Ludwig, Irish tenors, sing in the Opera House.
1883	Percy French, Irish songwriter and entertainer, performs in Corporation Hall.
1884	Oscar Wilde, playwright, gives two lectures at the Opera House.
1885	First public organ recital in St Columb's Cathedral by Dr Daniel Jones.
1887	Alexandrina Elsner first sings in Derry.
1888	William H. Collisson gives first season of Popular Concerts in the Opera House.
1889	Londonderry Orchestral Society formed by Edward Conaghan.
1890	The Guildhall opens in Shipquay Place.
1891	First series of H.B. Phillips' subscription concerts in the Guildhall.
1892	Inauguration of the new Guildhall organ.
	H.B. Phillips opens his first music business in Marlborough Street.
	Madame Albani sings at a H.B. Phillips' concert.
1894	H.B. Phillips opens his shop in Shipquay Street.
1895	Death of hymn-writer Mrs C.F. Alexander.
1896	H.B. Phillips' syndicate takes over the Opera House.
1898	Premiere of Edward Conaghan's *'98 Cantata*.
1899	The Londonderry Philharmonic Society is founded.
1900	The first Feis Ceoil (later the Londonderry Feis) is held.
1904	Payne Seddon takes over the Opera House from Phillips.
1905	Hempton's (now Graham's) Pianoforte Warehouse moves to Strand Road.
1906	The Opera House is renamed the Hippodrome.
	Irish tenors Plunket Greene and Denis O'Sullivan sing at Phillips' concerts.
1908	Guildhall is extensively damaged by fire on Easter Sunday.
	First performance of Thomas O'Flynn's play *Cahir O'Doherty* in the Opera House.
1909	John McCormack gives his first Derry concert, in St Columb's Hall.
	Corporation Hall demolished.
1911	Sousa Band gives two concerts in St Columb's Hall.
1913	Derry's first 'continuous' film shows, in the Opera House.
1914	'Hallé Band' (orchestra) concert in St Columb's Hall.
	New organ installed in the Guildhall.

Appendix 1

	First Saturday night 'Wartime Concert' in the Guildhall.
1915	First Londonderry Amateur Operatic Society founded.
1917	Cyril Cusack appears on the Opera House stage, aged seven.
1918	Dublin theatre owner Barney Armstrong takes over the Opera House.
1919	The Opera House is renamed The Empire.
1921	Death of Armstrong: the Opera House administered by Munster and Leinster Bank.
1922	First Feis Dhoire Colmcille held.
1923	Bohemian Male Voice Choir founded.
1924	Bradlaw–Morrison partnership buys the Opera House.
	Hamilton Harty adjudicates at Feis.
	Opera House Strike.
	Charles Doran's first Shakespearean Festival at the Opera House.
1926	H.B. Phillips' Royal Carl Rosa Opera Company visit to the Opera House.
1927	Feis Dhoire Colmcille's prize-winners' concert first broadcast live on radio.
1928	Sir Frank Benson adjudicates at the Feis.
1930	The Londonderry Dramatic Club founded.
1932	John McCormack's second concert in the Guildhall.
1935	John McCormack's third and final concert in the Guildhall.
1936	Fritz Kreisler concert in the Guildhall.
	Paul Robeson concert in the Guildhall.
	BBC Northern Ireland Orchestra Guildhall concert with Redmond Friel's music.
	Anew McMaster's Irish Theatre Company makes two visits to Derry.
1937	First of two amateur drama festivals in St Columb's Hall.
1938	Londonderry Corporation lifts ban on jazz playing on the Guildhall organ.
	Last live show at the Opera House.
	Belfast tenor James Johnston is 'discovered' at a Philharmonic concert.
1939	Last Londonderry Philharmonic Society concert.
	First Saturday night wartime popular concert.
1940	Opera House destroyed by fire.
1942	George Formby visits Derry to entertain troops.
1945	Dublin Gate Theatre Company visits Guildhall.
1946	City of Derry Drama Club founded.
	The Guild Theatre opens in North Edward Street.
1947	Londonderry Music Circle is founded.
1949	Templemore Male Choir is founded.
	Tyrone Guthrie adjudicates at Feis.
1950	Death in London of H.B. Phillips.
1951	Éamon de Valera opens a Week of Gaelic Culture in Derry.
	Derry-born Michael McTernan's play *Wee Mick* accepted by the Abbey Theatre.
	Hallé Orchestra concert at the Guildhall.
1952	St Columb's Cathedral Oratorio Society is founded.
1953	Douglas Fairbanks Jnr appears in a Variety Show in the Rialto.
	Brian Boydell adjudicates at the Feis.
1954	First visit of the Raidió Éireann Orchestra to Derry.
1956	Lawrence Glover plays Prokofiev piano concerto in Guildhall.
	BBC Symphony Orchestra gives a concert in Guildhall.
	The Little Gaelic Singers are founded by James MacCafferty.
1957	The first concert season of the new North-West Music Society.
1958	Guitarist Julian Bream in North-West Music Society concert at Magee College.
	Joseph Cooper plays Beethoven's *Emperor* concerto in Guildhall.
	Kenneth McKellar sings in Derry.

From Farquhar to Field Day

1962	The Londonderry Light Opera Society is founded.
	First visit to Derry of Dublin's Abbey Theatre, with Brian Friel's *The Enemy Within*.
1964	BBC Symphony Orchestra at First North-West Arts Festival.
	Joan Hammond gives a concert in the Guildhall.
1966	First Ulster Orchestra a concert in the Guildhall.
1967	The second North-West Arts Festival.
1969	Larry Adler, harmonica virtuoso, gives a concert in Londonderry High School.
1970	Dana wins the Eurovision Song Contest.
	Colmcille Ladies' Choir and the '71 Players are founded.
	The third North-West Arts Festival held.
1971	St Columb's Minor Hall refurbished as the Little Theatre.
1972	Actress Siobhan McKenna performs at the Shantallow Festival.
	Guildhall is bombed severely twice.
1974	Derry School of Irish Harping launched.
1975	Londonderry Arts Association set up.
	LAOS and Feis Dhoire restart after a three-year suspension.
1977	Guildhall reopened after bomb damage is repaired.
	The Foyle Singers win major competition at the Oireachtas in Dublin.
1978	Benjamin Luxon gives a concert at Magee College.
	Irish Ballet Company visits Derry on first tour to Northern Ireland.
1980	Premiere of Brian Friel's *Translations* in Guildhall.
	Field Day Theatre Company founded in Derry by Brian Friel and Stephen Rea.
	Phillips' Beethoven House music shop in Shipquay Street finally closes.
	The North-West Arts Festival revived.
1981	First City of Derry Drama Festival at Magee College.
	Premiere of Friel's adaptation of Chekhov's *Three Sisters*.
1982	Premiere of Friel's *Communication Cord*.
1983	ABC Cinema converted to Rialto Entertainment Centre.
1987	Premiere of Stewart Parker's play *Pentecost*.
	George Melly appears in the North-West Festival.
1988	Classical Music Series of concerts launched at Magee College.
1989	Premiere of Kevin O'Connell's composition *From the Besieged City* in Guildhall.
	Muriel Anderson's 'Molitor' Stradivarius violin is sold by Christie's of London.
1990	Premiere of Shaun Davey's *Relief of Derry Symphony* in Guildhall.
	Premiere of Seamus Heaney's play *The Cure at Troy*.
1992	The year-long Impact '92 festival.
	First Two Cathedrals' Festival and first Guinness Jazz Festival.
	Derry premiere of Frank McGuiness's *Carthaginians*.
	Poetry reading by Poet Laureate Ted Hughes in Guildhall.
	Playhouse Arts Centre and Verbal Arts Centre open.
1993	Octoberfest '93 held.
	Victoria de los Angeles sings in St Eugene's Cathedral.
	The Jacques Loussier Trio plays Bach in St Columb's Cathedral.
	Stage invasion at performance of *At the Black Pig's Dyke*.
1994	O'Casey Theatre Company adopts The Playhouse as their base.
	Vandals damage St Columb's Cathedral organ.
1995	Death of James MacCafferty.
	Last Field Day play in Derry: McGuinness's version of Chekhov's *Uncle Vanya*.
1996	Derry Theatre Trust is formed.
1997	The Echo Echo Dance Theatre Company adopts The Playhouse as its base.
	Plans for the Millennium Forum are announced.

Appendix 1

1998	First Maiden City Festival organised by the Apprentice Boys' Clubs of Derry.
	Final Londonderry Feis held.
	Brow o' the Hill Choir gives centenary performance of Conaghan's '98 *Cantata*.
1999	Josef Locke dies.
2000	Julian Lloyd Webber plays at a Classical Music Society concert in Rialto.
	Cleo Laine and Johnny Dankworth perform at last Two Cathedrals' Festival.
	Verbal Arts Centre moves to former First Derry school on the walls.
2001	Millennium Forum and Waterside Theatre open.
2002	The Rialto demolished.
2003	Centre for Performing Arts opens at Magee College.
2004	The Playhouse reaches the final of the BBC2 *Restoration* programme.
2008	City of Song Festival organised by Music 55-7.
	Blue Eagle Production's Farquhar Festival.
2009	Refurbished Waterside and Playhouse theatres reopen.
	An Croi Theatre opens in Irish Language Centre, An Cultúrlann.
	Cathal Breslin's first Walled City Music Festival held at Magee and Guildhall.
	First arts event at Ebrington Barracks: Dave Duggan's play *Still the Blackbird Sings*.
	Blue Plaque unveiled to George Farquhar at Verbal Arts Centre.

APPENDIX 2

DRAMA AND MUSIC SOCIETIES IN DERRY/LONDONDERRY*

* Bands and choirs have not been listed as their number during the period runs into hundreds.

Amateur Drama Groups

None known before 1870

1870-1900
The City of Derry Dramatic Club
The Star Dramatic Company

1901-1950
The City of Derry Dramatic Society
Londonderry Dramatic Society
The Dramatic Society of Derry Guilds
Londonderry Dramatic Society (second of same name)
St Columb's Guilds' Dramatic Society
The Derry City Players
The Foresters' Dramatic Club
The Derry Repertory Society
The Londonderry Dramatic Society
The YMCA Players
St Eugene's Dramatic Society
The Ebrington Players
The Tower Players
The Waterside Players
The City of Derry Drama Club
The Green Circle Amateur Dramatic Club

St Enda's Drama Society
The Christ Church Players

1951-2009
The Colmcille Players
Magee University College Drama Society
Mercy Convent Past Pupils' Union Dramatic Club
Kieran Club
St Columb's Past Pupils' Union Dramatic Society
The 'Sea Eagle' Players
St Enda's Players
Derry Pantomime Players
The '71 Players
The Theatre Club
The Derry Players
St Columb's College Drama Society
St Brigid's Music and Drama Society
The Waterside Drama Players (later The Workhouse Players)
The Craic Pack
The Crimson Players

Amateur Music Societies

1780-1850
Londonderry Musical Society
(The Second) Londonderry Musical Society
Londonderry Musical Association

1851-1900
Londonderry Harmonic Society
Londonderry Choral Union
Harmonia Sacra Society
Apollonian Glee Society
Londonderry Cathedral Bell-Ringing Club
Derry Philharmonic Society
Londonderry Choral Society
St Columb's Choral Union
St Andrew's Choral Union
Derry/Londonderry Musical Union
Londonderry Choral Society
Londonderry Orchestral Society
Presbyterian Musical Union
Waterside Choral Society
St Cecilia Society
Londonderry Philharmonic Society

1901-1950
Brian Boru Choral Union (also called Brian Boru Musical Society)
Joseph O'Brien's Amateur Operatic Company
The Londonderry Amateur Operatic Society
Derry Glee and Madrigal Society
Christ Church Choral Society
St Augustine's Musical Society
St Columb's Cathedral Oratorio Society (renamed as St Columb's Cathedral Musical Society)
North-West Music Guild
Londonderry Music Circle

1951-2009
St Columb's Choral Society
St Mary's Choral Society
Londonderry Light Opera Society (now Londonderry Musical Society)
Magee University Classical Music Society
North-West Music Society
Londonderry Arts Association
The Classical Music Society (later Music 55-7)
The Walled City Festival Group

NOTES

1. It remains open to conjecture whether Farquhar fought at the Battle of the Boyne in 1690, as some historians have suggested.
2. Coteries were small-scale dances which included card-playing and polite conversation, and were attended by a fairly intimate circle of people, while drums were larger, more public dances.
3. Foreign musicians, usually from mainland Europe, were quite numerous in the larger Irish provincial towns during the eighteenth century. They increased in number in Derry during the nineteenth century.
4. Later known as the King's Arms Hotel.
5. The Ballyscullion house in Mid-Ulster is the only one of Hervey's three houses which has been demolished. Ickworth in Suffolk and remnants of Downhill, outside Castlerock, are still extant.
6. Hereafter referred to as First Derry.
7. Handel composed the oratorio to celebrate the victory of the Duke of Cumberland over Bonnie Prince Charlie at Culloden in 1745.
8. This contrasts sharply with Armagh Cathedral, which had a succession of English-born organists until 1798, when the first Irish-born organist, John Jones, was employed.
9. Every press advertisement for the charity sermons mentions that the boys were connected with 'the meeting-house of this city'. Nonetheless, it has been suggested that Derry had, in fact, two schools of 'singing boys', one each in First Derry and the Cathedral. This point remains unsettled.
10. The 'Peep O'Day Boys' were later to become the 'Orange Order'.
11. 'Logierian Academies' were the brainchild of Johann Bernhard Logier, a former military musician who lived in Dublin. In 1814 he devised a method of group teaching for the piano, and his academies became widespread in the British Isles during the 1820s. Logier's second son, William Henry, arrived in Derry in 1843 to propagate the Logierian Method.
12. The writer of the review in the *Athenaeum* where these memories are recorded is anonymous, but may have been John Doran, a regular contributor to the journal and author of *Their Majesties' Servants* (1860), an historical account of the English stage.
13. Egan invented a cocktail (brandy, eggnog and rum) and called it 'Tom and Jerry' after the characters in his novel; it was the cocktail, so it is said, that suggested the names Tom and Jerry for the cat and mouse in the MGM cartoons.
14. In 1849, the hotel building became the Sisters of Mercy Convent, which it remained until 1997.

Notes

15 A pochette was a diminutive, four-stringed instrument carried in the breast pocket.
16 This moral stance extended to other social entertainments in Derry. The 'Races' at Ballyarnett had stopped in 1833 because of 'the drunkenness, gambling and prolificacy that always [took] place at them'.
17 Perois had lived in Derry and in Belfast since 1802, being violinist with the Belfast Anacreontic Society. He settled permanently in Derry from 1833 until his death four years later.
18 J.B. Logier's children – all music teachers, performers and church organists – spread throughout Ireland, England and South Africa.
19 The Logierian Method had been taught in Derry since 1819 by Cathedral organist John Walsh and in a boarding school by a lady 'recently trained in England'.
20 Joseph was the seventh generation of Logier musicians since the mid-seventeenth century. No members of the family remain in Derry, although a great-granddaughter of Henry Logier lives in Belfast.
21 Tonic Solfa was the method pioneered by Hullah and Curwen in the 1840s which bypassed the reading of conventional music notation. Instead, singers read 'simplified' music laid out in Tonic Solfa format, i.e. Doh, Re, Me, etc. Tonic Solfa remained a popular method of teaching singing well into the twentieth century.
22 In 1862, the *Guardian* suggested that it had 'amalgamated' with the Waterside Musical Association. However, rather than a full-scale, formal union of the two societies, it seems likely that remaining members of the LMA merely joined the Waterside society.
23 The Third Congregation in Great James Street was locally known as 'the Scots Kirk', on account of the large number of Scottish families in the congregation.
24 Gwyn's Institution closed in 1901. By then, the grounds had been landscaped and laid out as a public park through the bequest of James Hood Brooke. The building subsequently became a public library and art gallery. It was demolished in 1973.
25 German musicians were common in British military bands. Their numbers decreased with the onset of the Crimean War, when many returned home.
26 McCloskie also conducted an unnamed 'Amateur Band' in 1841; this may have been the same ensemble.
27 The evenings were so named because each member brought his own 'Bottle and Glass' to the celebration.
28 Before the specialist dealers emerged, church organists and piano teachers sold and tuned pianos. In the 1850s their role as sellers declined.
29 Hayes returned to Derry to give another concert on 1 March 1861, five months before her death.
30 Up to the 1840s, orchestras were led by the first violinist, who 'kept time' for all the musicians.
31 Reviews did not give authorship of the *Pastoral Symphony*, but it was probably Beethoven's *6th Symphony*.
32 Thalberg was nicknamed as 'Old Arpeggio' because of his habit of holding the melody with both thumbs and surrounding it with swirling arpeggios.
33 His father, Mossom, owned a bookshop in Ferryquay Street from 1823; his brother James ran a bookshop in Shipquay Street until the mid-1880s.
34 This Commission investigated street riots in Derry in April 1869, during a visit by Prince Arthur, in which three people died.
35 He left £3,500, his music shop, and several properties in Derry and Moville.
36 A descendant, John Donnelly, who still lives in Ballintoy, was unaware of this legacy but suspects that it allowed his great-grandfather to buy the family farm on which the Donnellys still live.
37 By 1873, Chamberlain Place was renamed Chamberlain Street; it was also colloquially known as 'Bog Street'.

38 The actual date of its opening lies between 1859 and 1862. The building was not listed as a theatre in Griffith's 1859 Valuation, indicating that it opened some time after this.
39 The three previous theatres had relied on Belfast and Dublin-based companies for their seasons.
40 The Christy Minstrels were a well-known American blackface ensemble.
41 Not one to miss a chance, she combined this with appearing her own 'Grand Miscellaneous Concert' a week later.
42 Belfast, which didn't have its own Cathedral until 1904, had its first full performance of Handel's *Messiah* in 1813.
43 Derry's first two organists, the Shannons, sold spinets, harpsichords and pianos; Presbyterian precentors Watson and Peterkin tuned and repaired keyboard instruments.
44 Mulholland was organist of St Eugene's from 1873 until 1888; he was succeeded by his son George, who was organist until 1902.
45 James Smyly was organist of the Long Tower church between 1836 and 1878, but there is no record of his participation in concerts, music societies or bands.
46 Farmer was a military musician who lived in Birr Barracks, County Offaly; his son, also Henry George Farmer, became a noted musicologist.
47 Glover was the Dublin-born Professor of Vocal Music at the Irish National Board.
48 By the mid-1870s, the *Journal* had become the public voice of Derry's Catholics.
49 Less so today, although he did coin the phrases, 'the great unwashed' and 'the pen is mightier than the sword'.
50 Frank Matcham designed Warden's Belfast Grand Opera House in 1895.
51 This society used either Derry or Londonderry indifferently in its title. At this time the names had no political or religious significance.
52 Lloyd was the first prolific songwriter for music hall, writing over 185 music hall songs, including the still popular 'Married to a Mermaid'.
53 The Abercorns were patrons of Derry's musical life for several decades. This 2nd Duke of Abercorn, James Hamilton, was Lord Lieutenant of County Donegal. His son, also James Hamilton, the 3rd Duke of Abercorn and later first Governor of Northern Ireland, became patron of Derry's Philharmonic Society in 1899.
54 From its opening in 1873, the Cathedral had stood on rough, unlandscaped grounds, without spire or stained-glass windows. Both were added in 1903, but fundraising continued to pay off the debts incurred by the work.
55 Warden died at his home, Shakespeare House in Adelaide Avenue, Belfast, on 9 March 1898. His large funeral was attended by the Lord Mayor of Belfast and 'many legal and commercial men of the city'. Many leading actors and theatre architects of the day sent wreaths.
56 It was, of course, historical larceny on the part of the *Journal* to treat the 1798 Rebellion and its commemoration as an exclusively Catholic event, when so many of those involved in the former, especially in Ulster, were Protestants.
57 Abraham McCausland Stewart was related to both the McCausland family of Drenagh, Limavady, and the Stewart families of Killymoon, County Tyrone, and Mount Stewart, County Down.
58 The Feis Ceoil Association was founded in Dublin on 29 June 1897, largely through the influence of Annie Patterson. Its aims were to promote the study of Irish music, to encourage the cultivation of music in Ireland, to hold an annual music festival, and to collect and publish Irish traditional music.
59 This was Derry's third Philharmonic Society; there were two previous but ephemeral Philharmonics in 1868 and 1871.
60 Jones died in Ballinasloe in 1911 after a long illness. His decision to become the society's accompanist rather than conductor may have been due to ill-health.

Notes

61 Henry M. Prior was born in 1834 in Walworth, Surrey. He was a keen amateur violinist, playing in several music societies. In the 1880s he was Honorary Secretary of the Government School of Art in Corporation Hall. Nettie (1881-1969) was one of seven children.

62 Its best-known line, 'Gone! Gone! And never called me mother!' is from a stage version of the story and isn't found in the original novel.

63 Vincent O'Brien, McCormack's early singing teacher, was brother of Joseph O'Brien, organist of St Eugene's Cathedral from 1912 to 1930.

64 By 1909, Seddon also owned theatres in Lincoln and Loughborough.

65 By this time, the Herdman family, mill owners of Sion Mills, were the mainstay of the Feis. Captain J.C. (Jack) Herdman succeeded his brother-in-law Captain Ambrose Ricardo as chairman of the committee in 1924.

66 O'Brien left Derry in 1930 to become director of the School of Music in Cathal Brugha Street, Dublin.

67 Henry Coleman (1888-1965) was organist at St Columb's Cathedral between 1914 and 1921.

68 By 1920, W. Payne Seddon was a successful impresario, with two more theatres and cinemas in Whitby and Hawick. He lived in London until he retired to Hapsford House, near Frome in Somerset, in 1923.

69 Armstrong (1872-1921), whose real name was Bernard McNamee, was born in Sheffield of Irish parents.

70 Bradlaw's original family name of 'Brudno' was anglicised after their arrival in England. The Bradlaws became one of Dublin's leading Jewish families, Izidore's father being instrumental in founding the St Kevin's Parade synagogue and the Dolphin Barn cemetery.

71 The identity of the 'non-union' musician was not given in the press, but was probably well known locally.

72 Kathleen Watson (1899-2002), Derry's legendary dancing teacher, came from an old city family, her father Thomas being a perfumer and hairdresser in Shipquay Place. In 1922, 'Miss Watson', as she was always known, taught dancing from rooms at Shipquay Gate and ran her own dances in the Guildhall. She continued to teach ballet in Derry for most of the twentieth century, tutoring generations of young girls first in Pump Street, then at her studio at No.73 Clarendon Street. One of her pupils continues to teach in Derry in the 'Mary Hill School of Ballet'.

73 Doran (1877-1964) and shortly afterwards Anew McMaster were the latest in a long line of actor-managers whose touring companies continued the tradition of Benson, Beerbohm Tree and Henry Irving. Doran was still acting in 1954.

74 Phillips bought the Royal Carl Rosa Opera Company in 1923. His daughter Ailne (1905-1992), known as Babs, was a founding member of the Vic-Sadler's Wells Opera Ballet in 1931, which later became the Royal Ballet. From 1942, Babs was a teacher at the Covent Garden Ballet School and later personal assistant to Dame Ninette de Valois.

75 Granuaile was the Gaelic nickname of Grace O'Malley, a legendary figure in sixteenth-century Ireland also known as the 'Sea Queen (or Pirate Queen) of Connaught', who had become identified in Irish folklore with resistance to the English.

76 Alexandrina returned for Feis Week every year until 1937. She died in Dublin in 1942 but was buried in Derry.

77 Willman (1918-1988) was the son of Romain Willman(n), an émigré from Alsace-Lorraine who had a hairdressing business in Derry in the early 1900s. His film credits include *The Man who Knew Too Much* (1956), *Dr Zhivago* (1965) and *The Odessa File* (1974). He also won a Tony Award in 1962 for his direction of the Broadway production of *A Man for all Seasons*.

78 Born in Belfast, Alberto Macari came from an Italian émigré family; his father Luigi was a musician, his occupation listed as 'organ-grinder'. The Macari family moved to Derry sometime after 1911.

79 Louis Walsh (1880-1942) was born in Maghera. His career as a solicitor was combined with an active interest in politics and writing plays. Objections to the title of the play led to a later name change to *Auction in Killybuck*.
80 Food remained relatively plentiful, given the proximity to Donegal, from where it could be smuggled across the border.
81 The wavelengths of IRA radio frequencies in Belfast were often chalked on walls and pavements in the city, allowing their illegal broadcasts to be heard in certain areas.
82 This phrase was coined by a presiding judge who had heard allegations of such child neglect at a sitting in the Derry Court House in November 1942.
83 Although this acronym stood for 'Entertainments National Service Association', servicemen usually translated it as 'Every Night Something Awful'.
84 Farren's speech predated that of De Valera in March 1943, which is often misquoted as referring to 'comely maidens dancing at the crossroads'. De Valera's actual phrase was, 'the contest of athletic youths and the laughter of happy maidens'.
85 CEMA was established in 1942 with funds from The Pilgrim Trust given to Queen's University to promote 'Music for the People' and 'Arts for the People'. It would later become the Arts Council of Northern Ireland and have a major influence on the development of the arts in Derry over the years.
86 Mac Liammóir (1899-1978) was in reality English-born Alfred Willmore, whose fascination with all things Irish led to his name change. He was a brother-in-law of actor, Anew McMaster.
87 Fred Logan remained a linchpin of CDDC and a passionate supporter of drama until his death in 2006.
88 Loughlin is still a member of the choir of First Derry, where a stained-glass window is dedicated to his contribution to the musical life of his home city.
89 In Irish legend, Caoilte was a member of Finn Mac Cumaill's warrior band. In the medieval *Colloquy of the Ancients*, he returns from the 'otherworld' to tell St Patrick stories of Finn and other heroes of ancient Ireland. Derry's Caoilte perhaps saw himself as a bearer of tales from the theatre world to the public.
90 This IRA campaign lasted between 1956 and 1962, and included the bombing of a BBC relay transmitter in Derry in December 1956.
91 There is a wonderful story in Marjorie Wright's memoir *The Rise and Fall of a La Scala Diva* of Johnston arriving late for a rehearsal of Mendelssohn's *Elijah* in the Guildhall, but coming in on cue with 'If with All Your Heart' as he came up the staircase. When the aria was over, Johnston turned to her and asked, 'in his down-to-earth Belfast way, "How are you doin', daughter"'.
92 Later he bought a pub in County Donegal and made occasional forays into Derry to sing at concerts for charity. His eventful life was later portrayed in the 1992 film *Hear My Song*, the title of which is derived from his concert encore 'Hear My Song, Violetta'.
93 Cafolla had spent the war years in Dundalk, where he developed a reputation as choirmaster and string teacher. He retired to Bray, County Wicklow, in 1976. The Cafolla musical dynasty is continued in his daughters Roma and Olivia, both professional musicians.
94 His grandfather William Glover had lived in Clarence Avenue and worked in Derry's Inland Revenue Office.
95 Glover died of cancer in 1988. The press reported that 'the entire Scottish musical establishment attended his funeral to mourn the premature death of a great pianist, musician and colleague' – a measure of the esteem in which Glover was held in his adopted city.
96 As late as 1983, cigarette manufacturer Gallaher's of Belfast was the major sponsor of the Ulster Orchestra, and the cover of concert programmes mimicked the colour and style of their most popular brand.
97 Brian Ferran (b.1940) had recently been appointed Senior Art Assistant Officer with ACNI and was eventually to become its Director.

Notes

98 The Goodman family has been associated with the Britannia Band as players and conductors since 1900.
99 Ann Hasson (b.1948) was daughter of local tenor Larry Hasson (1909-2011), who forsook an operatic career to return to his native Derry. He eventually owned Austin's store in the Diamond.
100 Aosdána, meaning 'people of the arts', was started in 1981 and is limited to 250 members. 'Saoi' means the 'wise one' and is limited to seven living artists.
101 Mullarkey (1938-2006) was born in County Fermanagh. In 1986, he designed the award-winning Ardhowen Theatre in Enniskillen.
102 By the mid-1980s, there was a change in that ACNI still brought 'outside musicians' but drama was brought to Derry by largely Northern Irish drama companies, as in Charabanc and Mad Cow Productions.
103 Moville-born Donal Doherty (b.1956) studied at the Cantorum Musica in Mullingar, where he was schooled in liturgical music under Frank McNamara. Doherty was also Head of Music at St Columb's College.
104 Derry-born Kevin O'Connell (b.1958) attended St Columb's College, where he studied composition with Redmond Friel. He is currently head of composition at the Royal Irish Academy of Music.
105 The original stimulus for Impact '92 came from Kevin McCaul, Director of Marketing and Tourism at DCC. His illness led to Doran's appointment as programme and artistic director in July 1991.
106 Doran (b.1960) was another St Columb's College pupil who studied music with Redmond Friel. After a music degree, Doran had a varied career, including conducting, arts administration and journalism.
107 Frank McGuinness (b.1953) was born in Buncrana, County Donegal. Since 1997 he has lectured at University College, Dublin.
108 When the year's accounts were finally settled, it seems that the final cost was in excess of £2 million, although the projected budget for the festival year was £1.5 million.
109 The schools were run by the Sisters of Mercy, and backed onto their convent in Pump Street, formerly the King's Arms Hotel and Italian Saloon.
110 From 1995, regional ACNI advisors provided advice; the Forum for Local Government and the Arts, an umbrella body of arts representatives, also had a co-ordinating role in arts provision.
111 In 1998, Field Day briefly re-emerged as a theatre company to jointly perform Stewart Parker's *Northern Lights* with Tinderbox at the Belfast Festival at Queen's. Its theatrical component is now described as 'suspended', although it seems that three Field Day plays will be staged in Derry in 2013.
112 Joe McKee makes this claim in his essay on 'Classical Music' in *Stepping Stones* (2001).
113 A nadir was reached in August 2007, when the *Journal* reported 'Sales Soar for Freak Circus Show' at the Forum. The appropriately named 'Circus of Horrors' featured 'Dan the Demon Dwarf pulling a Henry the Hoover across the stage with his privates'. There were precedents for this, of course, in the grotesqueries that people paid to see in the Queen's Theatre of the 1860s. And again, in keeping with nineteenth-century precedent, the performance was roundly condemned by a Baptist minister.
114 The present theatre manager, Iain Barr, has family links with the site that go back to its days as a shirt factory. His grandmother Margaret Barr was a seamstress and one of the factory workers who had to meticulously sew on shirt collars and cuffs in that same building almost one hundred years ago. Her work, and that of hundreds of female workers like her in Derry, was portrayed in Frank McGuinness's 1982 play *The Factory Girls*. A piece of public art permanently on show at the Waterside Theatre, thirty stoneware ceramic buttons entitled *Fastened Faces & Button Beauties* by Gail Mahon, similarly commemorates the theatre's industrial past.

BIBLIOGRAPHY AND FURTHER READING

Primary Sources

The Arts Council of Northern Ireland (ACNI): Annual Reports 1963-2005, Minutes 2000-2009
The Belfast Newsletter
Thomas Colby, *The Ordnance Survey Memoir of the City and Liberties of Londonderry and Templemore* (Dublin, 1837)
Concert and Theatre Programmes, 1892-2009
Council for the Encouragement of the Arts (CEMA) Annual Reports, 1942-1962
Derry Almanacs and Street Directories
Derry City Council Museum Service: The Eamonn Gallagher Theatre Collection
The Era
The Irish Times
Linenhall Library, Belfast: Theatre and Performing Archive
Londonderry Corporation Minute Books
Londonderry Journal, later *Derry Journal*
Londonderry Sentinel
Londonderry Standard
Londonderry Guardian
Londonderry Chronicle and Weekly Mercantile Advertiser
National Library of Ireland, Dublin: Joly and Additional Music Collections; Lawrence Photographic Collection

Further Reading

Ophelia Byrne, *The Stage in Ulster from the Eighteenth Century* (Belfast, 1997)
William S. Clark, *The Irish Stage in the County Towns, 1720-1800* (Oxford, 1965)
Mark Carruthers *et al*, *Stepping Stones: The Arts in Ulster 1971-2001* (Belfast, 2001)
Brian Fothergill, *The Mitred Earl: An Eighteenth-Century Eccentric* (London, 1974)
Brian Lacey, *Siege City: The Story of Derry and Londonderry* (Belfast, 1990)
W.J. Lawrence, *Annals of the Belfast Stage* (Unpublished mss, Linenhall Library, Belfast, 1891)
Wesley McCann, *The Man Who Brought McCormack, Kreisler and Robeson to Derry* (Belfast, 2001)

Bibliography and Further Reading

Marilyn Richtarik, *Acting Between the Lines: The Field Day Company and Irish Cultural Politics* (Cambridge, 1995)
Alistair Rowan, *The Buildings of Ireland: North-West Ulster* (Middlesex, 1979)
Avril Thomas, *Irish Historic Towns Atlas No.15: Derry~Londonderry* (Dublin, 2005)

INDEX

Abbey Theatre (Dublin), 198, 199, 200, 225, 239, 240
Abercorn family, 115, 117, 183, 246
Adler, Larry, 240
Albani, Madame Emma, 8, *116*, 117, 200
Aldridge, Ira, 44, *45*, 237
Alexander family (Boom Hall), 23, 47
Alexander, Mrs Cecil Frances, 111, 115, 117, 238
Allen, Tim, 216, 221, 224
Amateur drama, 94-5, 99, 118, 149, 161, 164-5, 171, 175, 177, 179, 203, 204, 207, 226, 230, 239, 242
Anderson, Muriel, 183, *189*, 206, 208, 210, 240
Apprentice Boys, 11, 50, 56, 57, 63, 72, 74-5, 84, 89, 91, 99, 169, *174*, 211, 224, 238, 241
Armstrong, Barney, 148-9, 239, 247
Arthur, Thelma, 204, 206
Artillery Lane Theatre, *10*, 29, 30, 32-46, 54, 55, 63, 216, 230, 237
Arts Council of Northern Ireland (ACNI), 187, 190, 192, 194, 195, 196-9, 203, 205-6, 211, 213, 217, 223-4, 229, 231, 232, 234, 248, 249
At the Black Pig's Dyke, 218, *219*
Atkins, Michael, 17-20, 32-6
Atlantic Philanthropies, 231, 232

Bantock, Granville, 157, 158
Barbirolli, John, 183-4, *184*
Barr, Iain, 249

Beethoven House (Shipquay Street), *127*, 131, 147, 192-3, *192*, 240
Beethoven House Orchestra, 131
Beggar's Opera, The 19, 33, 41, 237
Bellamy, Thomas, 36
Benson, Frank, 102, 119, 120, 153, 158, 239, 247
Blackface entertainers/minstrels, 72, 104, 246
'Bloody Sunday', 192, 195, 213-14, 226
Blue School (Blue Coat School), *10*, 27-8, 244
Boruwlaski, 'Count' Joseph, 30-2, *31*, 46, 237
Bradlaw, Izidore, 150-1, 160, 239, 247
Brian Boroimhe (opera), 37-8, 39
Brian Boru (cantata), 97-9, *98*, 238
Brodsky Quartet, 222, 231
Brooke, Gustavus, 58, 87
Buchanan, Sidney, 161, 173, 181, 190-1, 204
Burgess, Jonathan, 236
Burnside, Sam, 217-18

Cafolla, Orlando, 156-7, *157*, 176, 183-4, 248
Caoilte (theatre critic), 176-7, 190, 248
Carl Rosa Opera Company, The (Royal), 106, 112, 120, 152, 154, *155*, 158, 239, 247
Carson, Frank, 187-8
Carthaginians, 213-14, *214*, 240
Cassidy, Paul, 222, 231
Catalani, Madame Angelica, 37, 49, *49*, 60, 62, 237
Christophers, Harry, 8, 220, 227

Index

Cinema, 133-4, 138-41, 142, 146-8, 151-3, 160, 167, 168, 169, 170, 177, 202, 205, 214, 223, 240, 247
City of Derry Dramatic Club, 94-5, 104-5
City of Derry Drama Club (CDDC), 171, 175, 177, 179-81, 189, 190, 195, 198, *199*, 207, 239, 242, 248
City of Derry Drama Festival, 203-5, 207, 230, 235, 240
City of Derry Orchestra, 231
Classical Music Society, 202, 208, 217, 222-3, 226, 230-1, 234, 240, 241, 243
Collisson, William Houston, 113, 238
Conaghan, Edward, 114, 118, 121, *122*, 126, 150, 187, 228, 238, 241
 '98 Cantata by Conaghan, 121, 150, 187, 228, 238, 241
Conaghan, William, 150, 152
Cooper, Joseph, 185, 239
Cooper, Margaret, 136
Corporation Hall (the Diamond), 32, *49*, 50, 53, 55, 56, 60-4, 66-8, 71, 74, 77, 79-84, 87-90, 91-3, 95-100, 104-5, 107, 108, 111, 114, 237, 238, 247
Coulter, Phil, 193
Council for the Encouragement of the Arts (CEMA), 171, 177, 179, 180, 181, 183, 185, 187, 248
Courtney, Annie, 221
Croi, An (Theatre), *174*, 226, 234, 241
Cunningham, Albert J., 124, 130, 145, *146*, 152, 156, 158, 159, 165, 167
Cusack, Cyril, 200, 239

Daly, Father Edward (later Bishop), 187-8, 192, 196, 217
Dan 'The Demon Dwarf', 249
Dana (Rosemary Brown), 193, 240
Dankworth, Johnny, 227, 241
Davey, Shaun, 206, 211, 213, 240
De Los Angeles, Victoria, 220, 240
Derry City Council, 198, 199, 200, 202, 204, 205, 211, 213, 214, 221, 223, 224, 226, 227, 232
Derry/Londonderry Musical Union, 104, *105*, 114, 115, 116, 117, 222, 243
Derry Pantomime Players, 188, 242
de Valera, Éamon, 239, 248
Doherty, Donal, 208-9, 216, 220, 224, 227-8, 249
Doran, Charles, 153-4

Doran, Sean, 213-15, *215*, 220-2, 224, 249
Douglas, Barry, 229, 231
D'Oyly Carte Opera Company, 106

Ebrington Barracks, 67, 73, 232, 241
Edmundson, William, 9, 14
Empire, The (renamed Opera House), 106
Exchange, (the Diamond), 8, *10*, 14, *15*, 17, 23, 25, 50

Farquhar, George, 9, 11-12, *11*, *13*, 236, 237, 241, 244
Farquhar plays:
 The Beaux Stratagem, 12, 34
 The Constant Couple, 12, 17
 Love and A Bottle, 213, 236
 The Recruiting Officer, *13*, 16, 17, 36
Farren, Father (later Bishop) Neil, 164, 171, 248
Feis Ceoil, later Londonderry Feis, 111, 123, 124,*125*, 129-30, 131,136, 138, 139, *140*, 141, 143-5, *144*, 150, 152, 154, 156, 157-8, 167, 171, 176, 181, 183, 191, 193, 195, 196, 197, 198, 202, 228, 238, 239, 241, 246, 247
Feis Dhoire Colmcille, 143, 150, 154, 157, 171, 179, 186, 188, 195, 196, 198, 202, 226, 228, 239, 240
Ferran, Brian, 190, 223, 248
Field Day Theatre Company, 200-3, *201*, 204-5, 206-7, 213, 214, 215, 217, 224-5, *225*, 240, 249
First Derry Presbyterian Church (Magazine Street), 24, 27-8, 65, 66, 67, 69, 71, 88, 94, 105, 114, 146, 159, 222, 238, 244, 248
Fisk Jubilee Singers, *93*, 94, 238
Foyle Civic Trust, 218
Foyle College, 11, 74, 96, 108, 115, 217, 232
Franklin, Henry, 158
Franklin, Michael, 182, 187
French, Percy, 108, 227, 238
Friel, Brian, 18, 191, 193, 195, 197, 198, 200-3, *203*, 204, 206-7, 214, 215, 224-5, 227, 235, 240
Friel plays:
 The Aristocrats, 207
 The Communication Cord, 206, 207, 246
 Dancing at Lughnasa, 214, 225
 The Freedom of the City, 198, 207, 214
 Lovers, 193
 The Loves of Cass Maguire, 195
 Making History, 207

Philadelphia, Here I Come, 197, 202, 203, 207
Three Sisters (translation), 204, 207, 240
Translations, 200-2, *201*, 203, 204, 207, 224, 240
Friel, Redmond, 176, 179, 185, 190, 191, 196, 239, 249
From the Besieged City (music), 211, 240

Gaelic League, 118, 124
Gardzienice Theatre Group, 215-16
Gillen, Michael, 191, 198, 203-4, 205
Glendermott Presbyterian Church, 66, *66*, 237
Glover, J.B. (Joey), 168, 171, 179, 189, 195
Glover, Lawrence, 185-6, *186*, 239
Government School of Art (Corporation Hall), 107, 111, 247
Gramophones, 115, 133, 159, 160, 176, 179
Grianan of Aileach (music), 158
Guildhall, 16, 56, 108, 111, 114-15, *116*, 117, 120, 123, 127, 130-1, *131*, 136, 138, 141, 142, 143, 147, 150, 151, 152, 153, 156, 158, 159, 160, 161, 162-4, 165, 166, 170, 171, 172, *172*, 173, *174*, 175, 177, 179, 180, 181, 182, 183-4, 185, 189, *189*, 190, 191, 195, 196, 200, 203, 205, 206, 207, 208, 211, 213, 214, 215, 216, 218, 222, 224, 226, 227, 232, 238, 239, 240, 241, 247, 248
Guild Theatre (North Edward Street), 175-7, *176*, 179, 239
Guthrie, Tyrone, 181, 239
Gwyn's Institution, (later Brooke Park), 73, 74, 88, 237, 245

Hallé Band/Orchestra, 138, *140*, 141, 183-4, *184*, 227, 238, 239
Hammond, Joan, 190, 240
Harty, Hamilton, 157, 184, 229, 239
Hasson, Ann, 202, 206, 249
Hasson, Larry, 170, 202, 249
Hayes, Catherine, 76-8, *77*, 81, 116, 238, 245
Heaney, Seamus, 200, 202, 203, 207, 213, 240
Heffernon, Edward, 85, 87, 92, 203
Hempton, John, 75-6, 82, 83-4, *83*, 87, 126, 238
Herdman family, 123, 141, 198, 247
Hervey, Frederick, Earl Bishop, 24, *25*, 29, 244
Hill, Donald, 188, 189, 206
Hippodrome, The (renamed Opera House), 128-9, 131, 133-5, *134*, 138, 139, 238
Hughes, Ted, 215, 240
Hume, John, 190, 193, 200

Hunter, James, 54, 57, 75-6, 237
Ilex-urc, 232
Impact '92, 206, 213-16, 220, 222, 223, 240, 249

Jacques String Orchestra, 171, 181
Joachim, Joseph, 79-81, 158, 238
Johnston, James, 159, 165-6, 182, 239, 248
Jones, Daniel, 99, 104, 116, 117, 123, 124, 186, 238
Jullien, Louis, 79-80, *80*, 81, 238

Kalener, John, 21-2
Kean, Edmund, 8, 41, 44, 237
Kennedy Miller Theatre Company 119, 120
Kerr, William, 71, 88, 95
King's Arms Hotel (Pump Street), *10*, 32, 44, 50, 52, 54, 61, 244, 249
Kreisler, Fritz, 132, 162-3, *163*, 164, 239

Lacy, Michael, 37, 237
Laine, Cleo, 227, 241
Lally, Mick, 202, 206
Lind, Jenny, 8, 49, 60, 79, 80-1, *81*, *82*, 87, 116, 238
Little Gaelic Singers, 187, 188, 239
Lloyd, Arthur, 106, 119, 238, 246
Locke, Josef (Joseph McLaughlin), 170, 183, 241
Logan, Fred, 161, 173-4, 181, 188, 189, 191, 204, 206, 248
Logier, Johann Bernhard, 38, *39*, 63, 244, 245
Logier, William Henry, 38, *39*, 63-5, 67, 75, 95, 227, 244, 245
Londerriaires, The, 182
Londonderry Air, The, 163, 164, 184
Londonderry Arts Association, 196, 206, 208, 222, 240, 243
Londonderry Choral Union, 64, 71, 72, 243
Londonderry Development Commission 192
Londonderry Dramatic Society, 161, 171, 173
Londonderry Harmonic Society, 71, 75, 237, 243
Londonderry Light Opera Society, (later The Londonderry Amateur Operatic Society, now the Londonderry Musical Society), 188-9, 191, 196, 198, 206, 231, 240, 243
Londonderry Musical Association (LMA), 64, 65, 66, 67-8, 69, 70, 74, 91, 245
Londonderry Music Circle, 177, *178*, 179, 183, 239, 243

Index

Londonderry Musical Society, 21-2, 27, 48, 65, 188, 231, 237, 243
Londonderry Orchestra, 189, *189*
Londonderry Orchestral Society, 114, 238, 243
Londonderry Philharmonic Society, 91, 95, 111, 124, 125, 130, 131, 136, 138, 143, 145, *146*, 147, 150, 152, 157-9, 165-7, *166*, 170, 181, 182, 183, 206, 208, 222, 238, 239, 243, 246
Long Tower Church (St Columba's), 24, 71, 114, 118, 121, 150, 246
Loughlin, William (Willie), 176, 185, 248
Ludwig (Ledwidge), William, 106, 115, 123, 238

MacCafferty, James, 170, 185, 186-7, 188, 191, 195, 239, 240
MacCafferty Singers, 187, 188, 239
MacGabhann, Risteard, 191, 198, 227
Macklin, Charles, 15-17, *16*, 55, 203, 237
MacLiammoir, Micheal, 173
Magee College, 56, *174*, 177, *178*, 179, 181, 185, 190, 191, 195, 196, 198, 199, 203, 204, 206, 207, 208, 232, 234, 239, 240, 241, 242, 243
Magee Drama Society, 190
Major, John, 220-1
Malmene, Waldemar, 63, 88, 89-91, *90*, 95, 186, 228, 238
Marshall, Scott, 188, 189, 193, 195, 198, 204, 206
May, James, 47-8
Mayhew, Patrick, 220-1
McAnally, Ray, 202, 204
McCaul, Kevin, 211, 224, 249
McCormack, John, 133, 162, 183, 227, 238, 239
McGuinness, Frank, 213-14, *214*, 224, *225*, 235, 236, 240, 249
McKenna, Siobhan, 195, 240
McMaster, Anew, 161-2, 180-1, 202, 239, 247, 248
Melly, George, 206, 215, 240
Messiah (oratorio), Handel's, 47, 71, 95, 104-5, *105*, 117, 124-5, 143, 159, 165, 189, 190, 227, 237, 238, 246
Military/Garrison bands, 20, 34, 46, 67, 72-4, 87, 88, 124, 143, 148, 157, 159, 167, 171, 245
Millennium Forum, 8, *174*, 226, 227, 228, 229-31, 234, 240, 241
Moore, James, 182

Mulholland, George, 114, 121
Mulholland, Patrick, 95, 96-9, *98*, 104, 147, 232, 238, 246
Mullarkey, Tom, 202, 205, 226, 249
Music 55-7, 234, 241, 243
Murphy, Kevin, 231, 234

Neeson, Liam, 202
North-West Arts Festival, 190-1, 192, 205-6, 211, 240
North-West Drama and Arts Guild 175
North-West Music Society, 179, 185, 195, 198, 239, 243

O'Brien, Joseph, 149-50, 243, 247
O'Connell, Kevin, 211, 216, 240, 249
Octoberfest '93, *215*, 220-1, 240
O'Mara, Joseph, *154*, 158
Opera House, 8, 32, 44, 56, 92, 100-3, *101*, 104, 105, *105*, 106-7, *107*, 108, 109-10, 111-13, 114, 116, 118-20, 121, 126, 128-9, *129*, 131, 133, *134*, 139, *139*, 142, 145, 146-9, 150-1, 152-4, *153*, *154*, 158, 160, 161, 165, 168-9, *169*, 200, 218, 230, 238, 239
O'Sullivan, Denis, 138, 238

Pantomime 14, 15, 17, 57, 85, 86, 109-10, 121, 145, 149, 165, 186, 187, 188, 191, 193, 198, 231
Patriotic Fund Concerts, 69-71, *70*, 237
Perois family, 61-3, 227, 245
Phillips, Ailne, 154, *156*
Phillips, Henry Bettesworth (HB), 111, 115-17, 119-21, 123, 126-8, *127*, *129*, 130, 131-3, 135-6, 138, 141, 150, 154, 155, 158, 160, 162-4, 172, 186, 192, *192*, 238, 239, 240, 247
Piano wars, 75-6
Players, '71, 193-5, 198, 203, 217, 240, 242
Playhouse, *174*, 202, 216-17, 223-6, *230*, 232, 233, 235-6, 240, 241
Pollock, Mac, 204
Power, Tyrone, 120
Poyner, Michael, 230-1
Precentors (Presbyterian), 8, 60, 63, 69, 71-2, 88, 95, 124, 246

Queen's Theatre (Chamberlain Place), 56, 60, 85-7, 92, 114, 203, 238, 249

Raidio Eireann Orchestra, 184, 239
Rea, Stephen, 202-3, 204, 206, 224, 240
Regondi, Guilio, 61, 87, 237
Relief of Derry Symphony, 211, 213, 240
Rialto, The, 152, 160, *174*, 202, 204, 205, 206, 207, 213, 214, *214*, 216, 223, 224, 228, 239, 240, 241
Rialto Orchestra, The, 152
Robeson, Paul, 8, 162, 163, *164*, 239
Royal Agricultural Society of Ireland, 61-2, 77
Ross, Pauline, 193-4, 197, 203, 216-17, 224
Ryan, Vivian, 58-9
Ryder, Thomas, 15, 237

St Columb's Cathedral, *10*, 25-7, *26*, 47, 51, 56, 84, 91, 97, 99, 115, 117, 121, 124, 147, 159, 167, *174*, 182, 188, 190, 191, 195, 220, 237, 238, 240, 247
St Columb's Cathedral Oratorio Society, (later St Columb's Cathedral Musical Society) 182-3, 188, 190, 191, 195, 239
St Columb's College Union Dramatic Society, 225
St Columb's Hall, 56, 111, 113-14, *113*, 118, 121, 131, 133, 136, 137, 139, 141, 142, 147, 149, 160, 164-5, *174*, 177, 186-8, 191-3, *194*, 203, 216, 220, 222, 224, 227, 238, 239
St Eugene's Cathedral, *56*, 95, 96, 114, 118, 126, 147, 174, 183, 187, 208, *209*, 227, 238, 240, 247
Second Derry Presbyterian Church, (Strand Road), 189
Seddon, William Payne, 128-9, 131, 133-5, *134*, 138-41, 145, 148, 149, 151, 238, 247
Shannon family (organists), 21-2, 27, 52, 246
Shipquay Theatre, 8, *10*, 17-20, 29, 32, 33, 56, 237
Smock Alley Theatre Company, 11, 12, 14, 18, 237
Smoking concerts, 117, 185
Sousa, Edward, 133, 135-6, *137*, 227, 238
Star Dramatic Company 118, 242
Stewart, Alexandrina McCausland (*née* Elsner), 123-5, *125*, 130, 138, *140*, 141, 145, 154, 157, 238, 247
Stoll, Henry, 73, 74, 232
Story, Belinda, 188, 191
Stradivarius, The 'Molitor', 208, *210*, 240
Sullivan, Barry, 106, 112

Talbot, Montague, 36-8, 237
Thalberg, Sigismond, 81, 82, 238
Theatre Action Group (TAG), 198, 199, 204, 205, 223, 227, 235
Theatre Club, The, 193-5, *194*, 197, 198, 203, 204, 207, 218, 242
Theatre Royal, (Fountain Street), 54, *56*, 57-9, *58*, 87, 237, 238
Theatre Trust, The, 227, 231, 240
Third Derry Presbyterian Church, (Great James Street), 64, 71, 88, 89, 103, 159, 223
Thornhill 148
Tolson, Richard, 146, 159
Tonic Solfa, 60, 66, 114, 245
Two Cathedrals' Festival, 216, 220-1, 222, 223, 227-8, 240, 241

Ulster Hall, 96, 99, 131, 133
Ulster Orchestra, 190, 192, 205, 208, 211, 216, 220, 222, 240, 248
Ulster Youth Orchestra, *228*, 229

Verbal Arts Centre, *174*, 217, 223, 226, 236, 240
Verni Continental Orchestra, 152

Warden, Joseph Frederick, 92-4, *92*, 95, 100-4, 105, 106-7, 109-10, 111, 112-13, 118-19, 120, 121, *129*, 138-9, 246
Wartime entertainments, 143-7, *144*, *145*, 167-8, 169-72, *170*, *172*, 175, 239
Waterside Theatre, *174*, 226, 229, 234-5, *235*, 241, 249
Watson, Kathleen, 152, 153, 159, 165, 247
Watson, William, 65-7, *66*, 71, 246
Weir, Hugh, 161, 173
Wesley, John, 29
West, William (Billy), 195
Wieniawski, Henryk, 79-80, 238
Wilde, Oscar, 107-8, *107*, *108*, 120, 128, 180, 207, 238
Willman, Noel, 158, 161, 247

YMCA Hall (East Wall), 56, 148, 161, 177, 199, 208, 227
YMCA Players, 175, 177, 181, 190, 242